PART-TIME CRIME

PART-TIME CRIME

An Ethnography of
Fiddling and Pilferage

JASON DITTON

First published 1977 by
THE MACMILLAN PRESS LTD
London and Basingstoke
Associated companies in New York
Dublin Melbourne Johannesburg and Madras

ISBN 0 333 21466 8

Printed in Great Britain by
THE BOWERING PRESS LTD
Plymouth

Contents

47157

Preface

I am lucky enough to have a number of friends and colleagues. Probably not as many of the former, and perhaps more of the latter now that this book has been published. I don't expect that many of the men at Wellbread's will look too kindly on the cut in real wages that this work may mean to them, and my bakery self would agree with them.

One man who has been both a friend and colleague of the very best sort is Richard Brown. He is, quite simply and without exaggeration, the kindest man I have ever met. He supervised this research in a painstakingly thorough, detailed, and yet simultaneously helpful and sympathetic way. Philip Corrigan spent a great deal of time not only systematically scouring newspaper and literary sources to provide me with material, but also writing detailed criticisms of some of the chapters when they appeared initially as seminar papers. Donald Roy stimulated this work with his interest, and actively encouraged me from the sidelines, and Stanley Cohen provided the initial spur with his lectures on deviance. I am not going to go on and on. At various times, Brian Taylor, Gerry Mars, Tony Hill, John Winckler and Stuart Henry have advised, argued, assisted and aided, and I am grateful.

Hilary Hubery typed a faultless manuscript from my fiendish and virtually indecipherable handwriting.

JASON DITTON

April 1976
University of Durham

Acknowledgements

Some of the material in Chapter 2 initially appeared as 'Becoming a Fiddler: Some Steps in the Moral Career of the Naïve Bread Salesman', *Working Paper* No. 6, Durham University, 1974 and later as 'The Fiddling Salesman: Connivance at Corruption' in *New Society*, 28 November 1974, pp. 535–537. Chapter 6 has similarly appeared in the journal *Sociology*, vol. 11, No. 1, January 1977, as 'Alibis and Aliases: Some Notes on the "Motives" of Fiddling Bread Salesmen'.

The research and analysis reported here was carried out whilst in receipt of S.S.R.C. Grant No. 71/6682/S, and S.S.R.C. Grant No. HR 3603/1.

1 Introduction: The Wellbread Bakery

THE WELLBREAD BAKERY AND SALES LIFE

The Wellbread Bakery (a fictitious name) is a medium-sized factory-production bakery in the south-east of England. It is the major bakery of a small chain which includes two other production bakeries, and several smaller distribution depots. At Wellbread's, production staff make a variety of bread, rolls, cakes and confectionery. Despatch staff break 'runs' of production down into the individual orders submitted by the salesmen, and prepare for each salesman a bread rack with his completed order ready for him to load onto his van. Each morning, from 2 a.m. onwards, salesmen begin to drift into work, load their vans, and get out to their customers. The sales department at Wellbread's employs seventeen wholesale salesmen driving small lorries, who deliver bread, as middle-men, to shops for resale, and twenty-seven retail men, who are 'on the basket'. Retail men drive small vans, and they tour a 'round' of domestic customers either on suburban housing estates or in the surrounding villages.

The Wellbread chain began as a small, old-fashioned family baker up a side street, Deal Street, in the old part of the town. The owners, the Grundy family, went the way of many small and inefficient bakeries. Batch production technology cannot compete with modern conveyor belt methods. One employee recalled what it was like, and also remembered how the Grundy family had got into trouble:

> They used to have real coke ovens and everything, they used to have the coke stacked up in the bakery there! . . . well, it was originally Grundy's, see? . . . but what they done, see, they borrowed too much money off of —— [local flour miller] . . . until they kept lending it, you know, to expand and expand . . . until eventually they couldn't pay off their debts, and so, of course, the Mill took them over.

The Mill that took Grundy's over renamed the bakery 'Wellbread's', and moved the works to a custom-built plant on the commercial outskirts to the north of the town. Although the old management (with the addition of a few Mill personnel) was retained, other things changed:

> Well, it was a lot happier down there [at Deal Street] it was a lot more closely knit . . . I mean it was a lot more like a small community . . . there had only been about fifteen of us working in the place . . . and about six women . . . it was a really happy place to work in.

The Mill, in its new Wellbread guise, continued the old policy of allowing flour customers to get too deeply into debt, and then buying them out. The Wellbread chain began to emerge. The same man continued:

> Course, they expanded even further . . . they were buying all these small bakeries . . . the Mill was serving people . . . getting them into debt, closing them, and then opening them up again as Wellbread's, this is how they have grown right the way through.

At Deal Street, the despatch foreman looked after the salesmen as a sort of side-line to his regular despatch duties. His experience as a salesman actually ceased with the advent of motor transport after World War I. His first-hand experience with a horse and cart, and his executive abilities with the fleet of broken-down, second-hand World War I ambulances which the Grundys were operating was not the sort of go-ahead team that the Mill had in mind. As one man said 'As soon as the Mill started to get their feet in, they decided that sales managers were the thing of the future . . . so they sacked him off the sales side of things, and got a proper bloke in'. This was the beginning of the present sales department. It also marked the onset of increasingly obvious differences between the sales department and the rest of the bakery. Most other department heads hail from the old days, and are usually referred to as the 'Deal Street boys' to distinguish them from the 'blokes from the Mill' in the sales department.

The move from Deal Street, and the subsequent import of a hard-nosed production manager from one of the bakeries which the Mill had endebted, the increase in production size, and the not-so-subtle transmission from craft to factory production, brought some easily noticed changes:

> It was terrifically hard work . . . it was to get harder as time went on . . . as they increased trade, and as they increased the speed of the plant . . . things just drifted apart . . . whereas everybody knew everybody else by their first name at Deal Street . . . up at Well-bread's, you had different men coming in who nobody knew, and,

I dunno, things never seemed to be the same, it was more impersonal than anything, I suppose.

The objective conditions for unionisation increased, and the Bakers' Union got a foothold after one or two shaky starts. It was at this point that the sales department began openly to adopt an identity different to that of the rest of the workforce. At one time, at Deal Street, they had been part of the despatch-and-sales department. Now, new management steeped in progressive American sales techniques, and thinly glossed with anti-union paternalism, began to remodel the sales department. One employee remembered:

When they opened —— [a specially built production bakery in a nearby town], they hadn't got a *bit* of trade there . . . three weeks before they opened, they hadn't got *one* shop, but they moved a team of canvassers in there, and they got enough to run the plant within three months of opening . . . and there was a Wheatkist bakery nearby, and they took that over and transferred all the production to ——

The current sales force is run with the curious ideological mixture of strict authoritarianism and team-spirit. The salesmen are unorganised, and sporadic attempts from within by the most experienced and senior salesmen to organise the salesforce as a branch of the TGWU are ferociously and speedily quashed by the sales management. One salesman commented:

We had a meeting in a pub about it . . . an Irish fellow organised it, it was just when I was about to take over the wholesale round . . . well, about sixteen of us went along, and we all joined for a week, and it all fell through after that . . . this bloke kept saying 'If we all stick it, they can't fire all of us' . . . but I didn't see it that way . . . they couldn't cover us all from blokes they had at Wellbread's, but they could bring in supervisors from the depots, couldn't they? . . . anyway, the manager called us in, and accused me of starting it . . . that's always his way, he does that every time he gets a sniff of the Union.

There is a sense in which managerial antipathy to the Union is born out of honestly believed conviction that they really are on the same side as their men. Indeed, for the management, bakery life is as time-consuming as it is for the salesmen. As the sales manager put it:

Take me, I earn a reasonable salary . . . I worked hard to get where I am mind you . . . but I've got a responsible job, and I enjoy it . . . but . . . it's not just twelve hours a day you know, you've got that bloody telephone by your bed all the time.

His anti-union stance is partially supported by the supervisory cushion which he has placed between himself and his men. For some organisational purposes in the sales department the salesmen are arbitrarily divided into groups of four, for whom single supervisors have moral and technical responsibility. Salesmen, as they caustically remark along the loading bays in the early mornings, are those who said 'no' to the managerial offer to become a supervisor. Those who say 'yes', and become supervisors, do so 'on a promise'. That is, they fall for the rosy picture of future meteoric promotion glowingly sketched out for them in the sales manager's office. Inevitably, very few get promoted from supervisory ranks. For most, the job of sales supervisor is the most permanent step imaginable on an illusory promotion ladder.

Individual dreams aside, the supervisors act as relief salesmen for most of the time, perhaps leaving one or two days a month for 'proper' supervisory duties such as canvassing, checking on their group's performance, paper-work, and so on. 'They use them blokes', as one despatch charge-hand sourly remarked, 'like a piece of old rag'. This administrative set-up allows the sales manager to wallow undisturbed in a morass of pseudo-sentimental human relations mythology. He explained to me:

> If the Union recruit anybody here . . . it'll be my fault . . . we don't need a Union! . . . what we've got here is a *team*, *I'm* one of *them*, I'm *part* of them, I consider them out there as the family, to me, they're second only to my own family, if anyone's got a complaint, they can come straight to me, the man at the top, and *bang*! . . . we'll have it sorted out in two hours . . . [later] . . . we tell the salesmen that they are the most important people here, they're the ones with the direct contact with the customer and that sort of time is very expensive . . . any firm depends on its salesmen, they're the men that really count . . . sales representatives are the backbone of any firm . . . of course, they're not more *important* than the lavatory cleaner . . . we all have a part to play . . . however big . . . [*sic!*].

As I hope to show later, the main difficulties in the sales department, as far as the management are concerned, stem from the fact that none of the sales force shares this viewpoint.

A RESEARCH DIARY: GETTING TO KNOW ABOUT THE 'FIDDLE'

In 1971, Durham University accepted my Ph.D. proposal to embark upon a period of relatively unstructured participant observation research wherein I hoped that those studied would suggest the direction and substantive content of analysis. I decided to return to Wellbread's (where I had previously worked in undergraduate vacations) and concentrate upon whether or not workers paid by the hour exhibited logically similar actions to the patterns of 'output restriction' noticed amongst workers paid by the piece.

Although the graduate grant didn't start until October 1971, I worked through the summer of 1971 as a plant worker, *né* undercover participant observer, at Wellbread's. By now, of course, I knew most of the men, and had none of the usual problems of getting permission, getting into the field, getting accepted, or getting going. In fact (and this, I suggest, is perhaps the mark of the truly accepted observer) I had far greater problems in getting *out*. My every attempt to leave, each timid suggestion that I might discuss 'research plans', was brushed aside, and I was plied with furious pleas to stay and help the management out in the perennial summer labour shortage period!

Nevertheless, I *was* able to develop personal covert participant-observation skills. Right from the start, I found it impossible to keep everything that I wanted to remember in my head until the end of the working day (some of the shifts were over twelve hours long) and so had to take rough notes as I was going along. But I was stuck 'on the line', and had nowhere to retire to privately to jot things down. Eventually, the wheeze of using innocently provided lavatory cubicles occurred to me. Looking back, all my notes for that third summer were on Bronco toilet paper! Apart from the awkward tendency for pencilled notes to be self-erasing from hard toilet paper (sometimes before I could even get home), my frequent requests for 'time out' after interesting happenings or conversations in the bakehouse and the amount of time that I was spending in the lavatory began to get noticed. I had to pacify some genuinely concerned work-mates, give up totally undercover operations, and 'come out' as an observer – albeit in a limited way. I eventually began to scribble notes more openly, but still not in front of people when they were talking. When questioned about this, as I was occasionally, I coyly said that I was writing things down that occurred to me about 'my studies'.

Ultimately, I returned to Durham in October 1971 and wrote up some initial material (Ditton, 1972, 1972a, 1976a) based upon either direct bakery experience, or upon consideration of derived theoretical issues. But by February of 1972, I was beginning to hanker for some non-sedentary activity. A common case of participant observer's Pyles. A fate frequently experienced by those observers who, like the war correspondent Ernie Pyle (Roy, 1970, p. 219) study the 'action' from the thick of it rather than from the side, and get to feel a little empty when they are away from it.

Thus, from May to December of 1972, I worked solidly as a despatch operative at Wellbread's with just a few days refresher course on the plant. From January to June 1973, I interviewed all the despatch workers, a minority in considerable depth, and had them fill in two questionnaires, one general, querying ordinary demographic data, and one specific, elucidating preferences for the various jobs that despatch staff had to do. Regrettably, involvement with the first questionnaire gobbled up the analysis time which I had planned to occur between periods of participant observation. Although initially designed purely as a blind – so that attention would be drawn away from the participant side of things, and so that the workers would be able to divide my time into 'actual research' (distributing questionnaires) and just 'getting ready' to do it (all the rest of the time) – to side-track any deliberate attempts to mislead me from the research proper, the first questionnaire grew into a Frankenstein monster. Greedily, because I thought that I would have to spend a lot of time designing, producing, distributing and collecting it (even finally to throw it away, as I had originally intended), I thought that I might as well try to extract a bit of research value from it, and so spent more time on it than I otherwise might have done, and asked for more information (e.g. names of respondents) than was prudent.

A few salesmen and most of the despatch men, but none of the plant men, the confectioners, the packers, storekeepers, mechanics, fitters or cleaners would fill it in; although one (anonymous) respondent returned it with 'THE ONLY ANSWER YOU WILL GET IS FOR MORE FRESH AIR' scrawled across the first page in large spidery letters. Although I was considerably disheartened, this was no great loss as far as the original research plan was concerned. Whilst the information it might have garnered would have sketched the practical parameters of the sample, and allowed me a few demographic footnotes, the 'discovery model' of analysis which I have used does not require the routine discussions of standard sociological variables. But I had just concluded tortuous and difficult negotiations with the sales manager to work as a salesman and by then, June 1973, I had to start participant observation in the sales department. This left me no time to start analysing the data that I had accumulated from my despatch experience, but it was obvious that, if I delayed working in sales, I would never get another chance. Four hundred typed foolscap pages of despatch data lie unanalysed in my filing cabinet, although they have been thoroughly searched for any information pertinent to an analysis of the sales department.

But my experience in despatch *did* mean that I could start work as a salesman with some colossal advantages from a research point of view. I knew the ins and outs of all the despatch operations; in fact, I knew more about the internal workings of the bakery than most of the regular salesmen. Additionally, I had worked for nearly a year in despatch, and I had made many friends amongst the salesmen. By the time I came to do research in the sales department, some of the salesmen had known me as a casual worker and student for four years. Sometimes I almost felt I was doing research on members of my own family.

But I must confess that I began to work and observe in the sales department with less than a wholly open mind concerning the 'problems' on which the research there would concentrate. I almost knew that I was going to study 'the fiddle', although, coincidentally, it *was* both the central problem of sales life for most of the salesmen, *and* represented the particular form that 'making out' (the general category of which 'output restriction' is a specific form) took in that department. But ever since I first started working on the plant there was one topic which guaranteed discussion veiled in analogy, vagueness, mystification, allusion, euphemism and ambiguity. Some of the older plant-hands 'knew what went on' amongst the salesmen, but whenever I pressed them for further details, it was always: 'I can't say no more than that', or, 'Ah! that'd be telling'. Perhaps, if it had been discussed differently, it would never have caught my attention. But the mixture of awe, reverence, suspicion and ignorance with which the subject of fiddling was treated by the inside men absorbed my analytic curiosity.

In the despatch department, it was the same story. 'The wholesale boys', one said, 'are up to all the tricks.' 'They all', the others agreed, 'make a bit on the side', 'have their little perks', 'make their tea money', 'take the odd loaf'. And always the meta-communicative wink: 'Y'know?', 'know what I mean?' The management was deprecating, the managing director said to me (after sacking two 'dealing' despatch men) 'This fiddling is only a temporary thing. I've just sacked the two men involved, so it's all over now.' And the night manager just thought of it as tolerable shrinkage: 'I mean, you've got to allow for losses, you do get a percentage of loss in every bakery . . . you get the odd loaf being taken home and not being paid for, a box of cakes goes, somebody has a nibble.' But always the insidious 'You know [laugh] we all make a bit on the side . . . know what I mean?' No, I didn't, but by God, I was going to.

I must have been looking too hard, and certainly in the wrong direction, whilst I was working in the despatch department. For, three months before I was eventually to start as a salesman, two men with whom I had worked for seven months were sacked for stealing biscuits from the cake-store in the middle of the night, and subsequently selling them to wholesale salesmen. A third worker on the same shift (who had in fact been fully involved, but not on the night in question) left under a cloud of suspicion. I was later able to interview the two men extensively, and obtain very persuasive proof that there were not only regular instances of domestic stealing, but that large scale regular dealing involving most of the employees had been in progress for a long time.

It was not by chance that the sackings came as a surprise to me. The two men involved, one of them a charge-hand, had taken great care to ensure that I and the other innocent operative were despatched on wild goose chases to other depots to look for missing bread, or otherwise had our attention waylaid and distracted when dealing was in progress. It is somewhat ironic, but one of the sacked men later said to me 'I thought you knew all about it, we thought you knew what was going on, but had enough sense to keep quiet . . . we used to say: "Oh, Jason knows about it, but he won't say anything". . . .' There are good reasons why it is particularly difficult to spot the occurrence of this sort of activity without recourse to inventories or to jobs which involve checking the work of others (neither of which I had). Bread is not only 'fungible' (Henry, 1976, p. 75), i.e. it is indistinguishable from others of its kind, 'dealing' is also what Lemert (1953, p. 101) calls a very 'low visibility' crime, inasmuch as there is nothing visually or objectively criminal about it, the 'skills' of passing out stolen bread are identical to those required to issue legitimate goods. Although incidents like this can be embarrassing, luckily, by the time I had started work in the sales department, memories had blurred, and many of the salesmen firmly believed that I had known all along, and could be trusted. I thus not only had in-depth information about a recent and relevant case of commercial enforcement, I had something much more valuable: I predated the current despatch regime, and, even more, I was trusted.

And so, from June to September of 1973, I worked as a bread salesman, and for the rest of that year interviewed as many salesmen as I could. I was, by then, a fairly experienced interviewer, having already completed taping and typing in-depth interviews with all the despatch men. When I began interviewing salesmen I had developed a fairly useful interviewing technique. I managed to conduct most initial interviews at the home of the respondent, and was sufficiently skilful by then to steer wives and children from the room, and pacify any qualms about anonymity before starting. I had a rough check-list of topics which I needed to cover, although in most cases (apart from the inevitable occasional interview which was tortuously staccato) I put this back in my pocket after a few minutes and allowed each man to talk about whatever aspect of being a salesman most worried, con- cerned or interested him. None refused to talk about fiddling, many volunteering information far beyond the extent I dared to hope for. The verbatim transcripts which I made from these taped interviews provided me with data in a form particularly useful for illustrating the analysis given in the rest of the book.

In December 1973 I returned to Durham with a total of over 4560 hours of participant observation and thirty-four taped and typed interviews under my research belt.

Although my original intention to analyse all this data still stood, it soon became apparent that I had too much information. Analytic justice could not have been done to more than a third of it in the remaining year and a half of graduate study. I made no conscious decision about what to leave out, but analysis of fiddling in the sales department soon grew into an exclusive interest. Nothing had been written about fiddling from a sociological viewpoint although it seemed to me to be a particularly interesting case as it appeared to confront many of the taken-for-granted canons of traditional criminological research. Fiddling was practised by most, not just a few of the salesmen. Most interestingly it had neither practical nor psychological priority (it was physically and emotionally an irrelevant part of life), and practitioners were successfully able to conceive of it as non-criminal action. Finally, it was the most suitable substantive and empirical coat-hanger that I could find upon which a 'theorised ethnography' of bread salesmen might be hung.

I have nothing very significant to add to the ever expanding socio-logical literature on the experiences, morals, ethics and practices of the participant observer. I was partially open (after the unfortunate experience with the Bronco toilet paper), although I never fully declared that I was chiefly interested in fiddling. This is partly ethically excusable (and at least not unique; Quinney, 1963, pp. 211–12, never disclosed to his subjects that he was interested in their pharmacy prescription violation), as the decision to concentrate upon fiddling was not made until some time after returning to Durham. Nevertheless, towards the end of the field research, I had begun to think that an analysis of fiddling would be the basis of the proposed section on the sales department.

To present openly findings deceitfully gathered, to sell to one group the secrets of another, is to play the 'defrocked priest' (Goffman, 1959, p. 163). The end serves as the justification (how else, Polsky 1967 asks, is crime to be studied in its natural surroundings?) and the ethical offence is mitigated in various ways. In the first case, I have sought to protect the identity of both the bakery and of those studied by omitting names and changing other irrelevant facts. Although I did not fully disclose all possible intentions to those I watched and interviewed, final intentions were not clear at the research stage. Anyway, participant observation is inevitably unethical by virtue of being interactionally deceitful. It does not become ethical merely because this deceit is openly practised. It only becomes inefficient. However, the depths of ethical degradation that I reached amounted only to the use of a technique which Gerald Mars (in personal communication) calls the 'false question', with which I was able to note data on the fiddle whilst it was being discussed. If something that was said seemed important but likely to be swiftly dropped if I took written interest in it, I immediately interjected a wholly spurious question on job preferences or something and, under the guise of noting the answers, was able to make the notes that I wanted. Without reliance on some subterfuge the practices of subterfuge will not be opened to analysis. A perfect reminder of the penalties of ethical behaviour is available. Daniel (1963, p. 108) did not resort to any unseemly and unethical practices in his study of a bakery. Although the inside men in his study claimed that the salesmen were on the fiddle, the salesmen denied it when interviewed by Daniel. Daniel concludes that the fact that the roundsmen have cars and the inside men bicycles is to be explained by the fact that the roundsmen could have part-time jobs, and that different expenditure preference patterns might operate. This is the only conclusion which ethically 'proper' research could support.

There is a sense, anyway, in which *all* observation breaks hidden rules stricturing interaction. The researcher is, as Goffman (1957, p. 119) notes of the type 'conspicuously concerned to an improper degree with the way that the interaction, qua interaction, is proceeding, instead of becoming spontaneously involved in the official topic of conversation'. Observation, then, is not something restricted to sociologists. The sense, of course, in which some ordinary actions share this reflexive dimension legitimates the sociological variety. Sociological research, from this viewpoint, is more of an exaggeration of conventional social activities than something separately constructed and separately justified.

It would be a mistake for me to attempt to recapture the flavour of the research experience by encompassing it within the dry verification metaphor, and churlish to dress up the research in what Cohen and Taylor (1972, pp. 32–3) call the 'chronological lie'. The research was done intuitively, without textbooks clutched in the left hand: there is no current need to pretend otherwise. Ultimately, the ethical questions are not just the responsibility of the researcher. The researched must always face the risk that somebody will 'analyse' him behind his back, whether or not that somebody is gainfully employed as a sociologist. To subtract this responsibility from those studied is to ignore their everyday competences and abilities. I didn't deceive the subjects. As one salesman said to me, some time after I had finished working full time:

> I never approached you [for extra bread] down the bakery, you stood out, see? . . . and most people realised that you stood out, you weren't supposed to be there, . . . and that was it, you didn't look like a bakery person.

INTENTIONS

The research upon which this book is based was not set up to answer any empirical questions. Actually, in a strictly empirical sense, the data are patchy, and in terms of statistical significance also 'dirty'. I mention this shortcoming only because I have produced empirical novelty. Nothing has been written about fiddling, and so empirical issues (which are discussed in Chapter 4) are important. Nevertheless, I have produced a theoretical and not an empirical analysis of fiddling and, only secondarily, an analysis of the bread salesman.

In fact, this book does not provide a full blown ethnography of the bread salesman, although I believe that I have, if only by imputation, provided a complete 'recipe' of how bread salesmen may successfully go about fiddling. My intention is not, then, to 'do' bread salesmen, but specifically to explain theoretically how 'fiddling' (which is a criminal offence) can simultaneously be 'fiddling' (that is, practically and psychologically trifling). I have accordingly devoted analytic attention towards describing those general social processes by which a group of men can simultaneously break the criminal law, and yet fully believe themselves to be ordinary, good citizens. I will concentrate, then, upon exposing the nature of the 'enabling processes' (Rogers and Buffalo, 1974, p. 112) through which salesmen may simultaneously stay 'good' and yet deviate.

To do this, I have tried to relay the experiences of those studied (very strictly speaking) as *ordinary* ones. I have attempted to lodge the analysis spiritually somewhere between the inhuman accounts so often found in criminological literature, and the subhuman ones given by journalists. It is useful if, as Glaser and Strauss (1967, p. 3) have suggested, theorising grounded in specific empirical material should be 'readily understandable to sociologists of any viewpoint, to students, and to significant laymen'.

The aim is not categorically to type a new crime or criminal. It is rather to illustrate the utterly confusing normality with which the criminal enterprise can sometimes be clothed. In so doing, one learns not so much about 'them' (or even, come to that, about the rest of 'us') but that such divisions are false. I have tried to understand the fiddling salesman qua person, and not qua fiddler.

But how can I do this in a way that preserves their ordinariness? One way would be to write a novel. Consider, for example, Solzhenitsyn's (1968) 'day in the life of' treatment of the prisoner, or Bukowski's (1973) amazingly funny yet achingly serious description of twelve years as a postman.

Regrettably, the analytic version of this, which Lofland (1974, p. 104) calls the unframed 'then they do this' eclectic catalogue of vaguely assorted anecdotes, is rudely organised theory masquerading as pure ethnography. True or false, to believe that this style contains less theory (than 'analysis') is similar to the belief that some days display less weather than others! Theory, like weather, is a zero sum concept: it cannot be more or less there, only more or less recognised and reordered. Naked experience is strictly unpresentable as it stands, it has to be theorised in order to be communicated. Thus we are inevitably faced, as Rock (1973) astutely notices, with a programmatic tension between phenomenalism (naturalistic reproduction – ethnography) and essentialism (depicting fundamental social processes – analysis). Even description of the deviant world cannot proceed very far if solely based on constructs derived from that world. Perversely, this theoretical impossibility of producing pure ethnography legitimates the overt celebration of theory-impregnation. It is useless to pretend to produce pure ethnography: one might as well come clean and admit to producing a 'theorised ethnography'.

In producing such a consciously theorised ethnography of salesmen, I have followed the rule of grounding the interpretation of fiddling as an 'Everyman Performance'. That is, I have tried to depict sufficient conditions for a reasonable man to consider fiddling to be, under the circumstances, a rational performance. This specific rule is derived from the general axiom that an analysis which portrays a phenomenon as bizarre or strange has failed to understand that phenomenon. People never experience *their* worlds as bizarre or strange: they experience them as wholly ordinary. The bread salesman, as I have said (strange though it may seem to us), experiences his 'fiddling' as psychologically trifling. How on earth can he manage this? More importantly, how can analysis convey this experience? Bateson (1936, p. 1) offers the long-winded route:

If it were possible adequately to present the whole of a culture, stressing every aspect exactly, as it is stressed in the culture itself, no single detail would appear bizarre or strange or arbitrary to the reader, but rather the details would all appear natural and reasonable as they do to the natives who have lived all their lives within the culture.

Instead of presenting a whole culture, I have used the 'Everyman Performance' rule to render experience ordinary in key constitutive areas (socialisation, customer interaction, culture, role and motives) of bread salesmen's culture.

But in the absence of relevant empirical criteria of significance, it is a complex issue to assess whether or not the analysis which follows succeeds in making fiddling appear 'natural'. In all non-empiricist research of this nature, the analyst is faced with the procedural dilemma so astutely described by MacIntyre (1973, pp. 1–2). He asks how we are to decide whether or not an instance of a phenomenon is a counter-example, or not an example at all – a dilemma, I suggest, which inevitably arises when grounded theorising is coupled with analytic induction (as it is in this book):

> We use certain criteria to identify this or that as gold or as amino acid or a Christmas pudding. If certain characteristics are present and others absent, then this will suffice in all normal circumstances for the identification. But what if the standard criteria are satisfied and then it turns out that this otherwise normal gold emits radiation . . . or that this Christmas pudding talks? . . . Are we to say that this is not gold or not a Christmas pudding, or are we to say that we were mistaken about the properties of gold or of Christmas puddings?

This is an extraordinarily complex issue. In an attempt to avoid the pitfalls of ignoring it, I have attempted what Glaser (1965) calls the 'constant comparison' of ethnographic incidents, until it seemed that further research was merely bringing in repeated examples of empiri-cally the same matter. At this point, according to Glaser, the theoretical category in question is appropriately 'saturated'. I am not convinced that Glaser satisfactorily resolves the MacIntyre dilemma (or, indeed, that it is at all resolvable) and, rather than close any options, I have most probably over-quoted the experiences of the salesmen in the text. This seemed to be a wiser course than presenting a judiciously selected representative experience. The same dilemma arises again during theoretical work: are the typical socialising experiences of recruits to Wellbread's sufficiently similar to those of recruits elsewhere to warrant calling this experience a 'moral career'? Or, are the differences (which certainly exist) sufficiently great to warrant inventing a different theoretical tag? Further, should I say that it is not a 'moral career'? Or, perhaps, that it is a 'sub-type'? Or (finally) that this piece of research is sufficient evidence to change the definitive conditions establishing the presence of moral careers? Such questions can only be answered pro rata and ad hoc. This idiosyncratic decision is the theorist's contribution.

Grounding the interpretation of fiddling as an Everyman Performance involves the analyst in making what we might call the 'Hughes Assumption'. Hughes (1962, p. 25) asks what sense we can make of the involvement of the German people in the last war:

> How could such dirty work be done among and, in a sense, *by* the millions of ordinary, civilised German people? . . . You will see that there are two orders of questions. One set concerns the good people who did not themselves do this work. The other concerns those who did do it. But the two sets are not really separate; for the crucial question concerning the good people is their relation to the people who did the dirty work, with a related one which asks under what circumstances good people let the others get away with such actions. An easy answer concerning the Germans is that they were not so good after all. We can attribute to them some special inborn or ingrained race consciousness, combined with a penchant for sadistic cruelty and unquestioning acceptance of whatever is done by those who happen to be in authority . . . [but] I only want to close one easy way out of serious consideration of the problem of good people and dirty work, by demonstrating that the Germans were and are about as good and about as bad as the rest of us.

The concern is not merely to locate a context in which intelligibility for all the data can be found (although this is also the case); it is rather that we have to explain that good people do dirty work not because they are really bad people, but because, under the circumstances, dirty work is what good people do. Lemert's (1962) brilliant analysis of paranoia is a fine example of perfect analytic operation of the Hughes Assumption. Lemert delicately explains paranoia in such a way that both the accusations and feelings of paranoia become a wholly understandable Everyman Performance.

To operate the Hughes Assumption, we need to specify those social processes which may simultaneously allow successful infractions *and* permit the retention of the actor's societal 'goodness'. Of course, this is not a literally moral conception of good and neither, curiously, need the resulting analysis be empirically verifiable. Donald Cressey (1953) has successfully demonstrated embezzlement as an Everyman Performance. Following the recipes provided by Cressey would generate successful embezzlement without any infringement of the actor's moral societal status. Cressey certainly makes the activity 'reasonable': but can we, after Nettler (1974) add that *nevertheless*, it is empirically likely that embezzlement will occur for 'bad' (the traditional 'fast women and slow horses') rather than 'good' (Cressey's) reasons?

We may conclude that, whilst Cressey is certainly metaphorically correct, Nettler may well be literally so. However, metaphorical goodness (as a programmatic goal for research) serves to justify conclusions which run counter to the practical badness and moral imperfection assumed by enforcement agents and enforcement sociologists. I hope to do for the fiddler what (albeit in a different way) Cressey did for the embezzler. The assumption is that one's subjects are good: I have made it of the salesmen.

The analysis looks first, in Chapter 2, at the 'moral career' of the recruit salesman (how he is taught to fiddle), and then, in Chapter 3, at the everyday occupational structural support for fiddling which can be derived from the social context of 'service'. Chapter 4 looks briefly at the wider industrial and economic context of occupational theft, and at forms of 'part-time' crime at Wellbread's. Chapter 5 examines Wellbread's, to see how the salesmen seem to combine possible theft types in a 'portfolio' of techniques, the practice of which under the guise of one of variously available 'characters' protects their identities both practically and psychologically. Chapter 6 looks at the salesmen's motives and considers the effect that occasions of enforcements have on these 'partial' identities. Chapter 7 normatively locates fiddling as a subterranean subculture of 'business' itself and concludes with an examination of the type of deviance that 'part-time' crimes represent.

2 Process: Becoming a Fiddler

How do salesmen, from being naïve recruits, become adept and experienced fiddlers? To answer this question satisfactorily, we need to specify those conditions under which such a change might sound *reasonable*. But to what conditions could fiddling be a normal response?

Some measure of sympathy for fiddlers emerges from a consideration of their harsh employment conditions. For a six-day week, with some work days of over fourteen hours, salesmen are paid a very low salary, coupled with commission earnings for passing individual sales targets and bonus earnings for good sales records during special competitions. This structure produced an average salary (in the research summer of 1973) of £32.50 per week. On top of this, each salesman is held personally responsible for ensuring that the cash collected by him from his customers satisfactorily matches the value of the goods he takes out. To check up on this, the girls in the Wellbread's sales office prepare a weekly account for each man, called a 'reconciliation' sheet or 'rec.' sheet. The threat of deductions from the wage packets of those whose verdict is that they are 'short' of the required sum is used to back up the rule that accounts should balance. If the verdict falls on the credit side however, 'overs' are theoretically transferred to balance other accounts which are short. Each salesman has an individual page in the sales manager's 'big book' (where these transfers are made), and weekly verdicts are systematically recorded there, providing a cumulative running total of each man's financial 'biography'. Because the salesmen do not have sophisticated means of checking these calculations, they have no realistic option but to accept them. As one man commented sadly:

> They've got you by the short and curlies, and there's nothing you can do . . . look, in the office, they allow 'private' discounts that we're not supposed to know about . . . how can we check that? . . . all the discounts vary from shop to shop . . . sometimes, it's 12 per cent, sometimes 12½ per cent, sometimes 15 per cent, 22½ per cent . . . too

complex to keep track of . . . you haven't got the time to do it for a start, and you haven't got the facilities for another . . . then there's credits and extras, and returns, and shorts . . . how do you know there isn't a mistake?

The salesman is thus responsible for the financial destiny of his accounts in areas where he has neither access nor control. On top of this, in signing an employment 'contract' with the firm on entry, most men believe that deductions from the wage packet are legally enforceable. Such an employment structure might beg a more basic question than why employees begin to fiddle. Why do they join the firm in the first place?

Essentially, recruits join the firm because they are deliberately misled over basic job conditions and they are deluded into thinking that they will be able to avoid making mistakes. Why don't they leave when they discover the realities of sales life? Crucially, truthful information is only released to recruits in stages marked by increasing degrees of commitment of the new man to the organisation. Sales supervisors are responsible for ensuring that gradual corruption of the recruit nicely balances the extent of his bond to the firm. It is hoped that, by the time the newcomer realises quite what is expected of him, it will be digestible, and that any lingering doubts about the propriety of sales life will be dissolved by his increased commitment to the organisation.

In short, whilst learning the job, the recruit is gradually made aware of the fact that 'mistakes' (responsibility for which he has already agreed to) and thus 'shortages' are inevitable. Once low pay and long hours have become a reality for him, he is considered to be morally and technically ready for a demonstration that both problems may be solved by overcharging customers. For most men, the relief at finding a solution dilutes any remaining moral qualms, and many go on from here to make money for themselves in ways not explicitly accepted by the firm.

The processes of transformation of naïvety into sophistication rely upon successful absorption by the recruit of two operational premises of the Wellbread sales department. Firstly, that the department must make a *profit* (the sum of individual weekly accounts must not be in the red); and secondly, the occupational belief that the processes of converting bread into money are fraught with inevitable *mistakes* disadvantaging the department (customers are believed to be less likely to report mistakes to their advantage, than they are those obviously otherwise).

The sales department therefore requires its employees to 'fiddle' customers (and return fiddled income to the firm) to balance the contradiction between profit-requirement and mistake-inevitability. On top of this, recruitment is expensive (so recruits must both be brought to peak efficiency quickly and encouraged to stay as long as possible) and labour turnover breeds a distinct loss of customer goodwill. The ongoing solution to these problems for the management is to encourage roundsmen to cover mistakes illegally by fiddling customers which, in turn, by removing their presumed worries about deductions from their wage-packets on account of shortages, decreases labour turnover. Needless to say, whilst the management admit the need for an inflow of fiddled income, they avoid assigning themselves full responsibility for such requirement. A senior supervisor felt he was merely channelling deviant motives in a commercially social direction. He said 'There's fiddles everywhere . . . it's like a rat, if you block the hole up, they'll find another one'. In a similar way, the supervisors who train new men define the situation as one where the organisation needs 'bent' employees, but that the organisation should do the bending over a period of time, with great care, and in such a way that the employee thus bent will stay with the firm. The same senior supervisor also said 'You always have to tell a man the tricks of the trade . . . there's always an easy way to do the job and, if there's a fiddle, it's a bad thing if the man finds out for himself'.

Thus, at Wellbread's, we are not faced with a conventional example of blue-collar occupational theft. Usually, employees either adopt illicit means to rob the organisation which employs them (see, e.g., Dalton, 1964) or they utilise occasions of managerial laxity and tolerance to steal from customers (see, e.g., Mars, 1974). At Well-bread's, we have a situation where institutional socialising arrangements are deliberately constructed to coach recruits to conspire efficiently in systematic theft. The intention of these practices is to rob customers regularly and invisibly on behalf of the company. These activities are not willingly engaged in by employees, but are instead a nice example of what Leonard and Weber (1970, p. 416) call 'coerced crime'.

In its simplest form, 'fiddling' is overcharging. The salesman regularly overcharges the customer as a way of exerting control in, and profit from, customer transactions. The first stage of the fiddle ('making' money) exploits the trustful basis of customer relations specifically built up for that purpose, with the talent and poise of the con-man. The second stage ('taking' the profit) is engineered with the delicate positional cover of the embezzler. The 'fiddle' is normally clothed in the protective fiction of the legitimate ritual sales activity which provides operational protection for the fiddler and illusive satisfaction for the consumer.

Fiddling is defined in greater detail in Chapter 4. Briefly, a 'fiddle' is a theft by a service agent from his customer which is practised in such a way as to make it interactionally and inventorily invisible. Theft from the firm by a salesman (irrespective of whether or not inventories have been altered to cover the loss) is either 'stealing', when openly individualistic, or 'dealing' when it also involves the subversion of other employees. The bakery management makes a crucial distinction between 'fiddling' (which they encourage) and 'stealing' and 'dealing' (which they make periodic attempts to stamp out). The managerial attitude, which helps to normalise the fiddle for the salesman, is reflected in their treatment of those caught out. When I asked a sales supervisor why men were sacked for 'fiddling', he said:

Who? Who gets fired for fiddling then? I've never known anybody get fired for fiddling since I've been here . . . can you name anybody? [I did] . . . Ah!, he wasn't caught for fiddling, was he? He was *stealing* . . . I know it sounds funny . . . [but] they don't care what you do in shops, as long as the sales are O.K., and you don't come short . . . that bloke [that I had mentioned] was taking it from Despatch, and that's an entirely different thing.

Salesmen occasionally find that they can fiddle with the full knowledge, and even co-operation, of the customer! For example, one salesman said:

Some of them don't care, one of my customers told me this summer that he had to add so much on to one of *his* customer's bills to cover what I fiddled him . . . so he obviously *knew* I was fiddling him, but he wasn't bothered, he passes the fiddle on.

Because the salesmen do not usually have to cope with the additional problems of others attempting to malign their characters, they do not have to reconstruct a private self in accord with drastic changes in their public identity. Every recruit is allocated a 'round' of customers, each with a history of customer-roundsman interactions specifically coloured with the biographies of successive departed salesmen. They discover a 'situated self' (Goffman, 1961a, p. 41) awaiting them in the expectations of these customers, reflecting our ability, as Mead (1934, p. 142) puts it, to: 'divide ourselves up in all sorts of different selves with reference to our activities'. This identity develops separately from the real 'me' that each man constructs out of work hours, and as an 'elementary self' is not aggregated with other moral experiences in the production of a 'complete' self. Thus, fiddling is an activity supported by the *part-time* self at work, and thus has auxiliary or *partial* (rather than master) status in the development of each man's identity. Supported in this way, fiddling has an occasional quality for the practitioner's psyche. As Becker (1968b, pp. 335–6) suggests, it only becomes *part* of a way of life:

> Their 'criminal' activities are not, for them, the one overriding fact about themselves which they must never forget, which they must always consider, no matter what they plan to do. Crime is, instead, just another of their many activities, exciting and daring for some, routine and commonplace for others . . . [he] expects, at the close of the day's activities to go about his normal business like any other citizen.

Fiddling is thus primary deviation (in the sense of its implications for the self) and the actions of controllers actively prevent, rather than explicitly seek, the usual development into secondary deviation.

But learning to fiddle does have one irreversible effect: once he has fiddled, the salesman can never look at the world in quite the same way again. He may stop fiddling, but he cannot stop *knowing* about it. As Strauss (1959, p. 92) puts it, 'a person *becomes* something other than he once was'. One cannot go back in time and, similarly, one cannot go back in self. Once an illegal activity has been tried and learned, then it is always 'on' for the actor to re-indulge. Matza (1969, p. 110) nicely anticipates this point, but fails to follow it up in his discussion of the initial 'invitational edge' of deviance. It seems that the naïve actor is faced with a dilemma: the disjunction between his secondary, mediated and evilly stereotyped conception of the activity, and his primary, actual and ordinary invitation to indulge in it lodges him temporarily in an 'initial participation quandary'. Ironically, the blacker the stereotype, the *less* likely is it that the actor will identify the activity at hand as an example. In fact, if this 'quandary' *is* resolved in the direction of participation, then the actor (if he is to remain 'good') will either have to define the act as not-an-example of the stereotype, or the stereotype as not-accurate-on-this-occasion. At the bakery (as is the case with most alter-directed moral careers), arrangements are made to commit the recruit towards participation in the fiddle before he has resolved the participation dilemma. This is done to indicate to him that he can easily cope with the psychological implications of infraction.

Thus the recruit may be thought to be embarking upon a special sort of occupational career in a context of increasing commitment to the organisation. What concern us here are the 'moral' aspects of this career, which Goffman (1959a, p. 119) defines as 'the regular sequence of changes that career entails in the person's self and in his framework of imagery for judging himself and others'. Learning to fiddle is a moral career ('a standard sequence of changes in his way of concerning of selves, including, importantly, his own' ibid.) not because it has anything to do with morality but because it takes account of the effects of training upon the self of the recruit. In fact, the notion of a moral career is used not only in discussions of deviant skill-acquisition and self-reconstruction areas (for example, Becker's 1963 discussions of the changes in self involved in 'becoming a marihuana user'), but also in the analyses of the rehabilitative construction of conformity from villainy (for example, Trice and Roman's 1969 discussions of the psychological 'comeback accomplishments' of reformed alcoholics). Once the specific sociological reference of the word 'moral' to the actor's self is grasped, it neither becomes possible nor necessarily desirable, with fiddling as with other careers, to attempt to disentangle completely moral from occupational career. But at Wellbread's, the two career strands are not merely coincidentally connected; the occupational 'career' of salesman acts as practical cover and public legitimation for the moral career as fiddler.

Of crucial importance in any moral career is the presence of *significant others* (the sales supervisor) and *institutional arrangements* (the 'round') which negotiate the chrysalis self-in-transition through the identity crisis of status passage. As Goffman (1959a, p. 138) puts it:

> The self arises not merely out of its possessor's interactions with significant others, but also out of the arrangements that are evolved in an organisation for its members.

Critically, moral careers infused with occupational necessities have three separable stages: *recruitment, learning* and *practice*. These reflect general properties of self-reconstitution as outlined by Van Gennep (1908) and Sarbin and Adler (1970). Processes of 'beginning' have to be initiated; skills have to be learnt to the level of 'passing'; and development of post-existential rebirth practice denotes 'becoming'.

For the neophyte salesman, the typical situation is that the recruitment and practice stages of the career are left more or less to chance, and the learning stage is excessively organised and over-institutionalised by the sales supervisors. The crucial learning stage commonly has four arranged characteristics. Firstly, because one is not born with the relevant skills, they have to be learnt. Skills, as such, are hard to learn in isolation and impossible to learn instantaneously. Here, since fiddling is not a legitimated role, there can be no 'anticipatory socialisation' (Merton in Goffman, 1959, p. 79) such as that which precedes the adoption of standard roles like father or husband. The fiddler's career learning path has to negotiate successfully 'contingencies' (the 'sack') and 'dangers' ('mistakes'), both of which are often productive of

Goffman's 'moral experiences' which act as bench-marks in the career of the salesman.

Secondly, status differences must be arranged and suitably publicised. At Wellbread's, a supervisor (in a blue coat) always accompanies a new man (wearing a brown coat) to each call. A display of such marginal role-signs is crucial if others are to interpret correctly any mistakes that the recruit makes as unintentional (in the sense of identifying him as an actor not yet at the stage of sophistication that would allow him to be capable of making a deliberate and malevolent mistake). Whilst the signs of passage ease the learning path, they simultaneously publicly disqualify the marginal member from making any accredited statements about reality. For the learner, things that he defines as real will *not* be real in their consequences, as his definitions will have to be demolished in order to 'accomplish' the superior status of the supervisor. For recruit salesmen, whilst training publicly declares their learner status, it only does so in a *general* sense. As far as the public is concerned, status-publication refers to occupational rather than moral training.

Thirdly, progress through status-change must be ceremonially ritualised and made routine (through 'tests' at the end of the three-week training session). Fourthly, progress must be balanced with carefully handled strains and tensions ('failure' and 'readiness') that occur at the turning points along the career line, where identity and the self are particularly frail. Whilst there are no real 'passing out' ceremonies for salesmen at Wellbread's, the sudden absence of an accompanying supervisor significantly changes a man's status in the eyes of his customers.

Recruits are always more susceptible to suggestion when trained singly, and at Wellbread's systematic corruption of employees is managed through careful chaperoning by individual supervisors. In addition to being serially- rather than cohort-managed, fiddlers at Wellbread's describe a moral career pattern which we may characterise as voluntarily undertaken, informationally subtle, initially intention-closed, Fagin-type, and alter-managed. This is so because the status change is voluntary (in the sense of being a social rather than physical change like ageing), initially participated in willingly by recruits. It is informationally subtle because information about fiddling is released almost imperceptibly (as it is in the moral training of both nudists, see Weinberg, 1966, p. 243, and relief masseuses, Velarde, 1975, p. 252 et seq.) and not in the form of formal indoctrination. The eventual career intentions are initially concealed from the recruit (compare recruit pickpockets in Maurer, 1955, pp. 158–62, who are conversely socialised on an 'open Fagin-type' pattern) and teachers and pupils are numerically in a one-to-one relationship – reminiscent of Fagin and Oliver Twist. It is, in common with most moral careers, alter-managed; that is, staged by an experienced hand.

The next part of this chapter describes (via amalgams of several cases) the possibilities of normative management of identity change. I do not just recite the bare ethnographic description of normal cases, but instead describe what Rock (1973a, p. 63) calls the 'basic career' of the learner. Ordinarily successful novices become, in sequence: prospects; applicants; interviewees; recruits; novices; roundsmen and salesmen.

THE PRE-TRAINING STAGE: BECOMING A RECRUIT

Election to pre-training status is a necessary condition of, but not the first step in, the moral career. In fact, the essence of pre-selection procedures is rejection of the unsuitable, rather than selection of the suitable. The conditions of entry may thus be conceived of as a 'funnel' (Lofland, 1966, p. 31). In other words, 'a structure which systematically reduces the number of persons who can be considered available for recruitment and at the same time specifies who is available'. However, the entry funnel is not systematically institutionalised by the Wellbread's management, although they use both what Lofland calls 'direct disembodied' (newspaper advertisements) and 'indirect disembodied' (reputation for vacancies) recruitment channels. Of course, Wellbread's can publicly advertise vacancies only by referring to the occupational side of the proposed career. Similarly during training itself general signs are substituted for actual indicators of specific marginality. The embryonic fiddler might have symbolic 'L' plates, but he doesn't have 'trainee fiddler' emblazoned on his coat. In this respect, other occasions of moral training which share this particular oblique feature often use what we may refer to as the 'coy advertisement'. Employers advertise for, and potential employees apply for, a nicely worded euphemism of the actual job. Skipper and McCaghy (1969, p. 400) admit that many strippers initially applied for jobs as 'show girls' or 'exotic dancers' only to find that a little more show than was estimated, or rather more exotic dancing than was anticipated, is in fact required. Velarde (1975, p. 252) notes that many women at one time naïvely applied for jobs advertised as masseuses, and that:

> During the initial interview, the owner did not disclose any of the sexual activities associated with the job, his reluctance being due to strict soliciting laws. One owner started off by telling applicants that 'customers are going to be expecting you to jack them off!'. He was quickly arrested for soliciting a woman to perform a lewd act. The

owner's grapevine used this event for a rationale for evading that topic in subsequent discussions with the masseuse as to what was expected of her. An owner said 'I don't do things that can get me busted . . . I wouldn't tell a masseuse to give locals – that's soliciting. Let someone else tell her, like her first John [customer]'.

For the Wellbread salesman, prospective entry is classically 'adventitious' (Sherlock and Cohen, 1966) – spontaneous, fortuitous, and based upon situational pressure and contingency – a sort of random circulation within the ranks of the industrially dissatisfied. One man claimed; 'I just took the first job that came along, I just took it for the money at the time . . . I saw it in the paper'. Several others suggested that they just went down to the bakery 'on the off chance' and some remembered that they had 'heard that Wellbread's wanted blokes'. One man's reminiscence exhibited the classic random pattern:

I got stood off from the building, and I went up to Wellbread's and the Creamy Dairy about jobs . . . they both offered me one, starting the Monday, the dairy at 6 a.m., and the bakery at 6.30 a.m. . . . I thought 'Which shall I take? Milk or bread?' . . . and then I thought 'I'll go to Wellbread's, it's nearer'.

At the application stage, many prospects are rejected by unwittingly demonstrating character blemishes (like long or dirty fingernails and hair) or career stains (like a previous job with a higher wage than the applicant would get at Wellbread's). Those who get an interview get given what Brim and Wheeler (1966, p. 85) call the 'guided tour'. For the sales management, entry is a practical question of how to manage the advance preparation in such a way as to increase the probability of a successful outcome. The recruit, on the other hand, is denied any control of entry and merely participates symbolically whilst decisions are made about him and for him. Thus the interviewer paints for the candidate a jolly but fictional picture of sales life, often merely filling out the conventional delusion they attach to their usual newspaper recruitment advertisements:

IS THE OUTDOOR LIFE FOR YOU? If so, leave that stuffy indoor job behind and join the happy, healthy outdoor team of Wellbread's salesmen who daily tour our delightful town and countryside.

Simultaneously, however, seedy reality may be mentioned to weed out those with a vastly over-optimistic conception of life at Wellbread's. The manager, for example, thought that support for the local football team was a crucial test which disqualified the applicant because he would not be prepared to surrender his Saturday afternoons. A senior supervisor indicated:

> If I had to interview a man for the job . . . I would spend at least half an hour telling him the worst points, and then ask him if he's still interested . . . tell him about shortages, what he comes up against, there's a lot of snags in the job . . . shorts, the weather, the hours.

This ambiguity in the content of the 'guided tour' derives from the organisational rule to take on only those who display a certain 'worldliness' (a paradoxical state lying somewhere between righteousness and crookedness). The morally ideal applicant is one who is both good, and yet sufficiently worldly to be persuaded to go bad (to fiddle) in organisationally preferred directions. Thus the key assumption of socialisation at Wellbread's is that recruits are not initially willing or able to fiddle. Suspicion lingers around those who seem over-eager to fiddle, or who do so too early. One senior supervisor complained:

> You will always have the chaps who are out to make a bomb out of it . . . they kill the goose that laid the golden egg . . . the majority of them would do it whatever phase of life they're in, for the sort of person who's going to do this, he's going to do it from the word 'go' . . . the corruption is there in the mind every time, we don't corrupt people, we try to put them off, or warn them not to overdo it.

But any interview can be fixed. Most of the applicants who have got this far have done so elsewhere many times before. One successful candidate recalled how he had dealt with the manager's 'test':

> His main concern seemed to be 'If you like football, the job's no good to you' . . . although I was a footballer, I didn't tell him I watched it, and I was still playing.

The fiddle is never mentioned to candidates. Instead, fictional rewards like 'high commission' are offered. As one man recalled: ' *Then*, I was a goody-goody, a little honest, innocent little boy, I didn't know no tricks . . . no, I was just an innocent little boy . . . 20 years old.' This stratagem firstly 'cons' the man into accepting a position in the organisation (the fiction may be maintained until well into training, in fact, until the time is ripe for tuition in the fiddle). Secondly, it provides the recruit with an organisational memory separating the management from the fiddle, from which he can later select recollections to substantiate the organisational need for the denial of managerial complicity.

B

Abruptly, if selected, he will find that encounters designed to invalidate and dismiss him change to those intended to commit him.

TRAINING: BECOMING A ROUNDSMAN

During the initial stages of training, the supervisor concentrates on method and technique. Initially, the recruit has to demonstrate willingness and ability to be a learner and not a practitioner. The first 'test' for the recruit salesman is a preparedness to adopt a strict-rule model of action. As Goffman (1961a, p. 82) notes, a main part of the neophyte role centres upon over-emphasis of the prescriptive aspects of the final role. There is a ritual requirement that the recruit 'prove his competence, sincerity, and awareness of his place, leaving the showing of distance from a role to a time and place when he is firmly "validated" in that role'.

Exhibiting a similar socialisation rhetoric, Bensman and Gerver (1963, p. 591) describe the unnecessarily extended processes of accommodating novices to illicit use of the 'tap' in an aircraft factory. The 'tap' is a hard steel screw, officially outlawed in the factory, but widely used by employees to realign nuts and plate openings distorted in the assembly of aircraft:

> To most workers entering an aircraft plant, the tap is an unknown instrument . . . The new worker does not come into contact with the tap until he finds it impossible to align the holes . . . In desperation . . . he turns to his partner [a more experienced worker] and states his problem. The experienced worker will try every legitimate technique . . . [then] he resorts to the tap. He taps the new thread himself, not permitting the novice to use the tap. While tapping it he gives the novice a lecture on the dangers of getting caught. For several weeks the older worker will not permit his inexperienced partner to use a tap when its use is required. He leaves his own work in order to do the required tapping . . . if the novice demonstrates sufficient ability and care in other aspects of his work he will be allowed to tap the hole under supervision.

Successful judgements of competence in the strict-rule role allows the supervisor to introduce the learner salesman to intricacies and short cuts. Only when the neophyte can be defined as having absorbed and having 'served his time' obeying the strict rules will he be allowed to temper negotiation of situations with 'good sense'.

All moral careers reflect the tutor's search in the neophyte for some evidence of the particular career 'sense'. Supervisors search trainees at Wellbread's for indications of 'sales sense', which is ultimately the interpreted presence of sales-conducive personality characteristics. Supervisors either do or do not believe in the existence of 'sales sense', but in any case concur that it is neither teachable nor communicable. Teaching is instead a mystical 'bringing out' of such abilities. Like 'news sense' (Rock, 1973c, p. 74), 'grift sense' (Maurer, 1955) and 'larceny sense' (Sutherland, 1937, p. 214), 'sales sense' is believed innate, and judgements of its presence are fateful for recruits.

Although the training stage may have many substages, there is, firstly, a *public exhibition of marginality*, so that others may make suitable 'allowances'. Customers who are aware of the dramatic niceties of everyday sales life will thus be able to exhibit some tact in handling the new performer. This marginality is acknowledged as temporary, and is seen as a passing status, i.e. one to which only short term adaptation need be made by customers.

Secondly, *responsibility and liability for outcomes is temporarily suspended*. Strauss (1959, p. 104) suggests that this period of tolerance is a structural necessity, and is often enacted by phrasing trials in a rhetoric of 'make believe' or 'not for keeps', wherein performance is not recorded in the dramatic 'biography' of the novice. Such suspension of reality is not merely to absolve the newcomer from liability for his actions, but also constitutes a mutual discovery phase for both parties, who withhold full involvement in the joint construction of interpersonal change until satisfactory mutual understanding is achieved. These themes of both marginality and tolerance are summed up by Goffman (1961a, pp. 91–2):

> When an individual is first wakening to his role, he will be allowed to approach his tasks diffidently, an excuse and an apology already on his lips. At this time he is likely to make many otherwise discreditable mistakes, for this time he has a learner's period of grace in which to make them, a period in which he is not quite the person he will shortly be, and, therefore, cannot badly damage himself by the expression of maladroit actions . . . This temporary licence . . . [may be] institutionalised . . . [but] for a while it is possible to say that the [trainer's] role makes allowances for maladroitness in beginners.

Novices in the sales department are often verbally prepared for this status. One man remembered:

> Any mistakes I made, well, he said to me 'Any mistakes you make . . . we'll leave it for a month or so until it settles down' . . . more or less saying that if you can't get it right within a month, that's your own fault.

The actual staging of the fiddler transformation follows a rhetorical form typical of all moral careers. An existential death/rebirth cycle typified by, as Goffman (1961a, p. 155) puts it: 'alienation and mortification followed by a new set of beliefs about the world and a new way of conceiving of selves'. At Wellbread's, this pattern emerges in two stages: firstly, one of chaperoned mortification and alienation; and secondly, a short period of tension swiftly followed by self-transformation through the 'fiddle'.

Initially, the first stage of chaperoned mortification and alienation produces a tyrannising regime of *demonstrations* and *trials*. Generally, the demonstration and trial period of training absorbs only the first week of training at Wellbread's, but the period may be extended until a satisfactory assessment of technical readiness can be made. The sales manual recommends that supervisors explain 'easily, step by step', and a supervisor explained to me what this meant:

> The whole idea is to get the bloke to know where he's going, that's the main thing, you do this the first week, and try and sort of familiarise him with the procedure, the bread . . . yeah, the first week, I just have the chap follow me.

At first, then, concern is with technical issues. Most experienced men recall that in the early stages of training all they thought about was learning the bewildering number of types and prices of bread, cake, confectionery and biscuit, avoiding getting lost on the route, and mastering the complex ordering procedures at the depot. In the first week, one man remembered of his supervisor that 'all he taught me was where to go', and another, that 'I was just acting as a passenger really'.

Mortification, as the deliberate disorganisation and disorientation of the victim in order to make him more susceptible to moral reinterpretations of action, begins here. The novice begins to worry about his performance in what has been described to him as a perfect system. A salesman admitted:

> I was a bit nervous at first, I was nervous about meeting people, I'd never done the job before. I hadn't done the knocking on doors to women and that . . . and the moans and groans that some of them come up with . . . it was strange. I thought 'Christ! I wonder if I'll be able to add up?' . . . I was worried about what the job was going to be like, I didn't want not to be any good at it, I didn't want to be a fool.

At this point, supervisors concentrate upon providing reassurance. However, they have to balance technical resuscitation with a curious form of moral strangulation. As two supervisors explained, the strict-rule model is over-emphasised:

> Well, when you train a person, he should always carry a basket . . . I don't still carry a basket to the door, I would tell *you* that . . . but if I was training a man I wouldn't say that, I don't think you should do, I would say: 'Take the basket to *every* door' . . . but after a while he's not going to, is he?

> On the first week, I always drag a man out, I always fuck about, talk to people, and stop for about three cups of tea, so we probably come rolling into the bakery when it's getting dark, and the bloke thinks 'Bloody hell! this job is going to be terrible', and if the bloke's one of those who wants to finish at 2 p.m. every day, he'll give his notice in then.

A general process, the 'fictional rerun', is involved here. The fictional rerun is an elaborately stage-managed replay of the set of connected steps which, if put in their logically occurring sequence, lead the disbeliever through the preferred stages of an organisational rationale. It is explicitly enacted to ensure long term belief in the preferred outcome rather than mere slavish and short term obedience to and practice of it. Supervisors who lead novice salesmen through examples of those formal occasions (the formally rational solution to which would, if annotated in their logical sequence, lead *any* rational actor towards reasonable adoption of the fiddle) typically experience greater success in training than those who baldly announce the necessity to fiddle. Since, alas, it would be inappropriate (for reasons of maintaining continuity of price to individual customers) to allow recruits *actually* to experience this sequence of steps, the 'rerun' for fiddlers is necessarily 'fictional'. A supervisor explained the difficulty of temporarily abandoning the fiddle in order to educate the novice:

> I've gone to the door, and the woman says 'Here's the money for the small loaf, Baker', and she puts 7½p in my hand, and I've known that it's only 7p . . . but I've looked in the route book, and I've seen '7½p' marked right through it, so it's put me in a very embarrassing position, what do I do? If I tell the woman it's only 7p, what happens? . . . the new bloke has lost a customer, she's not going to think of the one halfpenny saved, but of all the other halfpennies she's lost in the past.

As Goffman (1974, p. 64) nicely notes, practice sessions are likely to involve a higher concentration of varied difficulties and mock emergencies than 'real life', making practice paradoxically harder than the real thing. Although the supervisor is fiddling the customer whilst the 'fictional rerun' is in play (for the good organisational reasons of profit and mistake), the novice is too busy to notice. One man recalled that the supervisor had been 'too quick' for him to 'pick up what he was saying', and another claimed: 'At the beginning of the job, when you start, you're sort of dim in a sense, when the job is new, and you don't sort of know anything else'.

When demonstrations become trials, it is both inevitable and essential that the novice 'latches on' to something. Sometimes the supervisor drops his guard and information about the fiddle 'slips out' (as one man put it). On other occasions, experienced salesmen take novices aside, and explain the facts of sales life to them. Alternatively, the novice may notice that the supervisor eats cake without paying for it, or is not so scrupulous with company cash as he has taught the novice to be. Two men recounted how the fiddle 'dawned' on them:

As we went round, I gradually took a bit more interest, and thought 'Well, there *are* fiddles in this', I *reckoned* there were before . . . [but] I was dim from the start, I just followed him round and, on the third day, I carried the basket up to the door, and he did all the money . . . it wasn't until the third day that I realised he was adding it on.

I didn't know he was doing it, until he got back into the cab . . . that was only because I counted it . . . I *twigged it*, but he hadn't told me, I thought 'Christ! that's a rum one, he's booked that, and we only had this amount of bread on'.

This process of latching on outmodes the earlier strict rules: latching on is a crucial turning point in the process of learning the fiddle. As one salesman put it:

Well, shortages, that was the thing to start with . . . he always seemed to be on about it at first, even if you wanted something to eat, off the van, he used to say 'You'll have to put that in', or something like that . . . I did to start with, but not after I caught him not doing it.

Although now judged as ready to transcend occupational basics, the recruit is not yet morally ready nor sufficiently committed for full disclosure of the fiddle system. If the novice gets a glimpse of things too early, then the fiddle will be denied. One man remembered that his supervisor 'didn't tell me about it, not at first, he just said to add a penny or a halfpenny on, he didn't tell me too much about it'.

The most likely outcome at the present stage is postponement of full understanding until the recruit is more heavily committed to the organisation. Typically, postponement is achieved by the instructor *side-tracking, stalling,* or using *joking references* to pave the way to smooth transition into the next stage:

> What happened with —— [a supervisor], we went to a call, I went with him, but he done the call, and when he wrote it in the book, I was watching to see . . . I was watching to see how he wrote it in the book . . . and I noticed he put the wrong price in . . . [laugh] . . . and I said to him 'That's the wrong price' . . . you know, green that I was, I said 'I'm sure you've put too much down there' . . . and he said 'I'll tell you about that later'.

> When I took the round over, all the farmhouse loaves were extra, a penny extra, I think, yeah, old Dick, who'd been on there for years had been doing it . . . the supervisor kept that one actually, he did explain to me, he said 'That's old Dick's doing, we'll carry it on'.

> I realised it because on the Friday, at the Post Office, I made the order up, and I noticed that he'd booked more than they had had, but when I queried it, he just said: 'You'll learn later on' . . . and as we went round, I gradually took a bit more interest, and thought 'Well, there are fiddles in this' . . . I *reckoned* that there were before, but it wasn't until that day, that I realised that he was adding it on, and he said 'You'll learn later on' . . . I was puzzled, it looked as if I'd made the order up wrong, but he wasn't going to tell me, that was his only comment.

> Introduce it as a joke, that's the best way, you can't say to a new bloke 'You've got to be a twisting bleeder to do this job' can you? . . . yes, you can always make a joke out of it, when you're doing the booking, you say: 'That's so-and-so, and so-and-so, plus a bit for VAT' . . . and pass it off as a joke.

Technical readiness produces occupational shock in novices not yet morally ready to absorb new meaning. However, organisational routine demands that this shock be so managed that it does not interfere with commercial life. Supervisors carefully chaperone their recruits through the latching-on experience. Judgements of character and ability are made, and sometimes specifically tested. Sometimes what Goffman (1974, p. 96) calls the 'training hoax' is used. Here, the neophyte is treated as though he was engaging reality directly, although in fact he is later informed that he was insulated from the world he thought he was contacting. At Wellbread's, one of the supervisors said:

> Eventually, one day, I'll stay with him to start with, and then I'll say 'Oh, I've got to go round the corner and see a customer', and

let him get on with it. And if you come back and the bloke is sweating and shaking, you know he's not ready for it . . . on the other hand . . . if he's further ahead than you thought he would be, you know he's got the idea and you let him have one day completely on his own.

If suitable judgements of *technical grasp* can be made, then *organisational commitment* must also be engendered. Moral must be added to technical readiness. Usually as novices begin to articulate basic routines with panache, they may give the supervisor the impression that they are 'over-ready'. Goffman (1961a, p. 83) notes that this is a form of role-distancing designed to demonstrate publicly that one is about to abandon a lesser status. However, the life of the novice must be so arranged that, upon raw discovery of the fiddle, neither organisational solvency nor customer routines will be upset unnecessarily. Becker (1960, pp. 267–8) calls this the process of making side bets:

A person finds that his involvement in social organisation has, in effect, made side bets for him and thus constrained his future activity . . . A person often finds that side bets have been made for him by the operation of impersonal bureaucratic arrangements.

When a side bet is made on behalf of an individual, it is a trap. At Wellbread's, supervisors conspire to engender decisive allegiance of the recruit's self *against* either leaving the firm or practising honesty. Negative commitment is created by unwitting collaboration in the fiddle by the recruit which, apart from convincing him that it can be done successfully, attempts to persuade him that he has less to lose by continuing than by stopping. This sort of intimidation is more important than positive commitment, as it is hoped that through it the newcomer will form a positive attachment to the benefits that are obtained. Of course, it is not always successful. But although the 'straight' may become more determined in his honesty, he will experience less and less *shock* as more and more of the game is revealed to him. The straight, then, *is* transformed in a similar way to most other recruits. In addition, though, he makes the hard decision not to practice what he has learned.

Recruit salesmen at Wellbread's are encouraged to increase their commitment in stages. In fact, the subtle side bet is often indistinguishable from the early stages of fiddler training. Supervisors often offer neophytes cakes en route, and a loaf 'for yourself' at the end of the day. During my first training week, when the supervisor and I ate an apple pie from the van, he said 'Remind me to declare it as "waste" at the end of the week'. When we had a packet of biscuits, he winked and said

'Remind me to check that the last bloke didn't put these down on his stock!'. The recruit becomes implicated by unreported association before a point of reportable clarity is reached.

At Wellbread's, a financial side bet is also often made:

> I never let a chap handle the cash the first week, because we've had too much trouble with these blokes who help themselves to the money . . . so I always wait until we've got enough money, until he's a week in hand, so if anything happens, they don't come up to me and complain.

The company hopes quickly to establish a psychological bond between the novice and the organisation and the threat of insufficient attachment is contradicted and documented in the employment 'contract'. One man told me:

> You need a bond, you see, you need a reference, and they always give you a bad one here . . . they try to keep the blokes that way, you see? . . . they're always saying things like 'I've only got to snap my fingers outside the door twice, and we'll have fifteen blokes up here after your job'.

The sales manager privately agreed that the 'contract' was just a gambit. He said 'Mind you, it isn't worth the paper it's printed on, but it's . . . persuasive'. Once there is perceived commitment, the path is clear to proceed to establish success at the next stage: that of 'moral readiness'. When this hurdle has been surmounted and acceptance offered, the recruit will be pushed into the second part of the mortification stage and taught what Becker and Strauss (1956) refer to as 'crucial trade secrets'.

Demonstrations and trials soon cease to mortify, and are then replaced by an *introduction to inefficiencies*. Ideally, this stage should be reached by the second week of salesman training at Wellbread's. The recruit is now ready for alienation precipitated by gradual awareness of structural deficiencies in the selling process. Until now, the supervisor has been coping with these problems invisibly. Of crucial significance to his moral career progress is the way that the learner discovers, firstly, the inevitability of uncorrectable mistakes (until now, he has only been tutored in avoiding correctable mistakes). Two supervisors explained to me:

> When you're adding up a load of figures, *everybody* makes mistakes, so you're going to lose a few coppers here and there . . . this is the best way to explain it to a chap.

Look, if you get a mathematician from the London School of Economics to try it, I guarantee that he won't come right . . . it's an impossibility.

A second crucial discovery for the learner is his *accountability* for any shortages in his 'round' account. One man said:

He said that I'd have to pay shortages and things like that, and I thought: 'Christ! I don't want to come short in the money'.

What is being pointed out to the new man here is not merely that for the time being his mistakes will be tolerated but, more importantly, that these mistakes are inevitable *and* will continue to occur long after the conclusion of the period of tolerance. As soon as these two points have been digested, the supervisor manoeuvres the roundsman into situations where it is likely he will 'catch on' to the *full* meaning of the fiddle. Whilst he copes with these problems, the supervisor precipitates a tense stage of identity crisis for the learner. Now he fully realises the situation, is he prepared to fiddle? Most men find this decision awkward, one said:

It shocked me at the time, he didn't tell me *why* we had to do it, not really, I knew it wasn't O.K., but it *was* . . . I'd never done it before, never.

This period of shock is a crucial socialisation limbo. If the learner wishes to stay with the firm, he must emerge as a fully fledged fiddler. How do the supervisors manage this identity crisis?

The second stage of the death/rebirth cycle begins here: a short bout of tension, abruptly followed by self-transformation through the 'fiddle'. The novice salesman has learnt techniques, methods and problems. He now has to put them all together, and arrive at the organisationally correct meaning. Recruits experience strains at this point (should they stay with a deceitful set of moral standards, or leave with standards intact? How should they psychologically cope with the knowledge that the supervisor is not the model of rectitude he once appeared to be?). No amount of careful chaperoning can wholly obliterate the 'moral experience' of fiddle discovery (together with the sense of personal turning point which it breeds). Typical misalignment – 'surprise, shock, chagrin, anxiety, tension, bafflement, self-questioning' (Strauss, 1959, p. 93) – soon fades as a swift succession of practical experiences prompts case-hardening. Most of the men *did* experience shock (one said 'that *did* shock me at the time, he told me to do it if I wanted to cover shortages') although this is normally resolved with only a little residual guilt. As one man put it:

It *used* to worry me in case I might get caught sometimes . . . when I first started, I was hesitant whether to do it or not . . . I was a bit scared . . . really the fear of getting caught . . . although I don't think nothing of it . . . really, that's nasty . . . I don't feel guilty about it now, although it still strikes me as a bit immoral.

Supervisors deliberately engineer interaction so that the recruit experiences these dilemmas in their presence, thus becoming highly suggestible to any proffered meaning. By now, the supervisor has become the main significant 'other' in the occupational life of the novice. The supervisor's 'answers' thus gather psychological weight precisely at the time when the recruit experiences the need for information and moral reassurance. Recruits are encouraged to ask questions as a means of calming the deliberately induced crisis of psychological status. A supervisor explained both the wrong, and then the right way of 'explaining':

Yeah, I made a big mistake with him [a trainee who left] . . . I just told him what we were doing, I put it to him that if he was short, he was responsible . . . and if it couldn't be found in mistakes in charges, it would be assumed that he'd taken the money, that he'd had the money out, and he'd lose it out of his wages . . . but, *this* is the way you *should* do it . . . you've got to get him on your side, you say 'I know how to get round that' . . . you give them the problem first, if you don't, they think it's money in their pockets . . . having explained that, I say 'Well, there *is* a way round it, providing you don't make a fool of yourself, or try to be greedy . . . there *are* customers, who don't check what they have, and by adding a couple of pence on, you can cover yourself, for any shorts you might have'.

The correct sequence of discovery is crucial. What counts is that the organisationally preferred meaning of fiddling will not appear to the newcomer until he has experienced its use as applied to some organisational problems, and reconsidered himself in his original light, and in relation to himself as a practitioner. It is also hoped that the resulting dishonesty will be practical and limited to stealing from customers. But although mortification can be established, and then immediately replaced by rewards and privileges, the final step lies with the candidate. Whilst the public doubting of the efficacy that the recruit brings to work increases the attractiveness of the means offered for self-reassembly, what counts (and Matza (1969, p. 122) puts it brilliantly) is what happens then: 'Accordingly, *he makes up his mind*, literally'.

Naturally, the supervisor has to convey the information about fiddling obliquely. To inoculate themselves against whistle blowers (novices also might report the fiddle), the arts of fiddling must be taught with an existentially aloof wink. In this way, the worker 'soon learns which message he is supposed to hear' (Becker, 1968b, p. 331). When I was being trained, a customer once refused a loaf, and we had to take it back to the van. The supervisor charged the loaf to her account and then said to me 'She's paid for that loaf'. He winked at me and added 'Well, you know what to do in future, don't you? . . . Don't say I told you though, I don't want to know anything about it'. A salesman remembered:

> Well, I personally was told, that the supervisor didn't want to know, the supervisor who was on with me, told me he didn't want to know anything about it.

The recruit's possession of knowledge of the fiddle amounts to a permanent *transformation*. William James (1902, pp. 198–9) defines a transformation in the following way:

> Our ordinary alterations of character, as we pass from one of our aims to another, are not commonly called transformations, because each of them is so rapidly succeeded by another in the reverse direction; but whenever one aim grows so stable as to expel definitely its previous rivals from the individual's life, we tend to speak of the phenomenon, and perhaps to wonder at it, as a 'transformation'.

For the roundsman, information denial swiftly transforms into information dumping. This is accompanied by a tension-relieving bout of demonstration, a phase common to most illicit moral careers. As two salesmen put it, supervisors become suddenly willing to offer frank and open descriptions of the fiddle:

> On the second week, we carried on the same way, but between calls, he'd tell me things like 'This one's an easy push, so naturally, the more cakes you push there, the more money you can make' . . . and he said 'If she's got a bill of 75p, push it up to 83½p, so it's not an even round figure, because they might think that there's an odd half there.

> Yeah, the prices were up on this round, and I said 'Well, why is this?', and he said 'If you don't charge over the price, you'll always be coming short' . . . and 'Your round will never work out right' . . . in other words, you were told to charge more so that you wouldn't be short, . . . yeah, so I said to him 'How much are those jam tarts?' and he said, 'Two bob' and I said 'Two bob? That's a dear old jam tart!' . . . the actual price of them was one-and-four [laugh]; and he

said 'Well, you must do it' . . . it was obvious he was getting away with overcharging on these jam tarts, and other various things above the price . . . and the customers thought it was the standard charge . . . and he'd done it, and I hadn't spotted him.

The sudden flow of information prompts some identity stock-taking, some self-revaluation. Ossification of the self in the present is aided by plotting and confining the graph of personal experience in the past. This reflex is, interestingly, typically different to that experienced by those following other moral careers. Rather than being retrospective reinterpretation to establish the meanings of current actions somewhere in the past (Kitsuse, 1962), or an alteration of total identity such as that contrived by public degradation ceremonies (Garfinkel, 1956), the addition of an *auxiliary* (rather than master) status, is the lamination or layering of a new set of attributes onto an old identity core. The typical accounting mode for newly experienced salesmen is apologetic: new-found knowledge allows the old self to be interpreted 'properly'. Rather than thinking '*This* is what I was like all along', salesmen think 'I was a fool then, but *now* I know'. As opposed to interpreting the past to understand the past, it is realisation *in* the present to aid the future. One man said:

When I first went in there, the supervisor showed me how to do it . . . he thought he knew it all, but I now realise that he doesn't know half of it . . . when I suddenly noticed the other bloke was doing it, I thought 'Well, I'll keep quiet' . . . I wasn't checking on him, but he'd fill in the book, and I'd look at it while we were going to the next call . . . so I thought 'Oh, that's how you do it' . . . that's how I noticed it, I thought 'Well, there's no need to ask him, I know now' . . . then I knew how it was done.

Unfortunately, for various reasons, some recruits slip the socialisation net, and are released upon the customer world with insufficient organisational commitment or technical knowledge to survive. Others fail training altogether and leave the firm. What accounts for these career problems?

Of course, successful socialisation depends on good supervision. At Wellbread's, this is often felt to be lacking. Two supervisors ironically blamed their own poor training for this:

I never had no guide about training other blokes or anything . . . I didn't let that bloke [first trainee] do enough on his own, and I pushed him too much . . . the second bloke I trained, we went through it bit by bit . . . but I showed him how to make a bit extra right from the start, which was a mistake with him . . . he was a good chap, but eventually, he got caught, and I had no choice but to give him the sack.

They just took me in the office, and sent me out to train a bloke, I hadn't got a clue, . . . I must have lost fifteen blokes on that round until I got one to stay any length of time . . . look, I know that if I don't tell blokes properly, I'm going to be on that round until kingdom come.

Typically, as these two extracts show, bad supervisors lose pupils by alternatively teaching too little and then too much. 'Good boys' is the term used by those who *did* learn the 'ropes' (Geer et al: 1968, p. 228) to refer to those recruits who, because of moral refusal to fiddle, or lack of technical training in the art, have been caught by inevitable mistakes, shortages, and deductions, and have left. One man, with great glee, told me:

They've just had a bloke on my brother's old round, but he only lasted three days. Apparently, they were at this shop, and whoever was with him took in ten loaves, and showed him how to do the booking . . . well, he booked twelve, see? . . . and the new bloke said 'I don't understand that, you only gave him ten', and the supervisor said 'Don't worry about that, I'll show you later' . . . and the bloke said 'Oh! fuck that! that's too confusing' . . . yeah! he left because of that . . . said it was 'too confusing'!

In the latter case, the novice left because of over-teaching (the omission of crucial stages in socialisation). Actually, under-teaching (information not dispensed readily enough) is a more common cause of failure. Practically all those who go on to become salesmen decide to leave more than once because of poor teaching in the early stages of training. Generally, though, the management change supervisor or round until a satisfactory combination is found. Those re-entering training (changing to a different type of round or transferring from another bakery) sometimes experience under-teaching of a different sort. Although the trained man has no moral problems, technical information may not be forthcoming. As one man put it 'If blokes come down here for a job, if they've been on the vans before, the first thing they ask is: "What are the fiddles?". If they haven't, it just takes a bit longer'. Another man recounted a personal experience:

When I started on wholesale delivery (after three years as a retailer), he took me into Woolworths, and he booked them about three trays they never had . . . I was so simple then, I didn't know what he was doing! . . . I even said to him: 'Hey! You've booked that wrong' . . . but he showed me how to do it.

Sometimes, even if training is not successful in the first three weeks, the point can be driven home later. The Wellbread management popularly stage a confrontation in the office in such cases, as two salesmen recalled:

When I first came here, you won't believe this, but for the first year, I never got a thing for myself . . . never overcharged even a half-penny, but then, one day, I was having the rec. out with the manager, and he said 'You've been here long enough, there's no need for you to come short all the time' . . . and I said 'What do you mean?', and he said 'You know what goes on, I don't have to tell you, you've got some calls where the people don't know what they're getting, haven't you? Need I say more?' . . . well, after that, I really started.

I started to come short, I never found out why, this went on for months, short each week, then, eventually, they had me in the office, he didn't say he'd stop me, he told me, sort of, 'Start charging people more' . . . more or less, in a roundabout fashion . . . he never told me *how* to do it.

Outside the office, supervisors may provide prompts, in the form of *deliberate hints* or *unintentional asides*:

There's one honest bloke left here . . . he comes two pounds short regularly, every week. One week, I told him 'Why don't you add a penny onto each bill, just to see if you can come over once?', but he said 'Oh, I don't know, I don't want to do that' . . . but he did it, or I think he did, because he came two pounds over that week, although he was two pounds short the next week.

One day, I had a different supervisor with me, and he said to me 'Whatever you do, don't hurt old Bill' . . . and I said 'What do you mean?' and he said 'Don't fiddle him'. He added 'He's alright, but it doesn't matter about the others' . . . that's when it really sunk into me! . . . I thought: 'Well, they must be doing it to the bloody lot of them!

When I went out with him . . . (to learn a wholesale route) it was totally different to the first time, when I was trained . . . he just said: 'Twist him, and twist him' . . . I knew about fiddling, but not on wholesale.

The firm will only tolerate honesty if it doesn't provide additional organisation problems. The accepted existence of untroublesome non-fiddlers testifies to the ambiguity of managerial values. But 'straights' can be awkward. One over-zealous straight began to report others for overcharging customers. Potential supervisors are hard to come by (many are selected, but few accept) so the firm promoted him. As a supervisor, he canvassed for moral rearmament even more vehemently until, finally, he had to be disposed of as a night packer in one of the depots.

At the end of the chaperoned training period, the novice has 'become' a roundsman. As I have shown, this period may be extended beyond the three weeks training time and concludes when the recruit accepts the need for the fiddle, and practises it. However, the primary justification for fiddling has only temporary relevance. Most men discard the notion of fiddling just for the firm in favour of a secondary one which specifies that only a basic percentage of money be left in to cover mistakes and prevent wage-packet deductions. But whereas initial corruption in training was managed by chaperoned *transformation*, in the post-training stages, perversion of such corruption now occurs at turning points of abrupt *conversion* created by class-based career contingencies.

THE POST-TRAINING STAGE: BECOMING A SALESMAN

Occupational 'success' is, of course, immediate for most men at Wellbread's. One man remembered that 'On the fourth week, when I was by myself, the first call was surprised to see me alone, *and I sold*, she was a customer who never had cakes . . . *and I achieved a sale* . . . I was really pleased'. This semi-mystical thrill is part, according to Howton and Rosenberg (1965, p. 282) of subscription to the 'cultic metaphor of sales'. Importantly, it demonstrates to the new man that he *can* make a success of a sales career.

Similar success with fiddling concludes training. Initially, however, the roundsman feels that his illicit actions are 'transparent' (Matza, 1969, p. 150). But as empirical success dissolves 'stage fright' (Lyman and Scott, 1970) and the transparency of the experience fades, *being* a fiddler (which has been a part-time occupational, but full-time psychological status during training) dwindles to an auxiliary, partial psychological status. Training is morally concluded when fiddle occasions lose their 'countability' (Sudnow, 1967, pp. 2, 38), when they are defined as ordinary.

Thus, successful solitary practice completes the sense of psychological status change. Success in fiddling customers allows the salesman finally to solidify his feelings that he is somebody 'new'. The reality of his ability to play a role that he once might not have believed himself capable of playing (had he conceived of playing it) is fully brought home to him. As Strauss (1959, p. 97) suggests, 'It brings him face to face with his potential, as well as his actual self'.

Ambiguously, whilst they officially condemn personal theft, the management *expect* the men to pass a final 'test' of directing some of the 'made' money to their own pockets. As the sales manager regularly says, 'They're not real salesmen if they can't make a bob or two on the side, are they?'. Although the management are relatively sympathetic towards 'personal' fiddling such as this (they used to be salesmen, they know that it keeps work force turnover down), they simultaneously fear that open encouragement from them would lead the men to become attached to crime (as well as organisationally committed to it) and thus steal from the company, or 'deal' with some of its more unscrupulous inside employees. But teaching the men to fiddle *does* carry the seeds of its own destruction in precisely this way. Right from the start, roundsmen see double standards. One said 'They seem to think that taking bread from them is wrong, and fiddling their customers is right'. A supervisor, who used to introduce the fiddle as a joke in training, realised that for most of the men 'It's probably in the back of their minds "I can do that for myself and make a few shillings" '. Occasionally, supervisors overtly suggest that the new man should 'take a dip in the bag', at least to cover those financial needs (cigarettes, tea) occurring during the day's work. One roundsman remembered that 'He told me I should do it to cover myself, just for a packet of fags', and another recalled 'He was also saying I should pocket it, whatever I could make . . . he didn't say any specific amount'. Another man said:

> *Then*, he near enough said 'This will help to run your car, and buy cigarettes', he'd sort of say it and laugh . . . say 'This'll put petrol in your car!' . . . so I said to him, at that point, 'How much can you make?' . . . and he said 'Well, you can have bad weeks, and good weeks, some weeks you won't make hardly anything.' . . . he reckoned about four or five pounds.

As the roundsman practises by himself, he will mix more with the other salesmen than with the supervisors. He will eat less of the goods, make fewer mistakes, and begin to build up (exploitable) trust with his customers. Importantly, he will develop sleight of hand at fiddling generally, and specifically learn the 'easy touches' on his route. The likelihood of him continuing to come short on his weekly reconciliation decreases just at the same time as his skills at fiddling improve. Two of the roundsmen commented:

Although I was still making mistakes after a month, I wasn't coming short . . . I was making a few . . . and then I used to do a bit too much, and cover myself too much, and that showed up as over.

You can't get away with anything . . . when you first start off . . . they're all a bit wary of you . . . but after a bit they trust you, and you can start fiddling them more and more.

Instead of commitment to organisational goals, the roundsman develops attachment to the possible profits and to the increased standard of living that they bring. Awareness of other uses to which 'made' money could be put arises in the process of 'trying out' the fiddle:

After a bit you got to know the ones what add up what they had, and the ones that didn't . . . I used to try them out . . . I used to think 'Oh! I'll put threepence on, and see if she says anything' . . . if the bill was four-and-sixpence, I used to say: 'That'll be four-and-nine please, Ma'am', and if she didn't say anything about it, I'd know she didn't add up . . . put a penny on this, put a penny on that, you try it, then you think 'Oh well, that's two or three pounds extra in my pocket' . . . that used to worry me at first . . . but it isn't pennies now, it's pounds.

If I can't make a couple of quid out of it, I don't bother . . . I wouldn't cross the road for a couple of bob now.

The roundsman thus emerges with a vocabulary of fiddle techniques and possibilities far superior to that needed to satisfy organisational ends. Sooner or later he will make a decision to use the organisationally taught practices for his own benefit. Commitment to the end of fiddling subtly transforms itself into attachment to the means of fiddling. Typically, the men look back and account for this rationalisation of the proceeds as precipitated by an abrupt, hostile act of class aggression by the management:

They started to say that I was short, and all the rest of it . . . and you haven't got no proof of anything . . . and I think it's *that* . . . it's the company what *make* you . . . what you are, because *they're* twisting *us*!

Well, I thought it would be handy . . . a bit of extra money . . . I suppose it was sudden, really.

One of the supervisors took over from me, and forgot to take any out, so we went to look at the rec., to see how much he had made, and he was five pounds over . . . I told him I would take it out next week, and split it with him . . . but when we looked at it again, it was only a few odd shillings over, the rest had been struck off.

[Roundsman who had helped the bakery out in a time of labour shortage.] When I came to get my pay for that week, they hadn't even paid me for the Thursday! . . . and I'd come to work! . . . I'd never had a day off or anything, that's just the way they treat you here, I told one of the blokes in Despatch about it, and he said 'I'll stuff extra on your rack to make up for that next week, don't worry, mate, I'll pay you back for them' . . . and he did . . . I got it all back.

You know, I was there for a year before I realised what was going on . . . yeah, it must have been a year before I knew what all the others were doing . . . when I was first there, I wouldn't have *dreamed* of what was going on . . . I wouldn't have taken a *farthing* . . . then [laugh] I saw the light.

I didn't know anything about it until after six months, until I really got in with the blokes, and I knew what went on . . . it was the firm that changed me, they made me feel 'Oh! right, if you're going to rob me, I'm going to rob you.'.

I remember when I started to take a bit out, I remember it clearly, funnily enough . . . my holiday pay was short, and I went to see about it, and they explained to me that although I'd been there a full twelve months, they take it from the April, and I'd only been there since July . . . I accepted this, but I was still short . . . he said 'We can't work that out now, you'll have to go on your holiday, and we'll work it out and give it to you when you get back' . . . I thought 'Why should I?' . . . and I had it out of the bag . . . that was the first time I'd ever done it for my own ends . . . Oh, yeah, I used to make a pint of beer, and a smoke . . . but I hadn't gone out particularly to make money to put in my pocket at the end of the week.

Whilst an aggressive managerial act precipitates the conversion it is more likely that the decision to pocket some of the illicit proceeds is a gradual one. The change is probably so mundane that it would pass unnoticed until an incident of great conceptual and personal signifi-cance is encountered. Such class-based 'moral experiences' are used at the time, and in later accounts, to justify the switch, to close another period in an individual biography, and to reconstitute psychological equilibrium.

3 Interaction: Managing Customers

I have looked at what conditions, under the circumstances of socialisation at Wellbread's, made fiddling a reasonable practice for recruits to adopt. What is there in their ordinary daily life as salesmen that might make *continuing* to fiddle reasonable? Although the organisational profit/mistake dilemma is still a reality even when the recruit passes from the highly homogenized training setting to the highly differentiated network of fully fledged salesmen, what interactional, emotional and psychological support for the fiddle can be gleaned from customer interactions? I have already suggested that one 'secondary adjustment', to use Goffman's (1957b, p. 172) term, which the roundsmen make to the increasing discrepancy between the need to fiddle for the company, and the ability to do so, is the 'conversion' to fiddling-for-themselves. Although partly based on the trial stage of the moral career, conversion occurs when the roundsman's main contact is with his customer. What *is* it about customer interactions that makes this fiddling reasonable?

That service occasions induce the server to put on some sort of performance ('*performing* a service') marks them off as a special type of interaction. One where the usual conventions don't apply, or rather, one where the usual conventions *do* apply, but where they simultaneously apply at both literal *and* metaphoric levels. As Goffman has suggested in his classic work (1959), there is an element of performance in all our strategies of self-presentation in society. But when we look, for example, at stage actors (another special type of interaction), they are not only performing in the metaphoric sense as we all, by analogy, unconsciously do, but they are also literally 'performing' in a special and conscious way. Although Goffman uses the more common model of the stage actor, his 1959 analysis was in fact directly derived from his observations of 'Shetland Hotel' – a service (and not a theatrical) context analytically identical to the salesman–customer context at Wellbread's. In a very real sense, then, the Wellbread salesman's customers are an 'audience' to his 'performance'. In a smaller sense, the salesman is, in turn, something of an audience to the management's 'performance', and so I shall sometimes use the more formal performer/ audience distinction where the analysis might similarly be informative both about customer interactions (where the roundsman is performer) and management ones (with the roundsman as audience). In analysing these 'special' interactions, care must be taken not just to portray the content of the interactions, but also (as Bateson et al, 1956, p. 194, put it) to attend to the way that the actors involved adapt themselves to 'multiple *levels* of message' in the interaction. Further, the sense in which the salesman is also a fiddler adds another (this time consciously false and concealed) meaningful level at which the salesman is 'acting'. Here, he is like Goffman's original (1952) model – the 'con-man' – one depending on Sutherland's (1937, p. 197) classic 'wits, front and talking ability' to deal surreptitiously with customers who are simultaneously victims.

But what *type* of service do the Wellbread salesmen give? They qualify as performers in the analytic sense as they engage as routine in direct communication with the public (compared, for example, with charladies, who don't) and because the service they proffer is executed 'in' public, as distinct, that is, from those sectors of the service industry where the work is carried on out of sight of the customer. The salesmen perform a fairly perfunctory and routine technical service (compared with the rational demonstration of expertise and competence given by doctors and dentists) and, crucially, travel to their customers who, as audiences, view the performance sequentially and individually. Structurally, the salesmen may be seen as (Goffman, 1959, p. 33): 'quite profane performers of the pedlar class who move their place of work between performances, often being forced to do so'.

Because they work singly, there is no competition for available customers, as there is for example in a department store (see Gale's typology of Macey's salesladies in Mills, 1951, p. 174). The repeated meetings of Wellbread salesmen and their customers breed continuous and lasting relationships, allowing the customers to become defined as unique persons and not just apprehended as instances of a particular type. The repeated meetings also mean that the Wellbread salesmen cannot practice some of the more open frauds which Caplovitz (1963, pp. 137–54) has noticed amongst door-to-door pedlars not thus constrained. Davis (1959) has shown that conversely, for taxi-drivers, because customers are relatively scarce and only met fleetingly and served once, each individual customer will have to be typed immediately so that he may be appropriately served.

Gold (1952, p. 257) captures an essential ingredient of all service relationships – status:

> When the salesperson and customer meet, each brings to bear on the other valuations by which the other's status category can be tentatively ascertained . . . the status relationship between them is always present . . . in the case of the physician and his patients, the plumber and his customers, the minister and his parishioners, and in others, there is a status relationship of which both parties are more or less aware and which influences the pattern of their interactions.

In status terms, service is an asymmetrical relationship – one that 'leads others to treat and be treated by an individual differently from the way he treats and is treated by them' (Goffman, 1956a, p. 53). But if status is an openly declared dimension of a relationship, a concealed dimension is the distribution of available knowledge of the relationship's ground conditions and consequences. Paradoxically, in the service relationship, knowledge is inversely coupled with status, transforming the situation into a *doubly asymmetrical relationship*. The customer's high status is coupled with scanty knowledge, and the server's low status is balanced by the considerable extent and scope of his interaction knowledge. Strictly, this may be referred to as a knowledge dilemma, and contrasted with the status dilemma of high-status specialists who have little knowledge of the particular problem affecting their clients.

In any situation, the knowledge dilemma produces a form of cynicism, generally emerging as 'subtle aggressiveness' (Goffman, 1959, p. 22) in the server. More specifically, to use James' (1890, pp. 221–3) distinction, we may suggest that the customer only has vague knowledge *about* the service relationship, but that the server has an explicit knowledge *of* intimate acquaintance with it.

Looking first at the *server's knowledge*, it seems to be of two distinct kinds. Firstly, the server has an ascribed *regional knowledge* derived from his multi-regimed and extended contact with service. For customers, in a supermarket for example (see Taylor, 1974), items for sale are laid out so as to obey semiological as well as physical rules. Fish are kept away from soap not only for olfactory reasons, but also because their proximity could breed a feeling of 'out of placeness'. But these subtle semiological concerns are irrelevant in the 'back regions' of supermarkets (the stock rooms) where employees work out of sight of the customer. To work on the employees' side of the counter automatically gives one ability to manage contradictory phenomena unconsciously.

Taboo, in this instance the uncomfortable convergence of normally separate categories, the 'out of placeness' which defines dirt, is regionally indexical. Orwell (1933, pp. 60–1) offers some beautiful examples from his hotel experiences:

> It was amusing to look around the filthy little scullery and think that only a double door was between us and the dining-room. There sat the customers in all their splendour – spotless table-cloths, bowls of flowers, mirrors, and gilt cornices and painted cherubim; and here, just a few feet away, we in our disgusting filth. There was no time to sweep the floor until evening, and we slithered about in a compound of soapy water, lettuce-leaves, torn paper and trampled food. A dozen waiters with their coats off, showing their sweaty armpits, sat at the table mixing salads and sticking their thumbs into the cream pots . . . There were only two sinks and no washing basin, and it was nothing unusual for a waiter to wash his face in the water in which clean crockery was rinsing.

Performers gain access to regional knowledge by virtue of occupational position alone. Thus regional knowledge is workplace-specific, although gaining it becomes a matter of course for an employee with multi-workplace experience. Regional knowledge is not only immediately ascribed to newcomers, it is also lost, or rather sublimated, upon return to audience status. This is not so much because regional knowledge is weak, but rather because the myth of 'cleanness' which pervades service washes over and penetrates the experience of *all* who adopt the customer role.

Service workers, then, are 'dirty' workers. They may not only handle dirt literally (like Gold's, 1952, janitors) but they may also consciously manage the metaphoric dirt of 'out of placeness' (a loaf that is ambiguously lying on the ground) with experienced sensibility and circumspection in front of customers.

A second and complementary form of specific knowledge is achieved *trade knowledge*. Performers are often conscious of their trade information, and accordingly protective and secretive about it. Thus 'trade secrets' are not only 'dark' (concealed from audiences) but also 'inside' secrets, whose possession marks an individual as a performer (Goffman, 1959, pp. 141–2).

Although both regional and trade knowledge are occupationally specific, a novice performer has to be initiated into trade knowledge which is, conversely, never forgotten. For example, audiences rarely recognise that the warmly familiar terms of address that they come to expect as customers are never used when performers talk of them amongst themselves. The salesmen at Wellbread's, for example, never refer to their customers by name, preferring abstract combinations of technical address and consumer rating (called their 'code title' by Goffman), such as 'No. 3 is a large brown'. Performers will always treat audiences this way, but the audience always believe that they are exceptional.

In the terms I have been using, *customer knowledge* (knowledge *about*) is, on the one hand, *media-ted* through *image-inary* data and, on the other, because of this, particularly rigid and inflexible.

To take an example from the bakery. While I was working in the despatch department, a woman came in one evening, and asked for a pink wrapped loaf. I remember smiling indulgently, looking for but not being able to find one, and offering her an alternatively wrapped, but otherwise identical loaf. She protested, and claimed that her son would only eat bread if it was in a pink wrapper. I suggested that there was no difference, but she steadfastly refused to believe it, saying 'They're *not* all the same, they're quite different'. The only way to understand this is to realise that, for customers, the wrapper image is all important, and the concept-content (important for servers) irrelevant. Thus the sincerity of the customer's belief is coupled with intolerance of anomaly or ambiguity. This contrasts sharply with the way that the roundsman's cynicism is allied with tolerance of anomaly. Where the roundsman would unconcernedly pick up the loaf lying on the ground, the customer would recoil with horror at such 'dirt'. However, the flexibility of the roundsman's knowledge (he knows, for example, that the bread is not always fresh and that the customer confuses freshness with pliability) itself contributes to the undiluted and jaded cynicism with which he views the customer.

Interactions, like service occasions, which are 'special' because standard rules apply at two levels have what Barthes (1957, p. 115) calls 'two aspects'. Such situations may be sincerely read as 'meaning' (by the customer) or just cynically as 'form' (as the server does). The customer dynamically consumes the service interaction as an inextricably vivid and meaningful whole message. Sales reality is felt as wholly ordinary and not as constructed.

For example, retail customers are never aware that they are being 'switched', even in establishments (Conant, 1936) where no other sales technique is used and where the furniture with which they are 'baited' is screwed to the floor to prevent obstinate customers from trying to buy it! As Caplovitz (1965, p. 241) indicates, those customers who *do* realise that they have been cheated only do so through accident. In fact, there is a sense in which the very belief itself renders analysis of it impossible to the believer. As Schopenhauer (in Taylor, 1974, p. 15) reminds us, 'what is signified at once suppresses consciousness of the sign which signifies it'. Barthes refers to this sort of customer reading as 'isological': a grasping of the associative total (of the signifiers and signifieds which constitute the meaning) in an indifferentiatable way.

Conversely, roundsmen have the cynical belief that what is reality for the customer is, in fact, sheer illusion. In sales interactions, the server, as Goffman (1959, p. 210) puts it 'is *ostensibly* immersed and given over to the activity he is performing, and is *apparently* engrossed in his actions in a spontaneous, uncalculating way'. Operative cynicism, then, is guaranteed in the unconscious feeling that the performance is 'only a front', or that 'it's all the *same*'. For roundsmen, as Barthes (1957, p. 117) puts it, 'meaning leaves its contingency behind; it empties itself, it becomes impoverished'. Thus we have, as Goffman (1974, p. 116) tells us:

> The understanding that persons such as janitors, stagehands, newspapermen, waiters and servants may be involved only in a very narrow aspect of a given undertaking, since they often have a right to treat the whole activity as merely one instance of the type.

To a service performer, interaction is just talk. And any talk will do. When accused of fiddling, for example, Wellbread salesmen claim 'give 'em any excuse and they'll believe it', or 'just pretend to look at your sheet and look surprised', or that one can say 'anything, make it up as you go along'. This sort of provision of an 'impressive story' is particularly cultivated by salesmen. Shoe salesmen sell shoes with remarkable leather which has 'give' in it, drapers sell coats with sleeves that 'ride up', and haberdashers undersized garments with magical 'stretch' in them. Invisible repair specialists – those who necessarily repair appliances out of sight of the customer – hone the impressive story to a fine art. Strodbeck and Sussman (1955–6, p. 606) report examples of nonsensical explanations (like 'inclement weather', 'body magnetism' and 'rough skin') being given to those overcharged for watch repair, and Riis and Patric (1942) also report fictitious 'analyser talk' from garage mechanics, when they toured America visiting garages in a specially doctored car. A crucial stage in the development of cynicism is the discovery by roundsmen that fiction is not only more reasonable and palatable, but also more *believable* than the truth.

But sincerity is an *impossibility* and not merely an interactional difficulty for servers. This is so as the very structure of service is apprehended by servers *as* drama in two ways. First, solitary experience breeds cynicism through sheer jaded reflection upon consecutive repetition. Road accidents, for example, out of the ordinary for most people, are just another occupational hazard for roundsmen. Secondly comes the amazing discovery of credibility, both of performing self and of product. As the roundsman learns that, in a very real sense, the product will sell itself through the weight of its image alone, and that nothing that he can give will contradict this given-off expression from the product, he will begin to get cynical not just of the customer-audience but of the whole performance, including himself. Most Wellbread salesmen use mundane grammatical decoys like 'I can recommend this, Madam', and most eventually realise (probably through sheer accident) that they can be quite perverse, and yet still sell the bread. My own favourite trick was to leave a nicely wrapped stale loaf in the basket on or near the back of the van and tell all enquirers that it was stale. This never failed to intrigue female customers who (naturally) thought that I was 'only saying that' and that really I was 'saving it for somebody else'. Nine times out of ten they would take it and, of course, they couldn't complain when it tasted stale! Another roundsman whom I once accompanied used to offer eggs and potatoes as a sideline, and his verbal sideline to any reticent customers was that they would be wise to buy as 'they talk about a world shortage, you know'! Another roundsman commented:

> I *like* selling, though, that's why I stay on retail and don't try to get a wholesale job . . . I like the challenge of selling to people who don't want anything . . . and selling them things that they don't want . . . I shout at them and tell them that it's stale, and they still buy it! I like it when they look in the basket and start pawing things about, I hate them fingering the cakes, but I know that they are going to buy something . . . so I show them things that get more and more expensive.

The discovery of axiomatic credibility of performance is analysed by the roundsmen, with a dash of irony, as intuitively derived from customer stupidity, rather than from the structural nature of the interaction. One Wellbread salesman complained 'The public is so bloody dense, they'll believe anything', another that 'they're all fucking thick . . . really!'. Sometimes, the stupidity of the customer is not only a source of derision but also of money, as another roundsman explained:

> Silly fucker! . . . the warehouseman signs it each morning, but he never checks it . . . he just counts the trays, I ask you? . . . what fucking use is that? . . . count the trays! . . . I don't know!

But assymetry is power: customers are audiences in the interactional rhetoric of performance. They are simultaneously victims in the underlying grammar of exploitation. Although the structure is not clearly and visibly a victim relationship, cynicism and sincerity are not merely dramatic modes as Goffman would have us believe. They are also political emotions. Selling bread may be metaphorically dramatic, but the money and the bread (and the profit) are real. However, it is not the salesmen but Wellbread's who get the profit. Although the roundsmen cynically view the 'service' that they give their customers as a set of rhetorical linguistic devices (such as those empty phrases based on the rule 'the customer is always right') masking a reality of selling, the roundsmen are in turn deluded by the firm. For the management, the sales reality, the sales 'team', is a similarly rhetorical device designed to mask their exploitation of the work-force.

Although knowledge is unequally allocated in 'special' performance interactions like service occasions, the moral dressing with which actors clothe their performances allows variations in personal competence partially to dilute and soften rigid structural differences. Fig. 3.1 shows

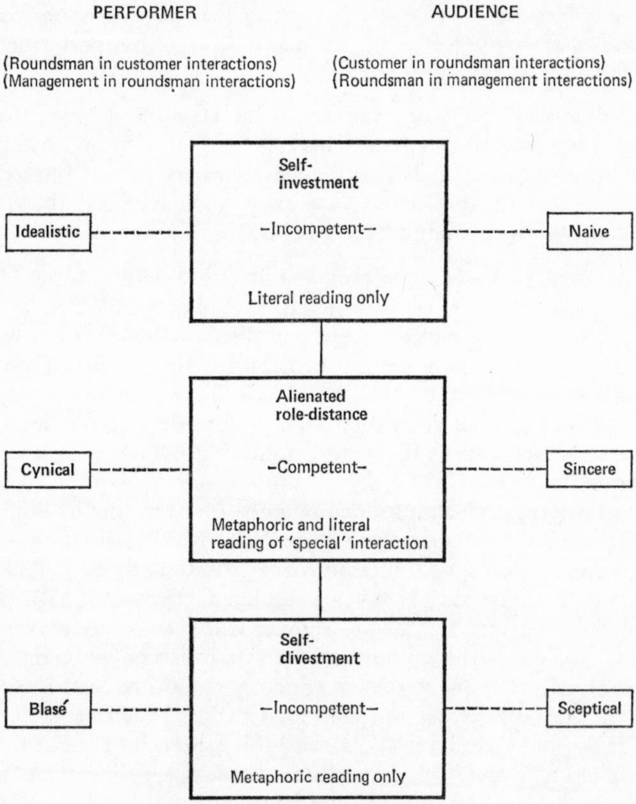

PERFORMER   AUDIENCE

(Roundsman in customer interactions)   (Customer in roundsman interactions)
(Management in roundsman interactions)   (Roundsman in management interactions)

Fig. 3.1   Personal competence

how three variations in competence can emerge in interactions and modify differences between performer and audience.

Theoretical competence, the middle horizontal line in Fig. 3.1, feels the pull of both the investment and divestment of the actor's 'self' in the situation. Also, the interaction is seen to be 'special' in the sense of having several levels of message. The resulting moderation, and relative lack of power, in fact masks the successful sublimation of contradictions between literal and metaphoric levels of communication and the production of what Marcuse (1964, p. 178) terms 'one-dimensional thought'. Competence reflects the perfectly socialised actor, who is, as Goffman (1961a, p. 91) argues, 'a juggler and a synthesiser, an accommodator and appeaser'. Someone, in other words, who exhibits a nice degree of 'role-distance' from the action – neither too much involved, nor too little. Competent audiences are perfectly sincere and are easily able to distinguish logically between different messages, and messages about messages, given by performers. As Bateson (1971, p. 260) puts it:

> An audience is watching Hamlet on the stage, and hears the hero discuss suicide in the context of his relationship with his dead father, Ophelia and the rest. The audience members do not immediately telephone for the police because they have received information about the context of Hamlet's context.

For performers, perfect cynicism requires that neither too much nor too little cynicism be expressed or felt. Goffman (1961a, p. 55) notes that 'only the manager of the store will display identification with his role, and even he appreciates that he must not throw himself too much into his calling'. On the other hand (Goffman, 1959, p. 208), performers 'must be taken in by their own performance to the degree that it is necessary to prevent them from sounding hollow and false to the audience'.

One exasperating form of incompetence (the top line in Fig. 3.1) is derived from over-investment of the 'self' in the situation – a role embracement, a disappearance into the situationally provided role – within which everything is taken literally. Goffman (1957b, p. 175) offers the nice examples of the parishioner who may try to live too much in and for the church; the junior officer who insists on going down with the ship; and the naïve audience which gets too involved in the play and even perhaps crosses the footlights to berate actors with 'nasty' parts. Incompetence here 'takes everything literally': such incompetents watching Hamlet might well telephone the police. The 'special' sense of the interaction is lost in the ignorance of the metaphoric level. Naïve customers typically demand more deference than they see themselves to be receiving – and, paradoxically, merely succeed in getting a greater *show* of it! This is essentially a misreading by them of the meaning of deference as something essential (rather than as something enacted). Such demands are particularly likely from those occupying a status category which is in uncomfortable proximity to the server. Gold (1952, p. 260) gives a neat example of tenants who earn less than their janitor and get particularly upset when they see the janitor's new car or television aerial.

A good example of an idealistic performer occurred at Wellbread's. A young supervisor took rather seriously the managerial directive that roundsmen should not come short on their weekly accounts. One of the roundsmen in his section said:

> He'll do anything for you, he'll help anybody out . . . he'll break his neck bringing all his rounds 'over', like when ——— was 'short', he helped him out by giving him cakes and bread, and by telling him to pay it in and come over . . . so it looks good on his record . . . he wants the manager to come up to him and say 'You're doing a wonderful job' . . . just as long as his job is done properly, he's chuffed.

A second sort of (sceptical) incompetence (the bottom line in Fig. 3.1) arises from misinvolvement of the self in the present – a withdrawal from and disdain of the situational role. Here, incompetence derives from taking everything metaphorically and nothing literally. Some customers prefer 'matiness' to 'servility', and are likely to mock the deferential display (qua display) by a server and demand a more blasé performance (one denuded of literal message content) believing this, of course, to be more representative of reality. This depicts the frailty of audience scepticism, and the irony. Sceptics are more at the mercy of performers than are the naïve – who at least are demanding the avoidance that they inevitably get, albeit under a different name. Demanding (as the sceptic does) to be treated with more 'matiness' on the grounds that this will mean less of a display will merely produce in performers a more (dumb insolent) deferential display. An example of taking a performance literally and objecting to it, rather than to the lack of it.

Audience scepticism, then, is not the same as performer cynicism nor, in fact, is it even a comparably knowledgeable position with, for example, the idealistic performer. Scepticism only brings an imaginary grasp of the performer's knowledge. The performer, however competent, has access to regional and trade knowledge which the audience, at best, can only guess at. For example, sceptical querying of the validity of a performance might make fiddling tricky, but it has an additional, paradoxical effect. Any warning story not only communicates some knowledge of trade secrets, but *also* communicates that the sceptic is unaware that cover is provided as routine. Scepticism is not that the interaction is *a* 'performance' but that, taking for granted that it is real, that it is the *wrong* performance. However, whilst the sceptic cannot guarantee immunity from the fiddle, she may, empirically, get it. I asked one of the roundsmen if he would continue to fiddle a customer who had caught him fiddling:

> Probably, if you could catch him once, you could hit him again, but I always think 'Well, if he's got me once, he might get me again' . . . although, as I say, he probably isn't even checking . . . just thinking that you think he is.

Every sales occasion, though, will be a matter of interactional co-production, rather than exclusively the effect of a single competence. The nine possible interactions crystallise into three conceptual forms (see Fig. 3.2 derived from Fig. 3.1). Firstly, *orthodox* interactions, where the created service 'facade' is thoroughly and typically ordinary to all concerned, and where competence, being balanced, does not alter structure. Secondly, *heterodox* occasions, where the performer/audience

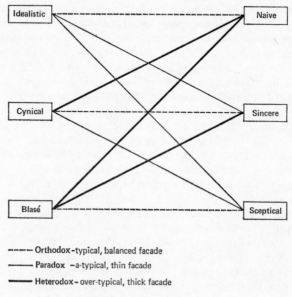

- - - - Orthodox – typical, balanced facade

———— Paradox – a-typical, thin facade

▬▬▬▬ Heterodox – over-typical, thick facade

Fig. 3.2   Facade forms

relationship is over-typical, and the resulting facade is thus 'thick' (for example, during a play the situation is 'thick' for that part of the audience who are totally engrossed in the production). A third possibility is that in which the performer/audience relationship is atypical. The fact that competence challenges the structural distinction between performer and audience warrants the term *paradoxical*. Under such circumstances, the facade starts to crumble and become 'thin'. For example, when one of the actors in a play requires a prompt which is loud enough for the audience to hear.

Using the formal dramatic analogy, the life of the bread roundsman includes both these sorts of performance. Sincere (audience) performances with the bakery management and cynical (performer) ones with customers. The reflexive outcome of these performances constitutes his work self. As Goffman (1956a, pp. 84–5) so eloquently and elegantly puts it 'for a complete man to be expressed, individuals must hold hands in a chain of ceremony'. The baker with one hand grasps his customers and by the other is held firmly by the management. His work self is thus created and maintained.

But the psychological demands that this makes on the Wellbread salesmen are incompatible. On the one hand the management demand that the men be an absurdly *idealistic* audience to over-selling of managerial idealism and, on the other, they allow them a measure of ordinary *cynicism* as performers in their interactions with customers. This creates rather troublesome contradictions, emerging as status disorder for the men, which may be characterised as the 'non-person dilemma' (Goffman, 1959, p. 150). Looking at the situation from the perspective of technical role, salesmen at the bakery are incarcerated within an awkward category which combines some of the elements of 'salesman' (the solicitation of orders from customers) with some of those of pure 'delivery'. This combination produces the paradoxical amalgam of 'roundsman' which, in status terms, combines both blue-collar and white-collar features. In blue-collar 'delivery' terms, the baker's roundsmen are existentially incomplete 'non-persons' (like domestics and children) as they merely deliver the bread in an invisible and unnoticed way. As white-collar 'salesman' the baker is the 'service specialist', whose dilemma is one already characterised as that of relative excess of status over knowledge.

PRESENTATION OF PRODUCT AND SELF

When the roundsman serves the customer, he is on show – a special sort of performer. Because he has to work in public, he is obliged to obey the customer's rules for ordering and selling. This is partly mercenary (it is difficult to sell loaves that fall on the ground) and partly symbolic. However, the roundsman *controls* sales interactions not only by subtly influencing the definition of the situation that the customer will make, but also by maintaining control in the situation of available information and knowledge. The selling setting is so arranged that even inquisitive customers can be well catered for; the roundsman's 'props' (his basket full of goods and his van) are especially prepared for those customers not satisfied with standard service, and who demand instead a more real image. Even those parts of the van which customers are not supposed to see are kept clean, fresh and tidy to give the impression that the whole presentation is palatable.

Service, then, is consciously *presented* to the customer. This presentation is not only of the product but also of the vendor. Looking firstly at product presentation, a basic organisational trouble with the service industries is that many otherwise hidden costs materialise and need to be transferred to the customer. Characteristically with bread, gaudy and eternally redesigned packaging is produced in order to reproduce dramatically the invisible costs of production. Unfortunately, this can demote the meaning of bread from necessity to luxury; from being the basic staff of life to just another inessential frippery. Thus short term competitive marketing generates a long term elasticity of consumer demand. On top of this, marketing trends towards more slicing and wrapping have translated the original basic concept of a loaf into a modern, clean, luxury.

The first product presentation problem for Wellbread roundsmen is bread *freshness*. Although a technical problem, it can be successfully managed with dramatic ability alone. The bakery management assume that the salesmen will master the arts of selling 'stales', and thus for planning purposes assume that all bread is saleable. When I first relayed customer complaints about the age of their bread to the manager, he said:

> Look, there's no such thing as stale bread at this bakery, so go back and tell them that. There's only fresh bread, . . . and bread which isn't quite as fresh as it normally is.

To avoid these confrontations with the management (and more awkward ones with customers) salesmen must learn to 'pass' stale bread. Mastering the arts of 'passing' is a long process of trial and error. Occasional initial attempts to rotate stales democratically among the customers are soon replaced by choosing customers on whom one might regularly palm off stales, thus eroding their criteria of difference by offering them continuity of stale experience. Some roundsmen manage to convince themselves (and sometimes their customers) that they have enough customers who actually prefer their bread a day old. One roundsman said:

> Funnily enough, I've got one or two on here who like bread a day or two old . . . well, if you get stuck with too much you have to know where to bung it on . . . I have bunged stale bread in a shop, but never in a small shop . . . mainly, because . . . this firm depends so much on the corner shop . . . also, you put them in a big store because there, you can get away with it . . . in the big stores that I do . . . we don't do sale-and-return . . . so the crafty fuckers can't push them back at me the next day!

Initially, roundsmen are only able to pass sliced bread as the waxed wrapper keeps the bread tolerably pliable. Learning the 'polythene trick' (uncut bread stored overnight in a polythene bag retains its pliability which, of course, customers, when they are handling the bread, can be led to confuse with softness and freshness) allows the roundsman to 'hold' any bread on the van overnight and successfully pass it the next day. The same salesman continued:

> Nowadays I hardly ever sell uncut bread that's a day old . . . if I'm pushed, I'd use it, but normally I'd chuck it off when I got back, even if it was in polythene . . . I don't try it too often, I think you can detect it too easily . . . sliced bread, well, there, in many cases, you can get hold of a loaf and it feels as good as a fresh one . . . and that's what I do with stale uncut ones, I try it, feel it, and think 'Oh, that one don't feel too bad'.

After a bit, the roundsman begins to rely less on technical manipulation (in the 'passing' of stale bread) and more on verbal dexterity, practising at first with absent customers:

> Well, I work a crafty one! . . . you get to know which customers are going to be out, that saves any arguments . . . [once] I only had one of yesterday's left . . . so, instead of taking it round the back, I put it in a bag, and left it round the front in the sun . . . when I got there next time, she said 'That bread felt a bit stale outside, you didn't leave it in the right place' . . . and I said 'It was probably the sun'.

There comes a time, naturally, when the very ability to handle customers verbally contributes to occupational cynicism. As one roundsman said 'Well, I'd tell them a lie or something, that the machine had broken down, anything', and I found personally that this can sometimes degenerate into the production of the most bizarre and absurd reasons, which cannot, quite frankly, make sense however you

c

look at them. I used to say things like 'Well, you can't really tell by feeling it' or 'It's all right really, it just *tastes* stale'. Another roundsman told me:

> Nobody used to say much about the stales, sometimes they would say 'Bread wasn't very fresh yesterday' . . . so I'd make up some cock and bull story that the machine had broken down . . . you've got so many excuses that you can use, I used to blame the weather . . . I used to blame that quite a bit, if it was cold, it would make the bread hard, and in the summer, the heat would make it go mouldy!

A final trick enabled one to use bread that was two days old. When the weather was particularly hot, even sliced bread used to go hard overnight. To counteract this, some of the more experienced men would place a day old loaf end-up on the floor and stand on it. It would be compressed to about three to four inches long, but by the time the driver had reached the first call, it would have concertinaed to feel beautifully soft.

A second product presentation problem is keeping the bread *clean*. To do so, the salesmen are taught product handling rules which forbid dirt on the hands, hair or overalls. Untidy hair is actually an offence and, in addition, one should not lick one's fingers when turning pages, pick one's nose, spit, smoke and so on. The idea, naturally, is to present a clean image, and not necessarily a clean reality. Thus, for example, loaves that are dropped on the ground in front of the customer are immediately thrown into a waste bin at the front of the van (to be retrieved for the next customer). A more difficult problem is keeping the hands clean when faced with perpetual handling of dirty steering wheels and van doors. One of the salesmen commented:

> When I want to wash my hands, I go up to the door *before* I serve her, and say 'Can I wash my hands please, ma'am, I got a bit dirty on the last customer's gate', never serve her first, they wouldn't like that.

A third product presentation problem is image *tidiness*. A loaf with a torn wrapper is as difficult to pass as one which is three days old. Held correctly, however, it can be sold without too much trouble. Even if returned to the bakery it can at least be rewrapped, and sent out to do duty again.

But the roundsmen have to keep their smile, as well as their bread fresh. Self, as well as product, must be presented. In the service trades, it seems that customer demands for nice demonstrations of attentive service pragmatically preclude the *actual* construction of what is displayed. Ironically, as Orwell (1933, pp. 71–3) bitterly tells us, so much time is spent on the show of the thing ('boulot' – the imitation of good service) that there is just not time for the thing itself. The self presentation rules that all salesmen learn (keep one's overalls clean, etc.), if obeyed, transform their action into an expression of service, and their work self into a 'whole image' (Barthes, 1964, p. 46) saturated with image meaning, if not with reality. But, for a Wellbread salesman, the service aspects of the sales 'front' are hard to control. Whilst his coat, van and basket act as a social licence for his presence on urban housing estates during working hours, actual selling takes place on the doorstep, where public reality dramatically intersects with private life. To maximise his chances of success, the personal aspects of presentation are highly stressed. Endless 'sincere' smiling is recommended, along with enthusiasm, courtesy, friendliness, cheerfulness, smartness and neatness. The salesman idealises his self in encounters with customers in various ways. A key technique is a thorough going 'personalisation' of each and every encounter with customers. Of course, this is primarily achieved just through smiling – the problem lying not so much in just doing it, but doing it in such a way that it will appear 'warm', and 'spontaneous'. The very fact that, for bread salesmen, customers are individually dispersed (thus making them what Goffman, 1959, p. 137 calls a 'weak' audience) allows them to present the same smile three hundred times a day, although they have to watch that sheer repetition doesn't turn it into a snarl.

As Bigus (1972, p. 153) suggests, the personalisation problem is generally solved by 'cultivating' a 'pseudo relationship' with each customer. The initially exasperating tendency of practically every customer to demand to be treated as the roundsman's favourite can, in fact, be accommodated. One salesman said 'You get to know the names, but you do find that you're saying all the same things to each customer . . . but still, you do get your favourite people that you can have a laugh and joke with . . . you've got to be happy-go-lucky, you've got to smile'. A senior supervisor explained that, in fact, there is really more to it than that:

There are no actual tricks . . . apart from the tricks of getting round the customer, to win the customer round . . . that is the only real trick of the trade . . . like dealing with children, you must never put a child off, or they'll never come to the door again . . . if they put their hands into the basket, you mustn't say 'Gerrof! you little bastard!' or you'll never get the mother's confidence . . . some of the blokes get to know the child's name, and the name of all the children on the round, so that they can make a note of their birthdays, and remind the mother to order a birthday sponge.

Exasperatingly, every customer is the same to the roundsman (at least, to the extent that he is cynical of the interaction) but differences in quite frivolous information, such as having birthdays on different days, have to be remembered. To do this requires phenomenal in-round chameleon-like adaptation, beautifully described by two of the men:

> You have to have a different approach for different people . . . it's off the cuff, on the spot . . . you say 'Good morning missus' but the next one, you have to say 'G'morning ma'am' and 'No ma'am' . . . and another one, you can say 'Morning, Doris, all right? All right last night, gal?' . . . these are the various ways you can go up to these people, and there again, you see, you have to get to know your customer.

> But they're all different, some you can stand at the door and tell her a dirty joke, and the next one, you wouldn't dare . . . you have to act different with different people, different types of customer as they come along . . . I adapt myself to each customer as they come along, I gradually get to know what they're like . . . I let them approach me first, to see how they do it, what they're like, see how they speak to me, I think this is the safest way, you're less likely to upset her then . . . I just think of them in my mind, as you go from one customer to another 'Oh yes, old so-and-so, I'd better be careful what I say to this one' . . . sort of rearrange myself as I go along.

Coupled with 'personalisation' techniques, is playing the 'memory game'. The game is to pretend to remember irrelevant instructions given by customers, such as 'call tomorrow', when this would be standard practice or, 'bring me a large white sliced one tomorrow', when this information is written in the route book, and would be done anyway. It is simpler and quicker to pretend to commit such orders to memory, than to explain painstakingly to customers trade secrets concerning how the round and the bread is really managed. Next day, of course, in the absence of specifically recalled information, the man will have to 'simulate a memory' (Joad, in Goffman, 1959, p. 58) and give the impression that he is well aware of yesterday's conversation, whereas, in fact, the three hundred customer conversations that he has had since then have irredeemably blurred his recall.

Wholly expressing the 'don't argue with the customer' rule which is commonly held by performers in all sales service situations is the 'rule of agreement'. Basically, whatever the customer says, Janus like, the roundsman will agree with her.

Actual selling, compared to performing the service, is relatively easy. For all service agents with naturally repeating customers the selling process is not problematic. Customer contact is purely a technical problem of catching the customer at home; the sales 'pitch' is, for regular customers, unnecessary; and the only problem with the 'close' is to complete it with sufficient speed to visit all the customers on the round in good time. Of importance here is that, in the same way that the colourful bread wrapper re-enacts hidden costs, the unnoticed rituals of customer interaction (like letting the customer, but not the roundsman, get into debt; handing over the bread before taking the money) dramatically recreate and express the background social relations of 'service'.

CUSTOMER INTERACTIONS

In his interactions with customers, the roundsman faces a major dilemma: how much of his 'self' should he psychologically invest in sales life? Too much invested, and he will have no time or emotion for an authentic home life. Too little, and the day's work will become so boring as to become totally unmanageable psychologically.

On the one hand, roundsmen are asked to identify with the product. As a senior supervisor told me:

> I teach them that they've got to sell themselves first, once you've sold yourself, you can sell them something . . . you've got to get yourself liked . . . you've got to think of little phrases to say to them that you'll know they'll like . . . like patting the dog, it doesn't matter how stupid it sounds, that woman loves her dog, so if you like her dog, she's going to think the world of you . . . you go to the door and chat about everything but business, and then at the last minute after you've patted the dog, cat or child, you pick up the box of cakes, and by that time, you've got her interested.

One of the roundsmen, on the other hand, reports what too *much* job involvement leads to:

> Strain . . . I can't stand the strain, the driving, the mileage . . . it's getting me down . . . it's also getting my wife down, when she gets back from work, she expects to talk to somebody, but I'm not available to talk to . . . I'm so tired, I just can't keep awake . . . for instance, some people came round the other night, and I fell asleep, and kept moaning, in my sleep, about stuff being out of code . . . I reckon that's time to quit.

The 'involvement decision' – a general problem for *all* workers, whether to invest the self *in* work (to see work as an end in itself) or to wholly divest the self *from* work (just viewing work as a means for the achievement of other ends) resolves itself for different roundsmen at Wellbread's in different *styles* of working. These styles (given in Fig. 3.3) reflect how variations in competence (see Fig. 3.1) emerge in the context of customer interactions. The three styles are chiefly distinguished by the way that they handle the three core problems of ordinary life as a roundsman: managing time, the route and various marketing problems.

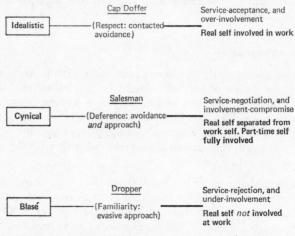

Fig. 3.3   Server styles: the baker and his customer

The competent *salesman* style reflects a continually engineered psychological compromise – one that can always spill over into over- or under-involvement. For example, competent inside production men at Wellbread's (Ditton, 1972a, p. 629) craftily mix involvement with disinvolvement and practice a sort of 'surface mental attention' as a solution to the problem of boredom. The 'salesmen' will firstly have to structure time. Doorstep interaction occurs at the intersection of roundsman and customer timetables, and experience produces a pattern of 'right times' for the baker to call. If the roundsman appears when he is expected, he will seem invisible or transparent – camouflaged by his ordinariness in the suburban drabness – and service may proceed unhindered. Nicely timed arrival is particularly difficult with wholesale customers, all of whom want a delivery at 8.30 a.m. Here the roundsman experiences the dilemma of having to resolve the problems thrown up by the firm seeking a competitive edge by promising arrival time which cannot be scheduled. It is only a slight over-characterisation of managerial action to say that they promise all customers an 8.30 a.m. delivery, and then leave it to the roundsman to solve the impossible time structure that this throws up.

'Salesmen' treat time conventionally. One commented that 'I used to make targets to reach on the round where you could relax . . . "cup-of-tea calls", or people you can have a talk with . . . you force your way to each sort of stage on the round, you can get to one of the calls, tell them that you're bloody cheesed off, and then start again'. Another 'salesman' suggested a more unusual strategy for managing his time-table:

> Well, I used to love to change the route . . . I used to start in the middle of the round sometimes, and work outwards, . . . I'm unpredictable, so that people can't say 'Oh, old Jim's coming at a particular time' . . . because I'd be there at 6 a.m. one week, and 10 a.m. the next . . . one or two used to worry about it, but I didn't do it until I knew them all, I used to look at all the little side roads, and think 'I wonder where they go?' . . . and one day, you experiment . . . to break the monotony, I might go round a different way to see somebody else first, and also I'd get the people who are going to stand there and tell you about their families . . . and you just naturally try and avoid people like that . . . by the time I got there, later on, I had the excuse that 'I'm sorry, I'm late, I can't stop'.

Route management (ensuring that one has customers by sufficiently balancing customer recruitment with customer loss to produce round regeneration) provides roundsmen with yet another problem area. However, 'salesmen' (almost by definition) generally manage to match gain with loss and produce, at worst, what the management define and tolerate as acceptable wastage.

Marketing, however, does pose problems for all. Marketing is managing to negotiate a daily fit between actual customer demand and actual bread supply. Embryonic salesmen are initially surprised that the fit is not automatic, and initially vastly over-react by increasing the supply order. As one man said of his first week:

> Well, the ordering was the only thing that I found peculiar, I always found that I used to order a hell of a lot more than I sold, I thought it would go . . . it was only when I brought a whole load of stale cake back, that they told me to cut the order down.

Each 'salesman' gradually learns to match supply with demand. One man reported 'I got it all sorted out by the next Easter, and on that holiday weekend, I only brought one loaf back the whole two days!'.

This is not a mathematical but a negotiating problem. Another man commented:

> You play this one against her . . . and you think 'I'll leave her out this week', and 'I'll leave her a Tin instead of a Farmhouse, but make sure that Mrs. So-and-So up the road gets one' . . . and normally, you get out like that . . . you could always sort of pull yourself by . . . *get by* on the round.

'Getting by' is not only skilful, but also covert. This ability is learned in parallel with that of being able to use fully yesterday's (bread) 'overs' as a solution to today's shortages. Without knowledge of the battery of stale bread management techniques, the situation is unmanageable. The salesman has to learn to 'hold'; to keep bread on his van overnight for future marketing problems. One man said 'I don't have too much over now because I keep the majority of it on, I found I was coming over and handing it in, and the management were bollocking me over the waste . . . but I just chuck it into my hospitals or contracts now'.

But 'getting by' is an anxious process, and never predictable in outcome. Each day requires constant and searching analysis. One 'salesman' claimed that he stopped 'for ten minutes' periodically to see if lasting supply matched probable demand, and another told me:

> You see, after you've done it for a few weeks, you look to see how it's going, and think to yourself: 'Cor! it's not going like it did last week', and 'Yes, I'm getting low here', and you go through your book, and you think: 'Christ! I could do with another 20 of them.'.

But not everybody has the ability to 'compromise' in this way. There are those who take *no* personal interest in work and those who, absurdly, 'live' there.

Cap doffers is the Wellbread name for the latter category – those who see all customers as being superior to themselves. This is an often noticed style of adaptation to the rigours of being a service worker, England (1973, p. 6) for example, commenting on a type of shop worker he calls the 'old school' who 'live vicariously through their customers' by basking in reflected status glory. Typically, at Wellbread's, deferential working class roundsmen adopt the 'cap doffer' style and gravitate to country rounds where, paradoxically, the classic collection of ancient landlords and simple folk have neither the need nor the call to make any status demands of their tradesmen. Accordingly, as one 'cap doffer' put it:

Well, I used to find that a lot of them used to think of me as their friend, rather than as a bloke who just calls at the door with the bread. In a country round, you *do* get more *personal* with the customers.

As a supervisor reports:

Generally (in the country) they used to treat me all right, and hardly ever as a tradesman . . . even the better class of people, funnily enough, I found the people who treated you worse, were your own working class people . . . especially in the towns.

In timetable terms, 'cap doffers' are plodders. Getting done and getting home are the least of their worries, although lateness may disrupt their interactions with their customers. Timing, for the 'cap doffer', is to be *on* time. As one said 'I'm so regular, that if I *am* ten minutes late, the old girls wonder what the hell is the matter'. Another claimed 'If I was forward, I would slow down', to allow the timetable to catch up with him. A supervisor told me:

Now, you take those old buggers, they *do* drag it out, yeah . . . if you go out with one of them, and you help him, it's a waste of time, because if you get done early, *he'll stop* . . . they all hang it out . . . if there's two or three women who say 'Don't call today' which puts him a bit early, ahead of his time, he'll stop . . . they won't go to Mrs. So-and-so until the normal time that they get there.

In terms of route management, rather than allow events to assume their *naturally* regenerative pose, 'cap doffers' deliberately ditch bad customers, even if they are good fiddle calls. Two said:

Well, if they buy a fair bit, O.K., but if they don't, I just lose them . . . I tell them straight 'You're wasting my time, and I'm wasting yours' . . . if they don't buy something three times in a week, I don't call there any more.

If I lose some, I always make sure that I gain some as well, I got four the last fortnight, and they're always the good ones . . . worth up to a pound each, some of them.

In terms of marketing, 'cap doffers' fulfil their managerial definition (sales manager: 'there are always the old men with what I call 'doffing the cap' sales, they always go to the back door, and they always touch their cap to the customer') by preferring to negotiate staleness with customers in face-to-face interaction, rather than deviously. When short, 'cap doffers' are usually too far from the bakery to have time to come back for more, and so either buy some bread in (as one of them said 'Just to satisfy the customers') from a nearby shop, or actually face the customer and explain the situation to her, possibly cooling out any inconvenience by offering bread at slightly reduced rates. Normally operating on a route a long way from the depot, 'cap doffers' inevitably come 'over' in their bread order. The standard practice for them is to hold large amounts on the van, and to sell off uncut loaves cheaply (when they are stale) to country customers with large numbers of dogs or pigs.

In total contrast to the 'cap doffer', the third style, the *dropper*, resists the idea of 'service' and sees himself as the equal of his customers. As opposed to the self-profaning deference of the 'cap doffer', the 'dropper' practices presentational rather than avoidance patterns. Whilst at work, like Jean-Paul Sartre's waiter, the 'dropper' manages subtly to convey the impression that he should not be there at all. Whilst 'cap doffers' end at retirement (as one man said 'Work is like a tunnel to them, and there's a little light at the end that they keep looking at . . . called retirement'), 'droppers' don't last long. Only those who change to wholesale work stay with Wellbread's. One who did didn't think that he could 'fetch and carry for people now', and another claimed:

> I couldn't go on the doors again . . . it's soul destroying . . . bloody soul destroying, up to each bloody door with a basket . . . 'What would you like today?' . . . and ten to one they want something that's on the bloody van.

'Droppers' have a distinctive style of timetable management, occasionally referred to as 'running'. Although 'dropping' refers to the submarketing strategy of leaving the bread at the door without bothering to knock, this is done primarily to save time. In terms of intersection with customer timetables, the 'dropper' is always early and concerned to terminate customer interactions as speedily as humanly possible. As one customer said to me about her previous roundsman, who had 'dropped' at her doorstep:

> Sometimes, I'd never see him for weeks on end, he never used to knock, or anything . . . and he hardly ever had what we wanted or ordered, he would leave us any odd thing . . . and he used to try and hide them, sometimes, we wouldn't find them for days . . . sometimes my husband would go out to the garage to do something, and he'd come back with a mouldy loaf, that looked as if it had been out there for weeks.

'Droppers' tend to view the job as just a piece rate one. Merely, as one man put it, 'seeing how you can get from A to B the quickest'.

Another added 'I just get done as quick as I can'. One of the most extraordinary examples of this under-involvement in anything not strictly necessary was relayed to me by a supervisor:

> He wouldn't even stop for a cup of tea, if anyone offered him one, he wouldn't stop to argue about it, he'd take it, and as soon as they'd gone, he'd pour it down the sink! . . . yeah! . . . that sort of attitude . . . if somebody offered us a cup of tea [when I was on with him] I used to think 'Thank God', but as soon as they'd turned their back, he'd be rid of it, and away.

Although not 'dropping' every customer, 'droppers' will at least 'carve' up the round by progressively alienating a sufficiently large number of customers to shrink the round gradually. Not bringing the basket to every door is a common trick. Relief roundsmen deputising for 'droppers' often find customers amazed to discover that Wellbread's supplies anything else but bread! Another trick is regularly to under-estimate consumer demand (on the basis of a few occasions when the call has been fruitless) and mark many of the calls in the round-book as 'E.O.D.' (every-other-day only). Those customers who waste too much time talking are dropped completely from the route-book, as are those who demand too much deference. One 'dropper', who had been reported by a particular customer for 'cheek', told me:

> When I went to that house the next time, she came out and said 'I hope your ticking off did you good', so I said 'Yes, ma'am', and I went and got the book, and tore her page out, and threw it in a little ball on her path . . . silly cow!

Unfortunately, the very customers who are undesirable are generally the ones who are exceptionally hard to ditch. As Bigus (1972, pp. 158–9) notices, both what he calls the 'holdover' (leaving 'held over', or stale produce) or the 'incompetence' tactic can be used to drive home the message. Since it is preferable that the customer terminates the relationship (thus avoiding any nastiness with the management) some roundsmen occasionally resort to the delightful but all too rare practice of 'posting'. Here a wrapped loaf is undone and posted through the appropriate letter box, slice by slice.

'Droppers' are traditionally poor marketers. They always prefer the less time consuming practice of leaving 'stales' to customers who are out to negotiating staleness face-to-face. When short, 'droppers' will either leave customers out altogether or, if facing them is inevitable, offer them two alternative loaves for the price of one. As one man said 'You'd lose a bit on it, but you'd get it back, either from them, or from somebody further up the road'. When 'over', a specific trick is to sell the surplus off at reduced price (to a shady café) rather than go to the trouble of returning it to the bakery or of holding it on the van. One 'dropper' said that one day when he was short, instead of buying-in Wellbread's from a nearby shop, or returning to the depot for more, he suddenly saw the Superloaf man:

> And I thought 'Well, bread's bread' . . . and I started off telling the customers that there had been a breakdown at the bakery, but I don't bother now . . . some of them even think that I'm the Superloaf man!! . . . after that, I never did bother to ring up again.

DIFFICULT CUSTOMERS

Of course, customers can be difficult. Sometimes, the service facade can be awkwardly 'thick' (see Fig. 3.2), as when customers take the idea of service more seriously than the roundsmen (this is called 'cantankerousness' at Wellbread's), and at other times disturbingly 'thin', when they don't, and produce what the Wellbread's salesmen wryly call 'flankers'. The different styles of interacting with customers produce different preferred ways of dealing with difficult customers.

A 'thick' facade produces 'non-person treatment' for the salesman. Here, it is not only too much deference that is demanded, but too much of everything. In interactions of this sort, the simple baker's roundsman is expected to be a baby sitter, postman, psychiatrist, friend and confidant. Most salesmen respond to such demands that they fulfil extra roles by subtly training their customers to be less demanding. This is an especial problem for beginners. When I started, I was told that customers would 'try it on', to see:

> How much you'll do for them . . . they ask you to run back to the van for them, and you have to do it for a bit . . . they want to know how willing you are . . . then, one day, you'll tell her to poke it.

Of course, every blasé roundsman will demand 'person treatment'. One Wellbread salesman told me that he would not let his customers call him 'baker' ('I hate that name, I make them call me by my real name'), and called them 'mate' or 'dear' in place of the official 'sir' or 'madam'. Another defined the customer as a 'cantankerous old bitch' just because she asked him to call at the back door.

Outright *'cantankerousness'* (always demanding more of whatever it is they think they haven't got, and always complaining when they don't get it) is a particularly seamy way of thickening the interactional facade. With the cantankerous, 'cap doffers' merely quietly persist. One, with some pride, told me:

I had a miserable old cow on the first round that I was on . . . everybody said the same thing about her . . . she was the most miserable woman I've ever met . . . when I eventually came off that round . . . she said to me 'Oh, I *am* sorry, I look forward to seeing you every morning' . . . I nearly fell off the doorstep!

'Salesmen', on the other hand, dislike such people but are determined to change them. One told me that:

You have to educate them, you have to train them . . . one I had, she was a sod . . . she was a right bitch . . . but as time went on, I could say to her 'I'm sorry, I haven't got a thick loaf, will you help me out, and take this one?' . . . and she accepted it . . . and I got on well with her in the end . . . there was even a cup of tea there for me . . . it was just a question of winning that woman over.

'Droppers', though, are less likely to go to such pains, and will probably just refuse to serve the customer or otherwise retaliate. It is not difficult to make the customer miserable without laying oneself open to reprimand. Orwell (1933, p. 101) illustrates the secret retribution enacted elsewhere, irrespective of how 'nice' the customer is: '[the waiter] told me, as a matter of pride, that he had sometimes wrung a dirty dishcloth into a customer's soup before taking it in, just to be revenged upon a member of the bourgeoisie.' This is not so much retaliation as self-definition.

Whilst not wishing to make too much of the fiddle as a way of generating psychological and secretive advantage in a sales situation, there *is* a sense in which retaliation of any kind is artful redefinition of asymmetrical status relationships. One 'dropper' at Wellbread's had his own inimitable style:

I used to keep the stale bread for the awkward customers . . . and I used to make them pay for making me write debt sheets out, and things like that . . . running back to the van . . . a sort of surcharge . . . one old bugger, if I went to the front door, she'd come to the door, but she wouldn't open it, she'd just shout 'Tradesman's entrance round the back', I gave her a stale loaf every time I delivered there . . . with some of the orders, I might get my revenge later, running over the cat, or something . . . [laugh] . . . I had one awkward one, she had a pebbled drive, she was a widow, and always running me back to the van for something . . . I used to put my foot hard down on the floorboards going out and try to scatter pebbles all over the grass to fuck the lawn-mower up . . . I used to apologise though.

Falling into the category of 'thin' facade are customer *flankers*; occasions of successful anti-fiddle – where, paradoxically, the customer fiddles the roundsman! Typically, 'salesmen' never quite know whether any particular action is a flanker or just plain stupidity. One said 'I've seen the girl on the cash desk take one before he's checked it in . . . I don't know whether she's just thick, or whether she's trying a flanker'.

'Droppers' (who are more likely to be experienced with flankers as they typically work in seedy urban areas where they are commonly found) will conversely tend to define *all* complaints as flankers. One 'dropper' refused a refund to a customer complaining of having been sold stale bread. He said:

Well, I thought she was trying to work a flanker, see? . . . I knew she was flanking, I'd sold her a Wellbread loaf, and she was handing me these slices in a farmhouse wrapper [he explained this to the customer, who looked in the dustbin for the correct wrapper] . . . her old man came out . . . and I left them there, going through the dustbin like a pair of ferrets, tossing old cornflake packets out, and snotty rags and all . . . dirty fuckers . . . I left them at it.

Conversely, 'cap doffers' may recognise a flanker, but will rarely be able to define it as actionable. One man had a particularly good example:

Yeah, they've tried it on me . . . and you won't believe this, but the one who *did* do me was the managing director's wife! . . . that's a fact! . . . she was known for doing it . . . I was warned about her, too . . . she had me for a packet of biscuits . . . usually, if you *do* have a customer who checks, and they can forget, then you have to say 'Do you remember me going back to the van to get it for you?' . . . and generally they do.

A 'thin' outcome to unequal interactional definitions is a necessary precondition for customers getting into excessive 'debt' (defined as money owing which the debtor refuses to pay). Although amounts owed are carried on to debt sheets by roundsmen even when they *will* manage to collect them, this is considered to represent a sale rather than a loss. All roundsmen are nevertheless reminded (in a note pasted to the back cover of each route book) that 'A sale which hasn't been paid for, hasn't been made'.

'Cap doffers' rarely have trouble with debtors, generally because they always define outstanding debts as collectable. 'Salesmen' similarly have little problem, but here mainly because they operate a firm rule of not allowing too much credit. It is the 'droppers' who find debtors the greatest hazard; 'droppers' seem to be unable to read the superficial enthusiasm of the intentional large debtor for what it will eventually come to be or, in fact, to maintain a service relationship with initially non-motivated, but eventually ensoured debtors. The Achilles heel of the 'dropper' is thus the intentional debtor; this perhaps results from his naïvety where actual selling is involved. Two 'droppers' said:

> One woman came out, all smiles, and asked me to serve her, she paid me to start with, but on the fourth week, she sent her little girl out for some cakes, she was a good call, six pounds a week, and I always got paid, so why worry? . . . a few weeks later, she gave it to me, the sob story, well, . . . I'm a sucker for that sort of thing . . . and I let it go up to twenty-one pounds . . . when I eventually caught her, she just turned round and said 'Piss off'.

> I'm too soft, if somebody builds up a debt, they've only got to give me a sob story, and I will accept . . . one got up to twelve pounds . . . and he started to dispute it . . . said it was nine pounds . . . he never did pay anything.

MANAGEMENT INTERACTIONS

In customer interactions, the roundsmen had to face the personal 'involvement decision'. In their dealings with the Wellbread's bakery management (where the roundsmen, in a formal sense, suddenly become the audience in a bigger, hidden drama) the roundsmen face another dilemma: to what degree should they technically *prepare* for customer interactions? Too much preparation, and selling will degenerate into a boring, mere 'delivery boy' function. Too little, and selling resources far beyond their capabilities will be demanded if they are not to become an occupational failure and either be grossly short or over in their estimation of customer demand.

The roundsman, then, is caught in the 'preparation dilemma'. As with the involvement dilemma which he faced as a performer, he somehow needs to come to a decision as to how he will construct his organisational, as opposed to his presentational, self. Preparation means, for the roundsman, submitting an adequate bread, cake and morning goods order so that, each day, he will be able to satisfy his customers without having too much produce over. One way of trying to cater simultaneously for both customer and management is to refine technically the otherwise rather hazy process of preparation by making out all one's orders from a sophisticated master bread order. This produces, for the roundsman concerned, an 'exact' amount of bread. I suggested this to the sales manager:

But you'll only go to the door with her loaf, and the packet of Crumbles, say, that she usually has . . . whereas what I would call a good salesman would be the person who tries to sell her something different each week, perhaps he still sells her Crumbles . . . but he also tries to sell her some Chocolate Weasels as well.

Curiously, then, over-preparation (like under-preparation) will lower sales. Too much 'kills' selling, too little makes it impossible. The ideal is a compromise: a bit of each. Fig. 3.4 – 'servant styles' (types of roundsmen in the management's eyes), again derived from Fig. 3.1,

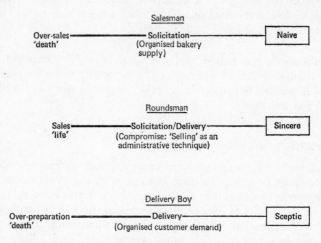

Fig. 3.4   Servant styles: the baker and the management

illustrates the specific nature of competence and incompetence in response to the 'preparation dilemma'.

For a competent, compromise *roundsman*, the positive side of sales reality (selling) absorbs its negative pole of preparation, and generates a tenuous and temporary existence. This category is empirically and not just theoretically temporary, as ever increasing profits must eventually level off, as consumer demand is locally exhausted. There is the ever present possibility that the 'roundsman' will concentrate too much on selling (and become a 'salesman', in the audience rather than performer sense), or upon preparation, and slide into the 'delivery boy' exit funnel.

One sure way of preventing this degeneration is for retail roundsmen to move to wholesale rounds, and there bask in the status reflected glory of association with early hours, large loads, big lorries and large profits. Becoming a 'delivery' *man* (rather than *boy*) allows the derogatory implications of the latter to be siphoned off. About a shop manager who had complained that a large order was a measly three loaves short, one man said 'This morning, I went in with six trays . . . I only deal in *trays* . . . not odd loaves'. Concern with the sheer effort of physically managing bulk orders excuses such men from too much concern with selling. For them, delivery *is* a socially and psychologically acceptable activity. As another wholesaler put it:

> Yeah . . . I just copy the orders out from the last time, unless I get a new call . . . if they give me one that is . . . I have to increase the order a bit . . . but I don't *look* for new calls [laugh] . . . not bloody likely! . . . I've got enough on my plate without going out canvassing.

There is the feeling that the lack of direct access to customers reduces, for them, the appropriateness of the selling ethos. But there is always the nagging feeling that they are, at heart, salesmen. I once overheard the following conversation between two 'roundsmen' delivery men:

> I never put the same order in week after week like some of the others, you know . . . I always start afresh and try to think what I can sell . . . I get all mine boxed up when I come in in the morning, and do all my box drops early, so I'm in the main town by 6 a.m.

> But that's not selling is it? . . . you're just delivering, aren't you?

> [Quickly] Look, I've put that round up by eighty pounds since I took it over.

But even some wholesale men manage to become *salesmen* (the absurdly incompetent response) by over-identification with the selling ethos. Life in this non-compromise category regrettably accelerates towards 'sales-death'. Over-concentration upon selling produces, ironically, its *own* exhaustion. Psychologically, this has the real effect of allowing, on some occasions, little sleep. One man recalled:

> I keep doing that, in the middle of the night, I wake up, and I can't see the clock properly, and I keep looking at it, and all of a sudden the hands look the other way round . . . and I think 'Christ! Half past four!' . . . and I run downstairs, still half asleep, pour the milk on the cornflakes . . . start eating them, and then all of a sudden, my eyes begin to open properly, and I notice the clock on the wall . . . and it's bloody midnight! . . . and I have to go back to bed again . . .

I'm always doing that just lately . . . my missus says 'That bloody job, it's playing on your conscience'.

Totally over-selling a round of customers pushes profits high, but the continued chances of ever increasing these profits dwindle. One top salesman recalled his early days:

> There *was* some incentive there, but you get your sort of level . . . I had one of the biggest rounds, even on retail . . . I was in the top six [salesmen] . . . but you couldn't go much above it, only by a few pounds . . . if there was a carnival, or a wedding, or something . . . you reached your level, and you just couldn't go above it . . . there wasn't any scope for any new calls . . . you couldn't fit *in* any new calls.

One solution to the problem of sales death is periodic change to a new round of customers (in fact, the last man went on to say 'that was why I decided to go on wholesale . . . I'd been on there for five years, and when you've been on a round for that long, a change is due'). More likely, it seems, is that the 'salesman' fails to see that possibility, and leaves. One such man, who left soon after I spoke to him, said:

> Well, I've got the highest sales retail round there is . . . but what can I do now? . . . I can't sell any more, I'm up to my limit now . . . I can't take any more customers on, it's *dead* now, isn't it?

One pays a price, then, for naïvety. But the sceptically incompetent audience – here of *delivery boy* style – the man who over-concentrates on preparation produces a similar occupational boredom, and an identical ending for himself. As the sales manager said:

> I'm against writing down too much in the route book, I'm against too much detail . . . if you have 'cake only Tuesday and Thursday' in the book, then he'll only get the basket out then . . . I have a lot of this trouble from the wholesale rounds, they write down a standard order for each shop and [never change it].

Most of the 'delivery boys' admit that they can write out all their orders from memory and that selling, for most of them, is a farce. One man I spoke to said (I'm just a fucking delivery bloke . . . a salesman tries to sell his stuff . . . [laugh] . . . I don't try . . . if they don't want it, bugger 'em [laugh]!'. But, unfortunately, delivery is boring. Two of the others said:

> The boredom is in the repetition . . . going to the same places every day . . . seeing the same people . . . going round the same old journey . . . you get to know where everything is . . . on retail, I knew where

every gate catch was . . . what was behind every door . . . if you saw anybody, you knew who they was, and what they were going to say . . . I'm a delivery boy, not a salesman . . . I'm more of a delivery boy than a salesman definitely.

They take you for granted after a time, they don't bother to get up, or come to the door to see you . . . you just drive up to the door, open it, put whatever it is they want inside . . . you don't talk to them any more . . . you're just delivering . . . so it changes from selling to delivering . . . which I find highly boring.

Ultimately, the result is the same for over-preparation as it is for over-selling. Occupational 'death'. A roundsman recounted why the previous man had left the round that he was then doing:

He had his run highly organised . . . he built it up so much, he involved himself in it, he messed himself up . . . do you see what I mean? . . . in the end there was no variety in it for him . . . because he'd got it so organised . . . he got too *involved* with the round.

DIFFICULTIES WITH MANAGEMENT

Some of the roundsmen take sales too seriously (put customer satisfaction above profit) and then feel righteously injured in dealings with blasé members of management. For example, although most of the men regard all the 'motivational' charts that the supervisors pin up on the sales office walls (they list sales, waste and profit performance) with undiluted scepticism – one man even feeling that they indicate a 'schoolmaster–pupil relationship, with a sarcastic ring about it' – there are those who, absurdly, feel that they are not being motivated enough. The same roundsmen (for whom the sales reality is 'thick') similarly feel embittered when orders that they fill in are not completely adhered to by despatch staffs, or when the management arbitrarily cuts the bread orders all round to reduce weekly waste.

But for most of the men, the management must struggle to solidify a precariously 'thin' facade. This is so because the bakery management are not always completely in control of the objective-supporting conditions of the sales reality. For example, when the firms which supply the bakery with cakes and biscuits fail to fill their orders, through no fault of the Wellbread's management, individual order shortfall for the roundsmen will indicate to them the hollowness of the managerial exhortations to sell. But, although the sceptics amongst the men deny any credibility to the sales facade (one of the top roundsmen said 'I never go to these sales meetings, they're a bloody waste of time'), money is a basic and material necessity. As one roundsman commented 'Let's be honest, what you're after is more money in the wage packet every week'. However, the manager perpetually tries to thicken the sales facade, referring to the sales force as a 'team' (a dramatic device for ensuring loyalty, Goffman, 1959, p. 208) and, as I mentioned in Chapter 1, by blocking every move by the men to organise themselves.

Managerial attempts to thicken (and worker reactions progressively to thin) the sales reality create an historical set of cycles similar to that of managerial 'efficiency' and the resulting shop floor 'fix' noticed so astutely by Roy (1955). Take pay, for example. The men are paid on a flat-rate basis with commission earnings (of 10 per cent and later 15 per cent) on all cash taken on each round over a certain target. The targets may have been set fairly and democratically in the first instance, but the situation has changed since then. Some rounds shrink, some grow, making it easy to make commission on some rounds and hard on others. Vaguely aware of the impossibility of setting a fair rate ('a lot of fucking guesswork' as a supervisor put it), see Ditton, 1975, the men begin to use one of the few bargaining weapons that they have – threatening to leave – to gain a drop in the target on their round. So what starts as a means of individually and divisively controlling the sales team 'efficiently', in the final analysis gets 'fixed'. The men then view commission no longer as an incentive but, instead, sceptically. It is only a short and easily recognisable step from here to quite falsely threatening to leave just to get an effective pay increase. One man claimed that you could just 'argue' the target down. Another remembered:

> I gave my notice in . . . but he came round to see me at my house and offered me [better] terms . . . [left eventually] . . . when I was working for the sweet firm, he came round again and offered more.

Eventually, of course, most of the men realise that commission is class based and that nobody will ever make a fortune out of breaking the target. One man commented sourly 'They make sure, even on wholesale, they make sure that you get about five pounds commission . . . to keep you happy . . . but not much more', and a supervisor reported the following case:

> When we took over —— [a small bakery] there was a bloke there getting about forty-five pounds a week . . . and this was in 1965! . . . they buttered him up, they said that he was the type of bloke that they needed to build the company up . . . all the old flannel, and they got him to take a job as a supervisor . . . he dropped about

twenty pounds in wages! . . . just so that they could re-target the round and bring the wage down.

Similarly, when recent governmental 'efficiency' barred sale-and-return, the men, who had depended on that system as a basis for inserting a fiddle, had to 'fix' it. One said 'That'll fuck me up good . . . most of mine was on returns . . . still, I won't lose, I'll have to put it on the booking now'. When the manager arbitrarily cuts bread orders when the waste gets a bit high, most of the men manage to anticipate and initially over-order to counteract the cut. Again, though, most read cuts as class based political action (as commission pay cuts) and not merely as acceptable profit expediency. Zeitlin (1971, p. 24) illustrates the added difficulties management can expect should they try to control remote interactions:

> Drivers for a retail bakery routinely turned over as many as 4000 loaves of bread a day to supermarket managers in return for kickbacks. Because retail prices were rising, the bakery couldn't tack the cost of thievery onto the retail price of the bread. So the company began charging drivers the full wholesale price [29c per loaf] for bread unaccounted for . . . Drivers countered by continuing their illicit sales and replacing the bread so disposed of with day old bread purchased for 10 cents a loaf from the company's day old bread store.

Several regular interactions reach a final charade stage in the eyes of the men, with the 'fix' going in, in some cases, before the 'efficiency'. Most of the roundsmen inflate their estimate of their weekly cake waste as they feel that they know full well that the submitted sum will be reduced by office girls, and perpetual battles are waged over the men's refusal to put their cash calls (which are essential for fiddling on wholesale transactions) on invoiced dockets.

A particularly relevant sector of sales experience for this analysis is the competitions which the management stage for roundsmen. Periodically, an outside sponsor (usually the agency promoting a high cost, name brand loaf) will support a competition for the highest sale of its product, and provide various cash and luxury goods rewards. This is particularly interesting as it provokes ideological confrontation between management and worker as the management simultaneously tries to motivate the workforce *and* test that motivation. Competitions are, then, in the reality sense, 'competitions'.

The men are immediately dubious of the supporting ethic of competitions. One commented 'I'm a bit suspicious . . . with the same bloke winning all the time', and most believe them to be a theoretically unsound idea. As one man frankly and cleverly pointed out:

If you're doing the job properly, they're [competitions] a farce . . .
you *shouldn't* be able to do any better than you normally do . . . to
tell the truth, I *never* take any interest in them.

Scepticism abounds. 'It's worked out on a most stupid system. A
system of points where you get four points for selling loaves over a
certain datum . . . it gets more stupid and complicated as it goes on . . .
at the end, they hand round a little catalogue, and you can choose
things to get with the points you've accumulated.' But this attitude is
not born in thin air. It is derived from hard, concrete experience that
every stage of every competition is a 'fix'.

The datum for any particular competition (the quantity which must
be over-sold to accumulate points) is usually set on an average performance basis taken from the sales record of each man during the four
weeks preceding the initiation of the competition. Bright 'competitors'
need in the first instance to discover when a competition is coming up.
It is said of one man 'He can go out, and he can take any prize that he
wants. I still say that he fixes it, because he's in the know with the
blokes at the bakery . . . and if something's coming up, they have to
know to order more flour and things like that'. Alternatively, the
roundsman can bribe the man setting the targets to do so, in one
instance at least, favourably:

> He came up to me and said 'I'm doing the targets for so-and-so
> competition' . . . this was last year, he said this . . . and he said 'Ounce
> of tobacco, and I'll drop it fifty' . . . there you go, look! . . . if he'd
> drop mine fifty, how did I know he wasn't dropping some other
> bugger's?

One man thought that the targets were not even set before the
competition began, but that instead 'they wait for the first week's
result, then they set the datum for about two pounds less than that
result', providing yet another example of class pay. Competitions
degenerate into a game, and not the sort of game that the management
intend. After a while, competitions begin to contradict, and not
support, the sales ethos:

> I only used to go for the Slimloaf competition . . . which was the only
> one I reckoned I stood a chance in . . . you get certain blokes always
> win certain competitions . . . like ——, he'll always win the Weatie
> Loaf one, it's a trick of the trade, you *know* when these competitions
> are going to come . . . he gets a tip off . . . and I always know that
> four weeks after that one, mine will come up . . . therefore, I drop my
> sales right down in those four weeks, and bump it right up during
> the competition.

The real business of the competition can be fixed too. A standardised practice is to 'stuff' the shops with the relevant loaf and even refuse to supply customers with near alternatives, insisting, instead, that they take the competition loaf. One man overcharges his customers for the competition loaves, but tells them that he is selling them at half price. Consequently the shop keeper sells more bread, customers get it cheaply, and the man's datum is exceeded. Everybody, at least as far as they know, is happy. Those loaves which fail to sell are either held on the van until after the competition is over, and quietly returned at a later date, or are slipped back into the bakery with the connivance of a despatch employee.

The winner is fixed anyway. When the figures are analysed after the competition is over, one man firmly believed that the supervisors concerned with checking results clip odd amounts off the submitted totals if 'they look excessive'. An experienced roundsman added:

Old —— had been coming short for some time, and he owed them quite a bit of money . . . but there was this competition, see? . . . with cash prizes . . . well, we should have had similar datums because we were doing about the same sales then . . . but he won the first prize of fifteen pounds . . . and of course, they took the cheque as the money he owed them . . . I said to him at the time 'Your target is twenty pounds lower than mine' . . . that was the biggest bloody fiddle going . . . they're just fixed . . . no doubt about it.

Several men have bitterly experienced survival at every stage of the competition, but yet, at the last hurdle, have failed to get their prize. At one level, the management just refuse point blank to hand the goods over. One man, who should have won five bottles of whisky, only got three. He said 'I went and complained to him, and he said that that was all they could afford to give me. He said that they'd only had eighty bottles for the whole firm. Well, I helped the bloke unload the whisky when the lorry arrived. Twenty crates with 320 bottles in . . . I went back and saw him, to complain, and he said "We've lost the papers for the competition now" '. The same roundsman had already had a similar experience:

They'd had a competition before, and I'd already won about forty pounds in the previous one . . . well, they forgot to take into account that the football was starting, and I came over my datum by thousands of pounds, and should have got about ninety pounds . . . well, to start with, they only paid me thirty pounds . . . when I complained about that, they gave me another twenty pounds . . . but what good was that? . . . eventually, I didn't pay my cash in . . . well,

he paid me the same day . . . out of a little tin he had in the office . . .
and he was the same bloke who said that the firm couldn't afford to
pay me.

ORGANISING SELF

The service relationship thus provides the psychological as well as the
material and empirical context for fiddling. Whilst there is an obvious
quantitative relation between fiddling and selling (in the sense that the
bigger the transaction, the greater the amount of the fiddle that can be
slipped into it), the sales manager at the 'Tiger' bakery noticed an
ironic convergence between fiddling and selling, as well as the symbolic
relationship:

> I know that if I've got fifteen salesmen out there, I've got fifteen
> fiddlers . . . and I've got this theory, and it's only a theory, that the
> top salesmen are the top fiddlers.

I shall examine this apparent paradox (thrown up by the analysis of
'service') in Chapter 7. How has this furthered the understanding of
salesmen who continue to fiddle customers when released from training
to practice on their own? It seems that the particular context of bread
selling demands the negotiation and management of a special 'service'
relationship. The very consciousness of this demand produces, for the
roundsman, interactional sense *as* performance. Reflection upon this
interpenetration produces only one satisfactory and permanent resolu-
tion of the stage dilemma of involvement in and reflection upon
performance; the 'sales personality' (as the Wellbread sales manual
refers to it) or the *part-time* self. Subsequently, it is *this* existential
partiality which acts as a psychologically insulating and legitimating
scaffolding for the fiddle. It is the *ordinary* experiences of daily life as a
salesman at Wellbread's that provide an enduring meaningful milieu
for fiddling.

4 Structure: 'Part-Time' Crimes at Wellbread's

Two basic conditions of sales existence operate to modify *how* the Wellbread salesman will use the moral licence for illegal activity he was coerced to adopt during socialisation, and persuaded to retain in everyday sales life. These two conditions are the differences in *scope* that his relations with customers will outline, and the variations in contexts of *opportunities* that are presented to him in his dealings with the inside bakery men.

Firstly, the form that his illegal activity takes depends partially upon the *scope* offered the roundsman by the type and size of the 'round' to which he has been allocated. The sales hinterland is divided into a set of forty-nine routes, nineteen of which are 'wholesale' (W/S), and the remainder 'retail' (Rt). A 'round' is a route specially coloured with a particular and unique history of salesmen and customers. Recruits are always trained on used rounds, and thus any situationally and charac- terologically appropriate choice of a 'correct' mode of fiddling will succeed or fail in terms of its ability to merge with historically accepted practices on that round. This 'situated self' found in customer expecta- tions strongly etches performance norms upon the *tabula rasa* of the neophyte salesman. As initial socialisation proceeds by example, recruits are accordingly encouraged by supervisors to fiddle by 'appeals to continuity', which may or may not be phrased as 'appeals to loyalty'.

So when training induces a recruit to practise the fiddle, it induces him to do it in certain ways. Salesmen failing to accept the need to curtail practice to fit pre-existing fiddle patterns that have historically occurred on the round experience particular problems. In fact, it is this discrepancy (or its absence) between recruit predilections and idiosyncratic, historically accepted practices which either entraps or protects salesmen. For example, it is said of some who have merely failed to follow literally in their predecessor's fiddle-steps, rather than over-fiddled, that 'He got greedy in the end', or 'He carved up that seaside run', or even 'He's what you'd call a shark . . . he just done everybody, left, right and centre'.

Differences in scope can also arise from the ways that the management organises customers into groups served by different *types* of round. W/S (wholesale) rounds deal in large quantities of goods, selling to a small number of customers (about thirty, but taking up to £1000 a week gross sales). Essentially, W/S salesmen deliver to resale outlets as middlemen, operating on a planned marketing basis. More time and care is given to each customer and the wholesalers, as a group, are an élitist band recruited from the best of the retail salesmen. One W/S man said:

> I *prefer* wholesale . . . I don't know why, you feel as if you're selling more . . . if you sell an extra bit of cake on retail, you get pleased with yourself, in a shop it's an extra *tray* . . . because it's bigger, it seems to give more satisfaction . . . On W/S, let's be honest, you don't go out to make a couple of bob . . . [on fiddles] . . . like retail, do you? . . . you go out to make four or five quid, don't you?

Rt (retail) salesmen, on the other hand, sell much smaller quantities of goods to a larger number (250–300) of customers, but only taking about £100–£250 a week in sales. Retail men act as door-to-door salesmen, and operate by 'pushing' the goods as front men. The most important difference for Rt men in organising fiddling is the type of customer and the sorts of treatment that the salesman can expect from different types. This is primarily seen as the difference between country and town people. One salesman claimed that country people had more 'character', and another offered a crucial effect:

> I wish I had a country round . . . much nicer, they treat you differently in the country . . . they greet you . . . like . . . you were coming round to *help* them . . . as an *equal* . . . whereas in the town, they just think you're a *servant*.

The typical result of fiddling customers is to add a bit onto the bill. In retrospect, this amounts to adding a *percentage* on. In fact, the metaphor of slight accretion ('padding', 'packing') adopted by fiddlers everywhere is commonly balanced by the victims' view of it as slight erosion ('chisel', 'cream' and 'skim'). At Wellbread's, with skill and finesse, the percentage can be as great as 10 per cent. Ultimately, however, the differences in the gross amounts that can be creamed off are dependent upon the size of the round. Two, fairly typical, examples, will do. Whereas a retail man told me that he thought two to three pounds a week on the side was 'pretty good', a wholesaler said:

I normally, on a good week, have about twenty-five pounds out, but I took an extra fifty-seven pounds out that week, because I was going on holiday . . . and I still came two pounds over on the rec!

Secondly, because rounds are scheduled to tie in with customer timetables and because there are not enough loading bays at the depot, every roundsman has a scheduled loading time. This produces variations in the contexts of *opportunity* that different salesmen have for stealing from, and dealing with, despatch employees. Coincidence of entry at different points on the despatch work pattern produces four distinct entry statuses for salesmen in the eyes of despatch workers: 'early birds', 'big boys', 'old stagers' and 'small timers'.

Three of the W/S salesmen arrive particularly early at the depot (about 3 a.m.) either to synchronise with early customers (ships leaving early from the docks) or to travel long distances before starting to sell. Their arrival coincides with the completion of normal duties by despatch staffs, who are still issuing or slicing bread, and who have not yet changed from stock production and stock distribution to stock control. At this time in the morning, greater areas of the despatch territory are open for free access by salesmen, although gradually, as the morning matures, these free access areas will diminish in size, and be replaced by large areas restricted to non-sales personnel. Despatch staffs are still, however, at this time in the morning, working at various points in the despatch area, and are not yet concentrated in the office at one end of the despatch area, where they eventually congregate to drink tea, and from which their collective view of what is going on in the territory for which they are responsible is limited.

Thus, despatch staffs' knowledge of the practices of 'early birds' is extensive, and their relations with them tend to be either extremely good or extremely bad. One 'early bird', who was subtle enough not to try to take advantage of despatch staffs' preoccupation with work rather than stock control found that he was allowed to take a few extra loaves each morning from the rack of spare day-stock bread which was situated a long way from his loading bay, and near the despatch office. He told me that he was able to do it 'openly', and that 'It's a sort of deal, really, they're easy with you as long as you don't go too heavy'. Another 'early bird' had broken this rule, and had so annoyed despatch workers with complaints and thefts that they began to 'watch him like a hawk' (as one of them put it). He told me, morosely, 'You can't even get a tray of bread now, you used to be able to get that at least'.

The 'big boys', wholesalers on large local delivery, begin to arrive at 4.30 a.m., but are normally loaded and away by 5.30 a.m. Their arrival coincides with the despatch tea break, which symbolises for despatch staff the change from stock distribution to stock control. 'Big boys' have typically good relations with despatch men, providing somebody for the latter to talk to and share tea with. Although, by now, the day stock is counted and out of bounds for 'big boys', control is only exercised mildly and haphazardly from inside the despatch office. As one said 'If you tell them you're short, they'll give it to you without too much fuss as a rule'.

Between 6 and 6.45 a.m., the 'old stagers' arrive and load on the top bays of the depot, furthest from the office. Accurate timing is crucial for them, as to successfully retrieve stale bread from the 'back passage' (a long passage, out of sight of the despatch office, running from the despatch area parallel with the plant, in which 'stales' which have come in from the outlying depots during the night are stored prior to being checked by the despatch manager) they need to be there after the despatch shift has gone home (about 6 a.m.) but before the despatch manager arrives for work at 6.20 a.m. Most of the 'old stagers' are middle aged retailers on large country rounds who rely upon selling a few stales to customers as dog food. Because, however, their entry time is close enough to the exit of the despatch staffs, they sometimes also deal in a small way with minor despatch men.

'Small timers', on the other hand, are not supposed to arrive until after the despatch manager. This is actually a rule. 'Small timers' comprise the rest of the retail salesmen, and their arrival between 6.45 a.m. and 7.45 a.m. precludes them from dealing with despatch staff (as they cannot synchronise with them for the 'payoff') and from any significant stealing from stock under the watchful eye of the manager. Some members of this group have occasionally tried to overcome these problems by earlier arrival, but the immediate suspicion that this places on them requires that they either substantiate their presence with an acceptable remark (such as 'getting a good start to get finished early to go on holiday'), or subject their vans to rigorous search. On top of this, salesmen's attempts to operate in off-limits or out of bounds areas will render them liable to report, challenge or suspicion, and may make them marked men.

The salesman's entry status thus acts as an invisible harness upon his illegal activities. In sum, the objective extent of fiddling customers (i.e. the weekly 'take' he may expect) will be, in the last analysis, ruled by the scope that round of customers offers. On top of this, the legitimate size of his round (and its type) will typically allocate him an entry status which will irremediably condition the nature of his relationships with despatch staffs; a vital condition both for successful stealing from and successful dealing with them.

STEALING FROM WORK

As I mentioned in Chapter 2, the Wellbread's management regularly make a distinction which puzzles recruits. As one put it 'They seem to think that taking bread from them is wrong, and fiddling their customers is right'. The rationale is obvious: the management are not so snippy about other people's losses. However, various strategies and processes operate in the bakery to reduce considerably the management's awareness of their *own* losses. Although the management is more concerned with calculating loss than with diagnosing its exact nature, even loss assessment is a hazy business. There was not even regular agreement at Wellbread's over what daily shortage figure was acceptable. One manager said:

> Anything up to a hundred pounds, but it's very hard to say, because on some occasions, we've been thirty or forty pounds short and they've not said a word, and sometimes, we're thirty five or forty five pounds short, and they'll say 'You're short' . . . you see, you can't really pin this down to a specific amount.

Actually, because some losses can be sustained without contributing to this daily total, the inventory implications of different types of theft by salesmen will be crucial. There are four different sorts of deliberate loss. Apart from loss of non-inventorised stock like plastic bags and clip boards, the management face accounted loss, *mis*accounted loss and *un*accounted loss. Only thefts in the latter two categories may escape detection. Firstly, *misaccounted* losses arise through classification error. There is often reticence at Wellbread's to label loss as due to malign rather than to understandably benign sources (for anti-defamatory as well as philanthropic reasons). When despatch staffs discover that goods are 'missing', an elaborately evasive vocabulary is used. Since inefficiency is as likely as theft, a non-stigmatising batch of terms which reserve final judgement is used. In the despatch department, absent chocolate fingers were said to have 'walked', bread to have 'gone astray' (if permanently, to have 'vanished'), jam puffs and other confectionery to have 'disappeared', and boxed cake to have 'flown'. These preliminary and kindly categories reflect later official inventory euphemisms, such as 'distressed' merchandise (Klockars, 1974, p. 184) or 'inventory shrinkage'. There is not only a permanent 'dustbin' ('damaged') category to absorb inexplicable loss but, also at Wellbread's, those with access to the inventories are sometimes those simultaneously doing the stealing. Quite regularly, inside dealer charge-hands not only checked the production sheets for errors they could use to their illicit advantage, but also sometimes altered totals to hide their thefts. Occasionally, other inside men dealt whole racks of bread which they then claimed *they* had been short delivered by the other production bakery in the chain. At other times, when straight despatch staff found 'extra' bread on salesmen's racks, they were told that 'inexperienced casuals must have made a mistake'.

Unaccounted losses, on the other hand, are 'invisible' to inventory search. They may either be permanently unaccountable (such as when customers are fiddled by salesmen) or temporarily unaccountable, such as when an employee 'covers' his thefts by carrying (rather than euphemistically resorting) his stolen deficit. Because customers have no collective (and often no individual) audit, they rarely discover their losses. When factory inventories are falsified to cover losses, the losses are theoretically discoverable, although they may lie dormant for long enough to make tracing the origin of the initial loss impossible. In these terms, of the forms of employee theft practised by Wellbread salesmen, 'fiddling' customers is permanently unaccountable loss, 'dealing' is temporarily unaccountable, except when it is unorganised (when the stock-sheets are not altered) which, like 'stealing', is accountable.

But employee theft is also situated in a different sort of economic context. British blue-collar employee thefts are currently estimated at £1305 millions per year (Ditton, 1976a, p. 25), and in the U.S.A., the total has been calculated as between $8.5 and $10 billions per year (Zeitlin, 1971, p. 22). These totals are considerably more than those lost to spectacular crimes like burglary and robbery. The cost of the latter has been recently estimated in Britain at £80 million per year (*The Times*, 2 December 1975). For the U.S.A., Sutherland (1949, p. 52) puts the disparity nicely in perspective:

> An officer of a chain grocery store in one year embezzled $600,000 which was six times the annual losses from 500 burglaries and robberies of the stores in that chain. Public enemies numbers one to six secured $130,000 by burglary and robbery in 1938, while the sum stolen by Ivar Krueger is estimated at $250,000,000, or nearly two thousand times as much.

But can we really see employee thefts as a 'loss'? Apart from the fact that it is sometimes difficult to decide upon the value of a stolen item (do you take retail value or production cost? How do you put a value upon damaged or surplus stock?), as Martin (1962, p. 115) rather nicely asks, what is the carpenter to do with the unneeded cut offs, the waiter with the half-empty bottles of wine? It seems to be more realistic to see those amounts pilfered and fiddled by workers in the same way as we look at the 'perks' of the executive – as an invisible part of wages. This is in line with how we conventionally treat corporate overcharging

– where the 'losses' to the customers are simultaneously the 'profits' of the organisation. This latter blurring makes white-collar and corporate 'crimes' increasingly difficult to cost, although Jaspan and Black (1960, p. 52) are probably summing up the proportions accurately when they say:

> Any white-collar employee is in a position to bite the hand that feeds him. The difference is that, while the ordinary worker may nibble on a finger or two, the executive invariably swallows the arm and sometimes the whole corporate body.

Nevertheless, the *levels* of blue-collar employee theft have remained surprisingly constant, with 'inventory shrinkage' normally settling at between one and a quarter and two per cent, varying chiefly with the gross figure to which the loss is contrasted. Wellbread's was no exception. Whilst the total weekly illegal 'take' that the Wellbread's salesmen made from fiddling, dealing and stealing was ultimately proportionate to the parameters of size and type of round and context of opportunity, the amount that an experienced and sophisticated roundsman would take hovered around the 'ten per cent of gross sales' level. This gave some of the 'big boys' an illicit income of over one hundred pounds per week, whereas most of the 'small timers' had to be content with a mere three or four pounds in a good week. Nevertheless, each man had an illicit income on top of his legitimate income amounting to approximately ten per cent of his sales. About a fifth of this illicit income (equivalent to two per cent of each man's sales) would have appeared in the next audit as a loss to the firm (i.e. was either stealing or unorganised trade dealing). The remaining four fifths of the illicit income (equivalent to eight per cent of each man's sales) was in the form of systematically concealed (and thus unaccountable and 'invisible') thefts from customers or from the firm. At least half of this (four per cent of each man's sales) was fiddled from customers.

The 'pilferer' is usually explained away with the rotten apple thesis; a morally defective individual, unable to resist temptation, liable to infect others. If the individual has failed to use or resell the stolen items he may be called a 'human magpie' (as a shipyard worker with a shed full of company tools was in the *Daily Mirror*, 10 September 1974). In fact, employee offenders rarely match the stereotype of the pitifully inadequate petty thief. Ironically, employee offenders (apart from their dishonesty) often resemble the stereotypically *perfect* employee, generally filling trusted positions, working hard (for nefarious purposes), coming early and leaving late, and when the occasion demands virtuously offering to remain behind to 'do' the yearly inventory. While it is usually assumed that the few corrupt employees steal large amounts, the (slight) statistical evidence could also support the contention that practically *all* employees *regularly* take relatively *small* amounts. To support this, consider the following data:

Spencer (1965, p. 348) has complete data for the Metropolitan Police area for 1957, when, of 4112 fraud convictions, only 122 involved amounts of over one hundred pounds. Zeitlin (1971, p. 24) relates extrapolated totals to staff numbers and emerges with the data that $300 per year ($1.50 per day) is stolen in retail establishments per employee, and that 'all the evidence' points to an implicated three quarters of all employees. Similarly, Jaspan and Black (1960, p. 236) admit that there was at least a fifty per cent dishonest employee rate even among those firms who had called in Jaspan's consultancy firm on quite different grounds.

There is extensive but scattered evidence that blue-collar employee theft is very widely practised at most places of work. Riis and Patric (1942) note that sixty three per cent of the garages that they 'tested' (218 out of 347) employed mechanics who attempted to 'gyp' them, and that sixty four per cent of radio repair men, and forty nine per cent of watch repairers were similarly dishonest. Laird (1950, p. 211) quotes the example of an American drug manufacturing chain who sustained a $1.5 millions loss in six months. The firm used lie detector tests on 1400 employees, sixty two per cent of whom admitted petty thefts before the tests were administered, with a further fourteen per cent admitting similar offences after test completion. Robin (1965, p. 7) quotes another firm where all those with access to money were tested, and fifty four out of fifty nine confessed to thefts. Yet another American firm discovered that eighty per cent of its employees were regularly stealing at least two dollars each per week; a supermarket study revealed that ninety per cent of those employed created shortages of $1.5 millions per year through thefts; eighty six per cent of parcel delivery men in Chicago admitted stealing packages from their vans, and Horning (1970, p. 60) found that ninety one per cent of factory employees had pilfered from their place of work. Cort (1959, p. 341) discovered that seventy five per cent of chain store employees steal, and Curtis (1960, p. 66) quotes a remarkable example of one store which he investigated where 150 employees were simultaneously but separately thieving. Robin (1965, p. 11) concludes that, on average, sixty five per cent of money handling employees steal cash, and that the thief proportions in work forces with merchandise access is even greater.

This evidence is impressive. Conventional explanations of 'pilfering' are certainly not relevant to these data. Accordingly, how can blue-collar employee theft (such as those varieties found at Wellbread's) be explained?

In short, what sort of crime is 'fiddling'? There are no obvious historical clues. Mayhew's (1862, IV, p. 25) extensive typology of criminal types is broad enough to include such highly specialised and defunct types as the 'dead lurker' (one who 'steals coats and umbrellas from passages at dusk or on Sunday afternoons'), but mentions no fiddler. However, fiddling seems to combine simultaneously two contradictory and irreconcilable features:

(i) It is a *mala prohibita* ('quiet') offence, given the occasional and partial psychological status similar to that typically felt by 'folk' criminals like traffic offenders (Ross, 1960–61, p. 326). Fiddlers do not feel stigmatised in the same way as white-collar criminals do not.

(ii) It is a *mala in se* ('classical') crime. The 'natural' crime of theft is regularly and habitually indulged in by salesmen.

Firstly, could fiddling be a form of white-collar crime? Sutherland (1949, p. 9) defined white-collar crime as 'a crime committed by a person of respectability and high social status in the course of his occupation'. However, Sutherland himself was vague as to what occupations this should include, and later (Sutherland, 1956, p. 58) he began to see 'white-collar' as a broader category, 'more generally to refer to the wage earning class that wears good clothes to work, such as clerks in stores'. This would fit the salesmen at Wellbread's, especially to the extent (some of them wear a collar and tie) that they see themselves as 'salesmen' rather than delivery boys. Thus, fiddling would be an example of white-collar crime, when the concept is extensively interpreted to refer chiefly to its logical, employee basis. Fiddling would, for example, be an occasion of Pepinsky's (1974, p. 229) 'challenge to an alleged use of private property', or Caldwell's (1958, p. 377) 'a breach of trust which is usually accompanied and consummated by misrepresentation'. Newman (1958, p. 737) considers the fact of occupation as more essential than its status:

The chief criterion for a crime to be 'white-collar' is that it occurs as part of, or a deviation from, the violator's occupational role. Technically, this is more crucial than the type of law violated or the relative prestige of the violator . . . likewise farmers, repairmen, and others in essentially non-white-collar occupations could, through such illegalities as watering milk for public consumption, making unnecessary 'repairs' on television sets, and so forth, be classified as white-collar violators.

D

However, it has become conventional to concentrate upon the status of the offender (rather than the fact that his offence is intimately related to his gainful employment) and to restrict 'white-collar' to those violators with a high social status. Thus, Shoemaker and South (1974, p. 193) omit clerical and sales positions from inclusion, as their status, although white-collar, is not any higher than many blue-collar skilled jobs. Levens (1964, p. 328) similarly comments:

A number of white-collar offences can equally be committed by persons of acceptably white-collar status (like solicitors, managers, clerks, accountants) and by others who would not normally qualify for such a description (postmen, general dealers, dairy roundsmen, shop assistants, etc.).

Together with this narrowing of the concept of white-collar crime, there has been a parallel movement to restructure the overall field on a more logical basis. Quinney (1964, p. 210) has introduced the logical alternative: 'occupational crime', which Robin (1974, p. 262) defines as 'non-violent vocational property offences'. He adds:

Occupational crimes may be defined to include all violations that occur during the course of occupational activity and are related to employment.

Whilst blue-collar crime would fall under this rubric, a further definition is needed to avoid the standard paradoxical compositions depicting blue-collar crime, such as Hall's 'embezzler in shirt sleeves, the truck driver and warehouse employee' (quoted in Robin, 1967, p. 691), or the standard paraphrase of Sutherland: 'A crime committed by a person of *low* social status in the course of his occupation'. Donald Horning (1970, p. 48) provides an excellent definition of blue-collar theft:

One form of blue-collar crime may be defined simply as the illegal or unauthorised utilisation of facilities or removal and conversion to one's own use of company property or personal property located on the plant premises by non-salaried personnel employed in the plant.

Secondly, because theft is *mala in se*, the blue-collar thief shares some characteristics with the full-time criminal. For instance, 'fiddling' (in the specific sense of *theft* from customers) would count as a 'racket' in Sutherland's (1937, p. 43) terms, as it involves the 'manipulation of suckers by non-violent methods', and as 'grift' in Maurer's (1940, p. 15) sense as it requires the 'skilled hand and sharp wit'. A crucial difference is, however, that the fiddler is practising an identical legitimate occupation within which he submerges his illegal peculations – a rather literal interpretation of Sutherland's specification that a 'racketeer' must be a good actor and a good salesman!

Fiddling is an occupational form of 'part-time' crime. Part-time crime is not simply the opposite of full-time crime, where, as John Mack (1964, p. 39) puts it:

> Although the people concerned have some nominal occupation which they practise more or less regularly, they are known to be engaged in or available for criminal activity at all times.

In fact, part-time crimes and full-time crimes have some similarities (practitioners are infrequently caught and rarely imprisoned). Nor is part-timeness a simple chronological matter. In fact, a part-time offender might well spend more hours and minutes breaking the law than somebody involved full-time in crime. The crucial distinction is that whereas the full-time criminal's legitimate occupation is perceived by him to be merely nominal the part-time criminal sees his *il*legitimate activities in the same way, as nominal. This distinction is forced upon offenders by qualitative differences in the societal reaction to different forms of deviant practice. In dire opposition to the malevolent general reaction to practices like robbery and burglary (forcing some practitioners psychologically and practically to embrace the activity full-time), part-time criminals experience a benevolent and excessively muted societal reaction. This societal normalisation allows them to continue at the theoretical level of secondary deviance, to classify psychologically the fact that they are law breakers as an auxiliary or 'partial' character trait. (Malevolent societal criminalisation conventionally transforms initial infraction for full-time criminals to the state where it becomes a psychological 'totality', a master character trait.) For part-time criminals, then, it is the nature of control which guarantees the psychological 'partiality' of the criminal activity in the actor's reflexive construction of his self. In theoretical terms, part-time crime may be defined as those forms of criminal activity which are psychologically unaffected by societal reaction, and which eternally retain their primary-deviation status in the eyes of practitioners. In this sense, societal reaction does not transform primary into secondary deviance, but instead entrenches it rigidly and ultimately as primary – and part-time.

The non-occupational and widely practised rareties of part-time crime include tax-*evasion*, fare-*dodging*, benefit-*scrounging*, and, perhaps most widely acknowledged, shop-*lifting*. The practitioners of these crimes all experience the same 'partial' psychological consequences of infraction. For example, Cameron says of the 'snitcher', the non-professional shoplifter (1964, p. 182):

Their crimes are peripheral to rather than central to their lives . . . [each] has a vocation which is legitimate. His career may be in merchandising, clerical work, teaching, machine operating, nursing, truck-driving, medicine. His major source of livelihood is from his respectable career and he identifies with the dominant values of society.

The Wellbread salesmen's fiddles are occupational part-time crimes. As a rule, part-time occupational criminals have a full-time legitimate occupation in which they are predominantly involved, both in terms of time and personal commitment. During the course of proper practice of that occupation, they surreptitiously and regularly indulge in minor illegal acts which are generally visibly indistinguishable from their legitimate activity. Examples from other occupations include almost universal instances of bribery, graft and corruption (Schuck, 1972), general expenses and pay-roll padding (Dalton, 1964, p. 109), prescription-violation by retail chemists (Quinney, 1963), 'ambulance chasing' by unscrupulous American lawyers (Richstein, 1965), 'adulteration' of foodstuffs (Clinard, 1969), embezzlement (Cressey, 1953) and so on. These activities are regularly and habitually immersed in standard occupational routines, and carried on as a side-involvement to everyday legitimate occupational activity.

Fiddling, stealing and dealing at Wellbread's, as occupational 'part-time' crimes, finally exhibit some of the technical characterisations of 'craft theft' as defined by McIntosh (1971, p. 102): a highly routinised, repetitive and skilled set of criminal techniques for taking small amounts from a large number of victims. Because people do not bother to take pains to protect themselves against such minor crimes:

> The salient feature of craft thieving is that the routinised patterns of behaviour make it a relatively safe way of earning a steady but rather low income . . . craft criminals aim not to be noticed while they are working, even though their victims may be present at the time. Indeed, many a craft theft is never discovered at all since it is hard to know whether things have been lost or stolen. This is the major way in which craft criminals reduce the risks of detection.

With these economic and analytic discussions in mind, I shall now try to characterise the nature, extent and types of 'part-time' crime at Wellbread's.

FIDDLING

Skill at 'fiddling' customers is a major criterion of unofficial status amongst Wellbread salesmen. In the absence of comparable historical clues, what does fiddling mean? It has a number of possible derivative sources, all of which probably combine to give it its current usage. It can mean a player of the fiddle (stringed instrument), and hence an entertainer; a small sum (originally one sixteenth of one pound on the London Stock Exchange); and probably derives from a strictly defined term in bookbinding, where to 'fiddle the books' actually meant sewing book sections together by hand with a type of cross stitch. The art of fiddling inevitably comes from a subsidiary meaning as sleight of hand: perhaps even indirectly from the Victorian art of 'fiddle-duffing' (Chesney, 1970, p. 229), where a 'drunken' violinist offers to sell his allegedly expensive instrument for a song. Currently, the practice has been noticed as 'finagling' (Davis, 1959), 'gypping' (Riis and Patric, 1942) or 'gouging' (Leonard and Weber, 1970) in the U.S.A., and as fiddling (Mars, 1973, and Henry, 1976) in the U.K. But few of these definitions coincide, so I have simply presented the standard Well-bread's wisdom: fiddling is of customers (and is trifling); stealing (sometimes objectively identical to the fiddle) is of management and is accordingly morally outrageous.

In transactional terms, a successful fiddle refers to over-charging: the practice by salesmen of invisibly altering the ownership of goods in transactions with customers to cover expropriations from a money (or equivalent) source within the fiddler's control. Such an extensive inductive definition is needed to take account not only of simple over-charging, but also the complex procedures needed on some occasions to obtain the cash benefit.

Even over-charging can be of two sorts. Firstly, the price is simply increased to unknowing customers; although the 'price of bread' is heavily invested with moral and symbolic significance, few people actually know *what* it is. Secondly, the price, but not the size of the delivery remains constant. Traditionally (Thompson, 1971), bakers rarely let an opportunity to squeeze customers pass by; sometimes literally, when all else failed, one sort of grinding was exchanged for another. Corn merchants and dealers engaged in adulteration and in 'forestalling' (selling by sample to restricted rings of buyers rather than on the open market). Millers were frequently, according to Thompson (1971, p. 104):

Accused of quaintly mediaeval customs – oversize toll dishes, flour concealed in the casings of stones, etc. . . . some millers purchased at half price damaged corn which they then mixed with the corn of their customers.

Further, the baker himself was frequently accused of making and selling inferior, adulterated, and light-weight loaves. Analytically, either the quality can be reduced and the price stay constant (under-weigh) or the quantity may similarly suffer (short deliver). Mayhew (1872, IV, p. 383) notes: 'embezzlement is often committed by journey-men bakers entrusted by their employers with quantities of bread to distribute to customers', and similarly, Kirkland (1911, III, p. 249) adds: 'as these barrowmen have to collect weekly amounts as well as deliver bread, it is not surprising that, particularly among the poorly paid ones, there is a good deal of trouble with petty thefts and embezzlements'.

Nowadays the situation is simple for retail salesmen: customers lose money in sales transactions in clear, simple and easily specifiable ways. The fiddled retail customer either gets the ordered number of items at a higher price (over-charge) or a reduced number of items for the standard price (short deliver). Whilst this is occurring, the customer may unwittingly accept insufficient change (short change). The percentage made is simply physically diverted from the cash bag (a large leather pocket hung by a leather thong from the neck down to the waist) to the salesman's own pocket.

Wholesalers, on the other hand, have a separate triplicate carbon, receipt/invoice docket for each call. The top copy of each docket is divided into six easily removed sections, each section consecutively representing a day of the week. Each week the salesman is given a fresh docket for each call by the Wellbread sales office. Each day, upon delivery, he fills in the daily section and tears off the section, or 'stub', and gives it to the customer. At the end of the week, the customer has six identifiable docket stubs, which he may later check against his bill. The salesman returns the remaining two complete carbons for each call to the sales office. The office girls price each invoice, after deducting discounts, and the salesman normally returns one priced carbon to each customer the next week as a bill. As the office thus has a complete and accurate check of how much cash is required from each wholesale customer, none can be diverted by salesmen. Since the customer has a collection of delivery docket stubs, which can be checked against the returned bill, the roundsman cannot add fictitious amounts to daily invoices after he has delivered the goods.

It seems to be a very closed and tight system. However, most whole-sale rounds have 'cash calls'; customers who, for various reasons, prefer to pay in cash rather than be invoiced. The Wellbread's sales office thus has no record of how much is paid in by these customers to the salesmen each week. Additionally, the assumptions that the customer is com-petent to check that the bread given to him tallies with that listed on the delivery docket stub which he is given at the time, that the amounts on this stub tally with those on the returned invoice/bill, and that the office addition and discounting has been done accurately are theoretically satisfactory, but (as we shall see) wholly impractical.

Calls, for the fiddling wholesaler, are thus divided into 'make' calls and 'take' calls, and the process of fiddling (instantaneous in practical terms for the retailer) has two practically separable stages; fiddling 'make' calls provide cover for complete or partial withdrawal of funds from 'take' cash calls. The 'take' has no argot name at Wellbread's, and this is rather unusual. Mars (personal communication) has discussed the use of the word 'turnover' by bread salesmen in London, the 'weed' in English fair-grounds, the 'dropsy' amongst waiters, and the 'sparrow' by dustmen. At Wellbread's, the crucial difference between wholesale and retail fiddling lies in the theoretical possibility that sales office staff might check up on the absence of cash inflow from cash calls that they know about. However, as one supervisor put it when I questioned him about the difference between wholesale and retail 'if somebody *wanted* to catch you [on wholesale] they could more easily'. But he remembered the case when:

One of the women in the office started comparing the amounts of ordered bread with the returned dockets, . . . she said that she had to check one off with the other when a bloke was 'short', so why shouldn't she do it when blokes came 'over'? . . . the blokes got together, and they soon told her to stop doing that.

The two stages of fiddling (theoretically for retailers and empirically for wholesalers) that I have described, analytically exhibit dramaturgic characteristics of both 'con-men' and of embezzlers, as described by Goffman (1952, p. 483):

The con is practised on private persons by talented actors who methodically and regularly build up informal social relationships just for the purpose of abusing them; white collar crime is practiced on organisations by persons who learn to abuse positions of trust which they once filled faithfully. The one exploits poise; the other, position.

Unlike the 'con', however, there are no practices designed to make the fiddled customer aware of what has happened to her, and the success of the transaction does not rely upon her greedy collaboration. In fact, it is essential that the customer *never* discovers her loss, so that the fiddle can be practised again under the cover of the legitimate work transactions on the baker's next visit. In interactional terms, the fiddle emerges as a delusive interaction undertaken within the sale, but wherein the fiddled (the customer) is unaware of her role and thus an unwitting partner to the fiddle.

There are three crucial symbolic preconditions of fiddling: trust, identity control, and customer typification. Firstly, trust. Although the Wellbread salesmen are basically and initially distrusted by their customers, they fully recognise both the need for trust as a structural basis for successful fiddling and the peculiar clues that typical customers rely upon in establishing trustworthiness in salesmen. One roundsman claimed that 'respect' was crucial and that a recruit he had trained 'doesn't say "Good morning", just "Eh?"'; they'll never trust him, *he'll* never make anything'. Ironically, whereas customers see trust as natural and unalterable, salesmen see it as supremely man made. Another roundsman said:

I never give my customers a *thing* for themselves, not a *thing* . . . that was the way I started, and I've never given any of them anything . . . it makes them trust me funnily enough . . . you don't want to let them think you can cover anything.

Salesmen even believe that core traits, like 'genuineness' are systematically acquirable. In fact, simply 'performing' as a salesman *is* to induce the customer to experience him trustingly. The dramatic nature of the sales situation prevents the otherwise natural development of trust-corroding hypocrisy. The salesman's 'body gloss' (Goffman, 1971, p. 162) is overwhelming: he positively exudes trust. Accordingly the salesman gains interactional control of sales occasions by so controlling the customer's view that she will voluntarily act in ways that make fiddling easier.

The fiddle is thus slipped into standard interactions in subtle ways that serve to clothe it in protective fictions. The fiddle is a socially invisible and technically non-existent act. There are neither tools nor booty to be concealed from the gaze of the victim, and the financial losses to the customer are strictly unaccountable. If the fiddle 'fails', it will be immediately apparent, and the rent in the delicate interactional fabric that failure produces can be invisibly and verbally repaired.

Secondly, in the sales act, legitimate selling emerges as the 'dominant role' (Gross and Stone, 1970, p. 179) of the fiddler, or his 'virtual' social identity (Goffman, 1963, p. 12). The fiddle itself is an 'adjunct' role, a disguised and hidden 'actual' social identity, a side involvement knowingly performed only by the fiddler, in parallel with his dominant role performance. However, it is a side involvement that must be concealed (treated as a 'dark secret' in the baker's occupational culture) because it is incompatible with the conception of 'service' that the sales performance wishes to foster.

Looking at this in game terms, a precondition of fiddling is that the salesman be a routinely successful practitioner of an obscure version of what Scott and Lyman (1970b, p. 58) refer to as an 'information game' which arises 'whenever one actor wishes to uncover information from another who wishes to conceal it'. In these terms, the checking process of the customer might be seen as a 'control move' (information seeking), and the routine ways that the salesman prevents discreditable information leaking out during checking as 'covering moves'. 'Moves', as such, are not necessarily perceptively and sequentially organised in that way. In fact, neither participant need be aware of the game-like structure of the proceedings at all (Scott, 1968, p. 158). Nevertheless, the salesman's awareness of his fiddling identity transforms him (in game terms) into a career deceiver or, as Scott and Lyman (1970b, pp. 58–9) put it, one who 'must play information games almost all the time, or as part of [their] occupations'.

In terms of identity, the fiddler has to 'pass' his self, perhaps as well as his 'stales', in front of customers, although he can drop this strategic self for short periods in dealings with his peers back at the depot. Successful sealing off of unmanageable biographic facts produces a 'closed awareness context' (Glaser and Strauss, 1964, p. 10) wherein 'one interactant does not know either the other's identity or the other's view of his identity'. This context is basically unstable because successful uncovering moves by customers are always theoretically possible, however empirically unlikely.

Thirdly, the baker's round of customers is subdivided into those who are disqualified from being fiddled (generally disabled, e.g. blind pensioners, or excellent game-players, e.g. hefty ex-salesmen – both of whom would provide problems as victims, one psychologically, and the other practically) – and the rest, who qualify as 'fair game'. This is important. Not all customers are fiddled, merely those who can be fiddled without infringing the psychological or practical status of the part-time self. Being selective, giving the world a chance to defend itself in this way, allows the salesman to redefine fiddling from the unremittingly exploitative, to the fair game context.

Rock (1973, p. 78) summarises the situation succinctly. 'The deviant thus lives in a world which is populated by the knowing, the unknowing and the too knowing.' The fiddler lives in a world where customers may know nothing, too much, or just possess that little knowledge that qualifies them (in the game sense) for play.

The customer varies considerably in the sort of 'interest' he has in checking the sales transaction and it is sometimes necessary for the fiddler to use sophisticated distracting techniques to waylay accurate checking. Structurally, however, retailers are faced with customers who are simultaneously checker, consumer *and* payer. Wholesalers, on the other hand, experience selling situations where one or more of these functional roles is not played. The consumer role is never present during the checking situation for wholesale salesmen and at some calls, such as hospitals, payment is on a national basis, consumption is by inmates, and checking is enacted by disinterested bureaucratic sub-ordinates. St. Mary's Hospital was such a call:

> St. Mary's Hospital used to be a hell of a call, they used to over-book, ditch stales, deal with the chef . . . the lot . . . nobody checked the bread in, we were supposed to go into the kitchen, and see how much bread was left in the cupboard . . . and make it up to twenty five sliced, and ten smalls . . . well, they used to chuck a couple of stales in, and book them the full amount . . . not every day, of course, they used to knock one or two off now and again, to make it look good.

Customers also initiate different means of checking which have to be understood before fiddling can proceed unhindered. The 'single check' is to check either the amount of bread coming in, the number of loaves on the docket stub, or the office addition on the bill. 'Double checkers' might check the bread in against the bread billed (fiddler would overcharge); the office addition against the bread in (fiddler would add bread onto the bill, or short deliver); or the office addition against the bread billed (where the fiddler would overbook). 'Treble checking' checks all three, and if this is combined with a systematically closed system (i.e. one with no occasional slips) fiddling chances dwindle. However, most checking systems, of whatever complexity, are relatively open in this sense, thus allowing occasions for large amounts of money or goods to be added invisibly to the bill. As one wholesaler put it:

> A lot of the calls, they think that you make it on stale returns . . . they wouldn't *dream* that I book extra bread in! . . . but they check my returns religiously! . . . and if I leave a single loaf off the returns, they'll leave me a note the next day.

Salesmen find checking procedures more time consuming than insulting, as most wholesalers have very tight timetables and probably other, very loose, calls. One salesman remembered a call that took half an hour to do because the manager checked thoroughly. He continued:

> Sometimes I say to him 'I'll give you a fiver if you can find a mistake' . . . hoping that he'll say 'You can put it up' . . . [put bread on display] . . . not because I've fiddled him, just to save time.

Establishing whether or not a call can be fiddled is the outcome of a delicate process of *'trying out'*. For wholesale salesmen, once a call has been successfully tried out, it is regularly and effortlessly fiddled. For retailers, on the other hand, calls are tried out and, if they prove to be what the men refer to as 'easy touches', attempts are regularly made to '*try it on*' with them. A retailer and a wholesaler explained this process:

> After a bit, I got to know the ones who added up what they had and the ones who didn't . . . I used to try them out . . . I used to think 'Oh, I'll put threepence on and see if she says anything', and I used to say, if it was four-and-six, 'Four shillings and ninepence' . . . and if she give me the money, I'd wonder if she'd say anything the next day, and if she didn't, I'd know she didn't add it up.

> He [the previous roundsman] . . . never used to give credit for returns from the shops, that's how he used to make his cover, . . . or sometimes, he'd make twelve loaves look like fourteen on a tray, if you hold it up high, or grip it close to your belly, they don't know that you haven't got fourteen on a tray . . . that's the best way, you walk past, and say 'here's a tray', and carry it above your head . . . I often do that.

Rather than having specifically inefficient checking procedures, some customers are just generally careless or incapable, and some salesmen are phenomenally quick witted and dexterous. One retailer admiringly remembered a roundsman practising an ancient technique called (Giles, 1954, p. 220) 'ringing the changes':

> You know, I once went with this bloke from the Superloaf bakery . . . he said 'Short change them, yeah, but never overcharge them, you're daft if you do, it's against the Trades Descriptions Act' . . . he'd been on that round for about five years, and he was a fly bugger! He used to count the change so fast . . . then he'd say 'Sorry, ma'am, it's a shilling short', she'd give him the other shilling, and then he'd turn his hand over, just to me, and he'd have it tucked between his fingers underneath . . . and he used to take the money, and then ask if she had a pound note, as he had so much change, and then he used to take the money *again*, and give her a whole load of two bob bits to make up for it, . . . you know, so it looked a lot! . . . he made five pounds in a morning, think what he made in a week.

Such processes are generally applied by salesmen in situations which separate analytically as three basic strategy types. These strategy types (standard techniques, techniques particular to specific control checking systems, and techniques to exploit sporadically occurring, or one off occasions) in fact apply to the analysis of the commission of *all* part-time crimes undertaken by Wellbread salesmen.

Firstly, just in terms of fiddling, *standard techniques* of fiddling are applied universally to all the calls thus, in fact, constructing a price system which is related to criteria other than cost or profit concern. Regular bread price changes provide temporary learning problems for the salesmen, but almost continual ignorance for the customer. During inflationary periods, there is no time for a regular price to become stabilised in consumer culture. Thus, ineffectual moaning by customers replaces effective checking and (as we shall see in Chapter 6) the fairly pointless 'warning story' on most occasions replaces the long term or lateral check on the salesman's honesty. Each salesman is able to carry a personal price list with official prices sufficiently rearranged to cover uncalculable mistakes that occur to his disadvantage. This is fiddling in the way that supervisors intend (see Chapter 2), and is sufficiently and customarily recognised in the food retail trade to be known as 'buncing'. 'Buncing' is minimal standard over-charging to cover small but inevitable loss. For Wellbread's retailers, this means marking up specific items. As a supervisor once put it to me:

Look, you can make it a bit easier on yourself, anyway, you always charge a bit over for the small tin loaves, everybody does, so instead of 6½p, charge 7½p, . . . that makes it easier, doesn't it? . . . rolls are 20p a dozen, and not 19p, and if you sell four, charge them the same as a packet, 8p.

In wholesale selling, standard over-charging emerges as up-pricing unpriced goods, such as cakes and confectionery, as bread prices are stipulated on the dockets that the customer sees. Similar techniques are used in other service industries, although bakery salesmen differ inasmuch as some of the 'made' money is left in the kitty to cover mistakes.

The second major technique is the application of regular techniques differentially to *specific control checking systems*. Differentially exploiting various control checking systems is the chief modus operandi of the wholesaler. In retail selling, this is replaced by the gambit of 'doing' the 'easy touch'. At one wholesale call (on a round on which I was being trained), the supervisor murmured that he had forgotten the price of the large fruit slabs. Quickly and accurately, I replied '46½p'. In tones of utmost horror, he turned to me and said 'Good God! No! . . . not the real price . . . what he charges them here . . . I think it's 60p, yes, we'll charge them that . . .'. Another wholesaler related his experience at an army camp on his round:

Yeah, and cakes too, I had to drop their stuff off in three separate places, and I had to give them the big cakes, and charge them for three small ones . . . in the end I was even doing it with swiss rolls, and charging them for fruit slabs.

The final basic strategy type concerns the development of a sophisticated fund of 'bent' knowledge to *exploit sporadic or one off occasions*. Retailers regularly fiddle casual customers in ways that their regular calls might easily detect. Not only are casuals charged more (justified as a surcharge for inconvenience) but also they are often duped with 'stales'. The price ignorance and non-return of casual customers makes them easily exploitable in most service industries. Mars (1973, p. 205), for example, reports that in the hotel dining room trade, only casuals (called 'chance') are eligible for fiddling as residents charge meals to their bill.

Wellbread's wholesalers have to rely either on the ignorance of a substitute checker or upon uncharacteristic slip-ups by the regular man. One reported:

> Some calls you just can't do . . . I've got one call like that on my round . . . he checks everything, it's just not possible to do him . . . mind you, I had a field day when he was on holiday.

Dimensions crucially distinguishing the fiddle from other ways of making money on the side are, firstly, tolerance of it or even overt recommendation of it by management because, secondly, the loser is exclusively the customer and not the firm. In terms of these two criteria, *stealing* is defined quite differently from fiddling at Wellbread's.

STEALING

Stealing refers to the application by Wellbread salesmen of illicit skills roughly similar to fiddling to the firm and not the customer. Such thefts are unambiguously defined as 'pilferage' (see Ditton, 1976a): *all* thefts from the firm by salesmen are unequivocally treated as 'stealing'. This is different from the managerial encouragement of fiddling (as we have already seen), and quite different from their treatment of production workers who have 'pilfering rights' to a daily loaf. Although extra bread is baked to cover this latter contingency, the bread is not freely distributed as a 'perk'; the men instead have to 'pilfer' it. Salesmen are specifically excluded from this dubious privilege. It is assumed that production staff have no outlet other than domestic consumption for pilfered loaves, and that this empirical feature of the practice will de facto limit the amount of bread that they will take. Salesmen, on the other hand, are assumed to have guaranteed occupational access to facilities (a round of customers) which would encourage them systematically to escalate their thefts beyond tolerable levels. Thus, for salesmen at Wellbread's, we may define a successful steal as the removal of some sort of asset skilfully, unobserved, and without permission. Salesmen steal both convertible consumer goods for resale to their customers, and non-convertible assets, such as plastic bags and clipboards, which, as tools of the trade, make occupational life easier.

Transactionally, stealing is obtaining goods either for personal use or as cover for later cash withdrawals. Although changed ownership of goods is the outcome, the practice is in essence the realignment of responsibility frontiers between actors for goods for which they were organisationally responsible. In interactional terms, stealing is generally a solitary action, completed in the absence of other actors, but highly cognisant of their possible presence or sudden appearance. As opposed to fiddling, which has a functional role in the system of the powerful, stealing constitutes a marginal threat to the firm as the management see it. It is a threat because it involves the subtle rearranging of segments of official practices; it is only marginally so because the losses involved can either be predicted and planned for in production, or economically tolerated.

As salesmen are held accountable for accurate ordering, checking, loading and returning of goods, they are allowed some access to relevant stages of despatch work. Each day, on return to the depot, the salesman initially returns unsold bread, and credits his current bread order sheet accordingly. These bread order sheets are kept in the despatch office in a pile on the desk, and each salesman comes in with his returns, rifles the pile for his old order, and enters his returns in the appropriate column for the office staff eventually to credit to his account. He is then allowed into the despatch area, where the racks of orders are being prepared for the next day's selling, so that he can check and make minor adjustments to his next day's order sheet which is attached to his rack. Subsequently, he is supposed to complete separate orders for bread, cakes, biscuits and confectionery in the sales office. When this is done, these advance orders are passed to the office staff so that his round account may be appropriately debited. Figures for adjustments and returns are later passed to the sales office for reassessment of credit or debit.

When he arrives at work the next day, he checks that the bread that has been issued to him on his rack tallies with the order that he has made out. If he has been under-issued, he can complain to the despatch staff who, if in agreement, may complete his order. If his order is complete, but in his estimation either too small or too large, he may obtain 'extras' (for which he is debited) or hand back surpluses for credit. Cake, confectionery, and biscuit returns are tallied weekly and processed similarly.

Every stage of this process is regularly fixed by salesmen, using three basic strategy types similar to those used to fiddle. All salesmen (including 'straights') exploit specific errors in *standard situations*. Errors regularly occur in despatch work, and salesmen rarely report those disadvantaging them. More actively, some salesmen construct orders in ways they feel will make positive mistakes more likely (by, for example, writing figures which they hope the sales office will interpret as '7' and the despatch man as '9'), a tactic also noticed by Mars (1973, p. 204), or by adding figures after orders have been charged to their accounts. One salesman who 'altered his ticket' (he had surreptitiously changed '10' into '100') was caught and sacked by the despatch manager. The sales staff, had they been involved, would have been more lenient. A supervisor told me 'Pity we didn't see it, one of us could have seen him and told him not to be so bloody daft'.

Some experienced men hope to rely on double-checking laxity by despatch staffs, by first checking the stock racks (to see what stock bread is available) and then posting an appropriate complaint. Skilled despatch men are, however, aware of this gambit, although they regularly allow some salesmen to take small amounts in this way. One despatch charge-hand told me:

> I stick the spare stock in the bakery . . . nobody's ever short then!
> . . . take old Sid, he always comes over to the stock rack to see what we've got before telling me he's short of anything.

Skilled salesmen also regularly exploit *general weaknesses* in bakery control checking systems. Salesmen of different status have widely varying access to stealable merchandise, as I have already discussed, but even within relatively free access areas, the despatch acceptability of stealing varies with the sort of definitions that they have attached to various goods. As Table 4.1 (overleaf) shows, a knowledgeable salesman arriving at an appropriate time will experience less difficulty than the naïve late-comer. The variations in the organisational responsibilities for bread makes theft gradually more difficult to accomplish. Exploiting general weaknesses primarily refers to collection of stock odds and ends lying on the floor; removal of 'stales' and stealing of day stock bread from the stock racks near the despatch office (if this can be accomplished unseen); or enlarging credits on return sheets, and reducing debits that pass to individual sales accounts – the common technique of 'padding'. Returning cake waste on Saturday provides the best opportunity for making large regular amounts, as the process is relatively unchecked. One man suggested the opposing tensions involved in making money here. He said that on the one hand he always submits a waste figure of about nine pounds ('I keep it the same so that they won't suspect anything and cut it down') but, on the

TABLE 4.1   Merchandise categories

Responsibility	Type of stock stolen	Victim
Despatch responsibility	Counted (Future stock, tomorrow's stock, day sliced stock)	Impersonal property Theft *may* offend despatch workers (Organisation = Victim)
Stock of intermediate and suspended responsibility	*Un*counted (Other day stock, stales)	*Victimless* Theft offends *no*body until despatch manager arrives at work
Salesman's responsibility	Issued *and* counted (Issued bread)	Personal property Theft offends *every*body (Salesman = Victim)

other, he had to remember to 'book some figure like £8.79, or something' so as to appear more realistic.

General weaknesses may also be exploited passively. Rather than chance offence by placing despatch staff or other salesmen in awkward situations, some salesmen prefer to fix figures in the credit or debit columns of accounting situations within their control. Retailers are often particularly adept at fixing 'debts'. Every retail salesman has a debt folder in which he records weekly money owing to him by his customers, so that the office girls may accurately balance his books. If customers leave, they may be recorded as having 'flitted' with large debts, and wholly fictitious debts may be inserted to cover withdrawals necessary to allow particular expenses. This 'phoney debt' trick is also a common one: collecting doubtful debts but reporting them uncollectable seems to occur to most service agents. The possibilities and variations at Wellbread's are enormous. One man remembered having seen a supervisor write '£2 discount' on a debt sheet once, and then did so himself every week, thus simply adding two pounds to his 'make' kitty!

The third stealing strategy involves the development of a sufficiently experienced fund of knowledge so that potential *breakdowns* in bakery control can be espied and exploited. Sometimes relevant information is passed between trusted salesmen, as in the following case. When a relief manager began to book 'extras' in the 'returns' column (thus crediting rather than debiting the roundsman with the goods), the word spread down the bays like wildfire, and within five minutes a queue of roundsmen wanting 'extras' stretched from the despatch office.

More frequent, however, are potential control lapses that are simultaneously 'sussed' by several salesmen:

> Do you know what happened the other day? . . . I got back to the depot, and the Cake bloke was there . . . and he said 'How long am I supposed to wait here' [to be unloaded] . . . so I said 'Just stick them on the bay, mate' . . . didn't I? . . . and after that, the Packet Cake man arrived and unloaded, and after him the Fruit Loaf man copied him . . . well, I didn't know all this was going on, as I was in the canteen having my lunch . . . when I came out, I saw it all stacked up there . . . I couldn't take my eyes off it! . . . all the blokes were coming into the yard, they would walk past, not seeing it, say 'Hello' to me, and I would see their eyes move past me and see all this stuff lying about . . . well, three of us got together didn't we? . . . backed a van up, one of us inside, and two watching outside, we stashed the stuff at ——'s house . . . just as well, we nearly got caught you know, apparently, all the Fruit Loaves were date coded, and they [Wellbread's] returned the rest to the company . . . so we were the only ones with loaves stamped '13th' . . . I was planning to stick a few of them in as cake waste, you know, dirty them up a bit, stamp on them and pull them about, luckily [a supervisor] warned me, and I warned the boys, . . . lucky I did, or we would have been out for sure.

Occasionally, two or more salesmen will pair up as a team, for a one-off attempt. One or more to provide distraction, or look-out, and one to steal.

> I used to think that was the safest way, that way you were the only one who knew you had it [stealing as opposed to dealing] . . . I used to 'borrow' a tray from stock . . . [laugh] . . . you have to wait until the right moment, we used to work in a pair . . . '——' and myself, one would cover for the other one, if you come in here at the right time in the morning, you'd find them all drinking tea in the office, and you didn't have a lot to watch, if you positioned yourself right, you could make sure that none of them moved . . . we never went past them, we used to put it on the rack, and *then* pull the rack across.

DEALING

All stealing, however, implies the possibility of collision with agents of control. Such inherent dangers are deliberately removed in the third form of occupational 'part-time' crime practised by Wellbread's salesmen: 'dealing'. Dealing can be defined as meaning the careful and clandestine unofficial distribution of other people's goods to the mutual interest and profit of those covertly involved. Collision becomes collusion: separated organisational relationships become 'cosy' (Klockars, 1974, p. 181). This is not so much abetment (by one employee of the nefarious designs of another) nor just collusion (a fraudulent secret understanding between ostensible opponents), but specifically subversion by salesmen of inside staffs and of the organisational rule which legitimately distances them.

Transactionally, collaborative dealing between salesmen and others constitutes a central threat to the way that the powerful in the factory have designed the distribution of goods and roles. A deal is essentially a role change inasmuch as the same number of roles is present in the interaction, but they are assumed by *fewer* actors. In such a rationalisation of service, the firm loses its percentage of the 'action' to both the dealer (who deals) and the 'dealee' (to whom it is dealt). By assuming a role not officially allocated to him, the dealer distributes goods which may or may not have been deliberately manipulated by him to become 'invisible' at the next inventory. The sharing of standard roles between conniving incumbents crosses official work group boundaries and elevates the stealing team into a dealing plot.

At the bakery, the deliberate buying in of control agents simultaneously provides extra safety, but a smaller percentage of the illicit profit for the salesman. In addition, this percentage can be further reduced if the salesman indulges in multiple dealing (buying from bakery staffs, and selling to morally unrestrained customers as 'hot' bread) rather than mere single dealing (buying from a bakery dealer, i.e. collusive buying, and selling normally; or collusive selling, i.e. 'making' goods somewhere on the round, and then selling the thus covered goods covertly to a shopkeeper in exchange for cash or groceries). But whatever the cover bought by the dealer, the multistaged dealing process is similar.

The first stage in successful dealing is the '*set-up*' (Goffman, 1971, p. 210). This, the 'clandestine phase' of the operation, is initiated by a secretly signalled opening move. However, the penalties for rejection of an offered deal (from either side) have been defined so that an outright offer is acknowledged as being out of the question. Instead, the 'request' (Goffman, 1971, p. 145) or stimulated offer is substituted. This is necessary because one can neither offer to, nor accept a deal without the suspicion that it might be a 'set-up' of an undesired sort. One of the Wellbread's salesmen remembered that 'I knew something was "on"', because I used to see this bloody trolley coming round, and everybody was getting bread off it'. But knowledge is insufficient: this man did nothing because 'I didn't want to lay myself open'.

The initial individual set-up is generally the construction of a non-chance transaction from an everyday casual encounter by a particularly interested member who believes that others have similar interests. The deal is 'on' when both parties combine all the possible communicative elements of the interaction in the same way, thus elevating the 'conversation' to a new meaning structure. Thus 'putting out feelers' (Goffman, 1959, p. 188) may result in successful 'double talk' which only performers can read and understand. At Wellbread's, the object of this pseudo-conversation is to prevent the risk of the bakery transaction reaching the official end of charging the salesman. Classically, between sales and staff, the 'alerting phrase' for those 'in the know' is the demand for, or offer of, 'extra bread', or the query 'Is there any bread about?'. Such talk is straightforwardly legitimate (if partially absurd) for straights, but ambiguous for experienced men. Indeed, Henry (1976, p. 183) notes how amateur dealing of stolen goods is managed through what he refers to as 'the ambiguous presentation of goods'. Henry found that this sort of dealing is initiated 'with what members described variously as a "test line" or a "probe line" concerning the request for or offer of "cheap goods", "cheap gear", "cheap stuff"'. In the same way, at Wellbread's, the receiver fills in the meaning in his own way; the wise 'wisely' and the ignorant innocently.

At the set-up stage, such a request can mean either the legitimate booking of bread in the extras column of the salesman's bread order sheet, or that the bread should not be booked anywhere. I asked an inside dealer, who was well aware of the possibilities and traps involved, how deals get set-up:

> It's hard to say really . . . I don't know how it comes about, might be like '——' [a straight despatch man] . . . a roundsman asked him for two 'extra' trays of bread one morning . . . and he said 'Don't book them, I'll see you later' . . . 'course, '——' went right in and told the manager . . . but if you were inclined to make a few bob, you'd most likely say 'Fair enough mate', and start off like that . . . or, you can get asked for 'extra', like one bloke did, and he gave it to him, and he just didn't book it down, see? . . . and later, the roundsman said 'You didn't book that tray' . . . and the bloke said 'No, I don't think I'll bother' . . . so he said 'O.K.' . . . and it starts from there, it usually turns into a regular thing.

For the set-up to succeed, then the dealer must understand the dealee (and vice versa), and both must trust one another. In Glaser and Strauss' (1964) terms, set-up changes from a closed awareness context (wherein neither knows the other's identity) through a suspicion awareness context, to a final open awareness context. If the set-up is 'on', then the parties involved have tactically negotiated a successful and favourably judged awareness context change. Sometimes, however, such subtleties are dropped, especially by experienced dealers, when attempting to set up what they define as good prospects. Several salesmen offered accounts of blunt and surprisingly risky opening gambits by inside dealers. One roundsman remembered that once he had naïvely asked for extra bread, and the despatch man 'just said "You can pay me Friday." . . . just like that!' Another claimed having made a similar request, only to be told 'I won't book that one, you can make it right with me at the end of the week, right?'. Another roundsman illustrates that even the most devious approach cannot finally avoid the issue:

> It was funny how it started . . . one day I came in and found an extra fourteen on . . . well, I didn't say anything, just put them on the van . . . and the next day, the same thing happened . . . well, I happened to see '——' and '——' in the canteen, and '——' looked at me and said to '——' 'He's so tight, he'd sell his grandmother', well, I didn't connect the two at the time, but I saw them again, after I had found more bread on my rack . . . and they started saying that I was tight again, so I said to them 'What do you mean?' . . . see, I wondered where those trays came from, but you can't go up to anybody and say 'Have you been putting extra on my rack?' can you? . . . you have to wait until they approach *you* . . . so I gave him a quid, and said 'That all right?' . . . and he looked at me, and said 'You'll do'.

Behind the scenes, however, it occasionally happens that a salesman who is 'in' will recommend a friend of his not at that time involved. Alternatively, 'wise' salesmen may understand what is going on and pester friends who are currently benefiting to be allowed 'in'. Thus knowledge of dealing is neither a sufficient nor a necessary condition of its practice. Two salesmen gave examples of 'sidling' into dealing:

> One of the other blokes said 'Well, there *is* a deal going on, I don't know whether you want some' . . . one of the [inside] shifts worked like that . . . but the other one just put it on my rack, and then came round, quite open about it, and asked for the money . . . the other shift, you had to ask for it to be set up . . . but the first one just put it on the rack, and then came round after I'd checked the bread, if I hadn't said that I'd got extra.

Christ almighty! . . . he'd only been back two weeks [from being suspended for dealing] and he came up to me and said 'Could I get him into the cheap bread' . . . just like that.

Acknowledgement concludes the opening move, and allows the second stage of dealing – *'transaction'* – the 'covert phase' (Goffman, 1971, p. 304) to proceed. This stage is relatively unproblematic unless several despatch men are dealing simultaneously and, in extreme, with only one salesman. Double dealing is awkward, as a different 'drop spot' (on the rack, under the van, below the loading ramp) has to be found for each dealer. Generally, though, in simple deals, bread can be left inconspicuously on racks of bread legitimately prepared for salesmen.

Potentially far more visible, however, is the third and final stage, the *'pay-off'*. Traditionally, loose cash is never offered nor accepted, and all pay-offs are conducted in notes. Because it is difficult to find a sufficiently hidden place to accept and check the pay-off at the depot at loading times, and because the sight of such transactions has only one possible interpretation for uninvolved staff, most dealers stipulate a pay-off time and place, as one despatch man put it 'Down-town, or somewhere like that'. A salesman commented that he rarely started paying off until the dealer had proved his worth by dealing 'several times first, even then I wouldn't pay him until he was out of the way, if he came up to me when there was other people about, he wouldn't get it'. He told me how sophisticated salesmen even avoid legitimate dealings with those with whom they are dealing:

Same with '——', I wouldn't pay him unless I saw him elsewhere, and he knew that . . . I could trust him, but I wouldn't pay him where anybody could see us . . . I wouldn't even talk to him in the depot in case somebody got suspicious . . . even if I was short of bread, I might ask the charge-hand, but never '——', I'd avoid him and he'd avoid me, the moment the despatch manager sees you talking to somebody, he suspects . . . I'd never leave the money anywhere, I'd never give the money to anybody to give it him . . . you can't trust anybody.

For the salesman, varieties of deals are available, and most salesmen take advantage of all possibilities. Analytically, deals can be either *traffic* (a strategy, whereby the dealer purposefully plans the transaction and deliberately passes the inventory responsibility for the goods involved elsewhere), or *trade* (a tactic, or unplanned game without inventory cover, whose success relies upon successful immediate game-playing abilities by the players). Traffic deals tend to become regularised, whereas trade deals are specifically ad hoc, requiring renewed negotiation each time, even with and between trusted traders.

Inside traffic offers the greatest potential safety and profit to the experienced salesmen. Primarily, they involve thick sliced or thin sliced bread, dealt by the inside charge-hands and their associates. Only charge-hands have both the access to stock figures and the power to alter them to cover 'losses'. One salesman claimed that his dealing was (inventorily) protected because his dealer, a charge-hand 'knows what he's doing, he goes through those figures with a fine tooth comb . . . he knows what he can cover'. In the production bakery departments, those in charge regularly make out stock sheets. Despatch charge-hands have sanctioned access to these sheets so that they may regularly check that the amounts of products that they require match those they are about to receive. Charge-hands who are also dealers can change the figures recorded on these sheets to cover the products they are dealing. For example, a high waste figure for a particular run of bread may be pencilled in, and the amount added on can then be deducted and dealt without a loss ever becoming visible.

Inside traffic deals can also be set up with inside staff members not strictly concerned with the despatching process. Such deals are not so common, and usually evolve from personal ties which crosscut official work responsibilities. One salesman had got sufficiently friendly with his supervisor to convince him to allow the salesman to load his cake order, and then take the order slip back and attach it to another man's cake order. The salesman concluded 'Then *I* goes in, and asks another supervisor for "my" cake order, see?'. Another man got close to an office girl at Wellbread's, before he popped an unusual question:

> Then I gradually got round to the idea and the way she did it was, I would write out two orders, a small one for charging, and a large one that she'd pass through for issuing.

Individual despatch workers, if not embroiled in the trafficking of charge-hands, may decide to set up on their own, and trade with willing salesmen. Because they often do not have the power to order straights from the dealing scene, pay-offs cut drastically into their profit margins. Coupled with this, each 'trade' has to be situationally re-negotiated on a fresh basis, thus reducing the predictability and consequent value of trading for salesmen.

Outside the depot, traffic deals are called 'sidelines', and constitute more the use of work-allocated sales roles to make individual profit on unofficial goods than the subversive corruption of control agents to obtain standard produce illicitly. On occasions where sidelines are 'pushed', retailers concentrate on high bulk/high fragility items (such as eggs and potatoes), whereas wholesalers occasionally use their different type of customer access to fence high profit/low bulk items, such as stolen coats and radios.

Sometimes chances arise for salesmen to trade-deal with regular suppliers to the bakery. One man recalled

> I saw the Fruit Loaf man unloading at lunch-time, so I asked him if he had any 'spare' . . . he said 'Yeah, take as many as you want' . . . I took three boxes, and he said that he normally got 84p a box for them . . . so I gave him £2.52, which was a third of what they were worth.

Alternatively, these trade-deals may be set up with some of the official customers of Wellbread's, sometimes quite by chance. One roundsman got started by bluntly asking a shop manager 'Can you shift some for me?' when he had more cakes than he could sell, and adding 'I'll let you make a few bob at it'. Another claimed that a shop manager began with the test line 'Cor! I've got a load of stales!'. The salesman thought about it, and then said to the manager 'I'll tell you what I'll do, to cut your losses, I'll give you half credit'. He told me 'If you walk out with a quid's worth, you know you've made ten bob, I dreamed that one up myself, that was helping him, and me at the same time'. A third salesman claimed that setting up trade-deals is a long-winded and difficult process:

> Well, first you've got to know the person . . . and keep your ears open to what people say, once you know he's on the bent side, then you can approach him . . . I spoke to the Superloaf man about '——' [shop manager] and other bits and pieces came in, then, you're going in there daily, and you begin to talk to him, and then you say 'Would anything interest you?' . . . you have to come out with it sooner or later . . . anyway he ('——') was always coming up to me and saying 'Hello, baker, got anything on the van?' . . . [laugh] . . . and I knew the Superloaf man was dealing with him.

Dealing, however, is a chancy business, and although dealer and dealee have interests in common (the dealer can obtain the goods, but not profitably dispose of them himself; whereas dealees can easily dispose of such goods, but not systematically obtain them), such mutual interest is dissected by certain inherent structural work conflicts. The dealee (the salesman) requires regularity and predictability in the illicit flow of goods in order that he may plan extras into his ordering, thus rendering them invisible and protecting himself from exposure. Conversely, the dealer (especially inside bread traffickers) cannot guarantee what he can 'cover' prior to the transaction, and needs a certain flexibility in demand to prevent him risking under-covered deals. Sometimes, as one salesman explained, it is precisely these problems that breed inter-shift conflict amongst despatch dealers. He was paying the 'A' shift charge-hand (who was on days that week) to put 'extra' on his rack, but the 'B' shift charge-hand, on nights, was checking all the racks (to find surpluses he could deal himself) and taking them off again!

Another problem for the salesman-dealee is that of deciding whether or not to accept dealer offers. One salesman commented:

When that bloke '——' came up to me at first, he said 'Do you want any cheap bread?' . . . well, of course, I said 'No, I don't touch the stuff, don't want anything to do with it' . . . but he kept on at me, saying 'No, I'm on the level, how much can you take, three trays?' . . . eventually, I said 'Yeah, you can put it on if you like' . . . but that other bloke came over, you know, that one with the limp . . . and he said 'Do you want extra bread for 50p a tray?' . . . I just said 'No, I don't have anything to do with that sort of thing' . . . I didn't trust him, it didn't seem right, somehow.

A problem as tricky as that of making an offer to a 'straight', is dealing near them. Whilst straights are inevitably ignorant of the processes of set-up, they may come, quite by chance, perilously close to discovering what is going on. The covert phase of transaction may, under unpredictable circumstances, become opened in the same way that open pay-off can. One salesman recalled:

Cor! . . . it worried me sometimes, I remember once, I was late in, and the bloke had put the [extra] bread on for me . . . and the manager was helping me load it onto the van . . . I kept saying 'That's all right, mate, I can manage' . . . but he wouldn't stop, and I was trying to load, sweating like a pig! . . . I thought I'd had it then.

Occasionally, dealees chance exposure unwittingly and quite accidentally. Carefully stage managed aspects of depot reality occasionally become falsified by the background reality which normally plays no part in the fabrication. One despatch charge-hand told me:

I took the manager home, early in the morning once, that was when he'd just started, and didn't know what was going on . . . and we went past one of the big wholesale vans on the way . . . and he was unloading big boxes of tea and taking them into a shop . . . and wholesalers aren't supposed to carry tea . . . bloody great boxes with 'P.G. Tips' written all over them in bloody great letters! . . . he [the manager] didn't bat an eyelid, but I was shitting bricks . . . he didn't know what was going on then, see?

But satisfactorily and successfully concluding a deal is just the start of the salesman's problems. Crucially, he has somehow to prevent the customer finding out that she has become an unwitting accomplice (which is relatively easy), and the sales management from discovering that they have become unwitting victims (which is considerably harder). The next section of this chapter will address itself to this latter problem.

ORGANISATIONAL PROBLEMS

When initially taking over a new round, salesmen are faced with the problem of maintaining the *continuity* of fiddles in the face of the need to renegotiate a basis for being *trusted*. On the one hand:

It would have looked silly me taking over, and he had, say, been charging two shillings for a box of jam tarts, and me suddenly putting them down to one-and-four a box! . . . somebody's going to be for the high jump right sharpish, aren't they?

And then on the other:

He [the previous roundsman] told me to take some bread in, and take some of the stales, and add them onto what you charged her . . . but the old cow was checking me, just because I was new!

Even if, eventually, satisfactory 'arrangements' can be made with customers, salesmen will still have to solve the problem of equalising the potential *visibility* of fiddles, steals and deals with the *continuity* of sales. Simple over-charging, for example, doesn't show in weekly sales figures produced for motivational purposes by the sales office, but reducing the amounts of bread ordered to take account of the probable purchase of 'cheap' bread, or increasing cake waste to cover appropriations from the cash bag, becomes immediately 'visible' to a trained and cynical eye cast upon weekly sales figures. Fiddles vary in terms of their visibility in weekly salesmen's accounts, stealing is always highly visible, and the potential sales visibility of deals varies with the degree to which they are pre-planned.

In addition to the solutions to these sorts of problems, salesmen must also (for their own purposes) balance *profitability* with the *predictability* of fiddles. Generally, the predictability of deals makes up for their loss of percentage profitability, and in some cases, especially where whole-sale men wish to regularise their deductions from cash calls, predicta-bility becomes the overriding concern.

Risks of entrapment and probable *consequences* need also to be taken into consideration, sometimes in very sophisticated schemes. A wholesaler explained how he managed these problems:

> I don't go across and take any . . . I don't steal . . . I can cover all the cash on overbooking, I don't 'make' it to the extent of what some of the others do . . . for the simple reason that I haven't got the calls . . . it's pointless taking risks above your cash calls . . . although they haven't had a check of the vans recently . . . before, I was buying most of it from the dealers, and I wasn't hardly touching the customers at all . . . dealing isn't as risky as fiddling . . . the risk is the most important, if you didn't have the job, you wouldn't have any money at all would you? . . . it's worth losing a little bit for the safety.

Most of the problems mentioned so far in this section can be indefinitely 'solved'. A perennial problem for roundsmen is the *transferability* of fiddles, steals and deals to holiday reliefs. Without sufficient warning of what to do and expect, reliefs might unwittingly expose previous practices. One supervisor remembered:

> I took over a round once, and all the women kept giving me a shilling extra each morning for their order . . . I didn't say anything, I just thought that I'd ask him at the end of the week what it was all about . . . he was charging a penny on *all* items . . . and *six* pence on rolls.

Usually, however, salesmen confer and pass tips to each other either verbally or through coded messages written next to the customer's name on each page of the salesman's route book. More regularly, the transferability problem is that of passing a round to a supervisor who is either straight, greedy or incompetent. One salesman complained that a supervisor who refuses to 'add a bob or two on here, a few pence on there' can 'bugger things up for you, word gets round'. Alternatively, another moaned that although he always 'adds a few pence' on at a particularly 'easy' call, the relief supervisor 'really hammers them, he does them for a fiver, some weeks'.

Deals have to be maintained during holiday periods for the reasons given above, but often dealers are not prepared to work in consort with relief dealees. An inside dealer once told me:

> '——' is on holiday this week, and the supervisor who is on his round came up to me and said that '——' had said that I was all right for a couple of trays . . . I didn't know what to say, so I just left it open, and said 'I'll see what I can do' . . . and when I saw him again, I

told him 'Apparently, you have to put all extra bread on the sheet'
. . . and walked off.

Although there are quite specific and detailed systems available for
the transfer of deals, both parties are always very wary, as a famous
bakery sacking was once the result of such temporary collaboration.
The following strategies were instituted by the big inside dealers to
prevent this occurring again:

> When the bloke goes on holiday, he pays you in advance for the
> bread, right, that he will require for that week, to keep his books
> straight . . . so the bloke pays the bill before he goes . . . and whatever
> the supervisor makes is his, less the amount that the bloke has paid
> for the bread . . . so the supervisor never handles the money . . . the
> regular bloke pays the paymaster . . . and the supervisor 'doesn't
> know' it's on there . . . he don't 'check it', as far as he's concerned,
> he just comes in, loads his bread, and if anybody asks, he didn't check
> it, right?

An alternative for worried salesmen is to arrange the customer side
of things or, failing that, to resist all managerial attempts to be sent on
holiday at all! One man used to pretend that half his customers were
also on holiday (to cover up what he had been buying on the side), and
then try and placate them for the temporary lack of service on his
return. Another told me that he had even told the sales manager 'I
never want to go on holiday! I never want a holiday again!'.

These are some of the practical problems of occupational theft. But
with them come some moral problems: what psychological effect does
routine solution of these problems have on the Wellbread roundsmen?
How can they ensure that 'part-time' crimes don't turn, psychologically, into full-time ones?

5 Characters: Public Identity Negotiation and Managerial Reaction

MORAL CHARACTERS AND PRACTICAL PORTFOLIOS

The Wellbread salesmen are trapped in an organisational dilemma. Whilst they have no realistic alternative but to make money on the side, doing so is sometimes punishable by the very people (the management) who demand the practice in the first place. As I have just shown, there are also several minor organisational problems. The salesman has to walk a narrow tight-rope between customer trust and the continuity of sales; the visibility of fiddles and the continuity of sales; the profitability with the transferability of fiddles; and between the risks of various fiddles and their entrapment consequences. Obviously, some form of practical organisation is needed: technical competence in fiddling, stealing and dealing skills is not enough in itself. Sometimes salesmen solve the practical problems thrown up by these difficulties by simultaneously practising several 'part-time' crimes.

Sometimes this can be protective, such as when a salesman subversively deals with a customer who is also being fiddled. One man couldn't believe his luck when a shop manager (without a sale-and-return contract) asked him to take back some spare bread at half price. The salesman had a field day 'Well, I just doubled the order on the second run, and got them all back at half price the next day!'. Whilst stealing from customers is acceptable because it doesn't threaten the cohesiveness or stability of the sales group (one salesman reported that he not only used to steal coffee and butter from an army depot he served, but he took it in such quantities that he was able to redeal it to his other customers as a sideline), stealing from other salesmen or inside dealers, or double dealing, is wholly divisive. When a salesman stole 140 loaves one morning, the inside dealer searched all the vans until he found them, whereupon he charged them to the thief's official account. He told me 'He'd conned me, I didn't like that, I said to him "If you'd come and asked me, I'd have *given* them to you for a couple of quid, but you went behind my back" '. Those salesmen who try to deal with individual despatch men as well as with the inside dealers are warned off, or even punished. When double dealing got too prevalent once, the inside dealers put their collective foot down. One salesman remembered:

'——' [charge-hand dealer] caught one or two of the blokes at it once, he was livid, . . . I had asked one of them to go and get me some rolls, and '——' came up, furious, he was, flinging his arms about . . . I thought he was going to put one on me! he said '*I'm* in charge here, don't you deal with anybody else . . . I'll get you the sack if you do . . . and don't you forget it' . . . he stopped all rolls then, everything, they used to be free . . . buckshee, but not now . . . it's 'pay for everything'.

Obviously, whilst this sort of practical organisation deals with the need to make money, it fails on two counts. Firstly, the criminal activity is not sufficiently protected against exposure, and secondly, there is no structural guarantee that the implications which illegal activity has for the salesman's self remain minimal. The 'part-time' practical status of fiddling, stealing and dealing needs 'partial' psychological support. Accordingly, salesmen require an operational basis for their illegal practices that will simultaneously provide the requisite invisible material benefits, *and* practical and psychological protection.

Principally, at Wellbread's, management *proto*type the salesmen into good or bad categories. Paradoxically, semi-official processing within the firm, coupled with the men's reactions and remoulding of this labelling endows each man with one of a variety of available *arche*typal 'characters'. The employment of these characters in sales life produces a 'portfolio' of relevant techniques of theft; a practical selection of 'part-time' crimes whose linking structure automatically and practically protects the salesman. A batch of techniques is selected by each man in order that exposure in the practice of one will not inevitably escalate to general exposure as a thief, as the rest of the portfolio may continue to be practised unseen and unhindered.

The 'casting' procedures of the sales management at Wellbread's allocate salesmen to particular rounds of customers. The particular strains of the round (set against the strains of the job in general) can be seen as a conflict between the 'situated activity role' and the 'role title' (Goffman, 1961a, p. 86) in the name of which the job is carried on. Specific practices become embedded in the expectations of customers, providing a work specific 'situated self' for the roundsman.

But this situated self that the roundsman has does not necessarily concur with the conceptualisation of 'me' that the individual holds. In fact, for most workers, work roles have an essentially apparent constructedness, that Burns (1953, p. 654) calls their 'fictive character'. For most of the Wellbread salesmen, what they do and how they feel at work has no relevance to the 'real me' that is constructed out of work hours. As Mead (1934, p. 142) puts it:

> We are one thing to one man and another thing to another. We divide ourselves up in all sorts of different selves with reference to our acquaintances . . . there are all sorts of different selves answering to all sorts of different social reactions.

We might profitably view the salesman's round as a *situated activity system* (Goffman, 1961a, p. 49), providing the individual on most occasions with a *part-time* self distinguishable and distinguished from that self upon which the individual relies for the development of his 'real' or 'complete' identity.

This part-time self is the psychological context of intelligibility for the practice of the part-time crimes described in Chapter 4. But not only does the salesman's round generate a situated, part-time self, the exclusiveness of the 'work me' in turn curtails and stunts its impingement upon the complete *me* of the individual. In addition, then, the 'work me' has significance only as an elementary, or *partial* self. Publically, it is unconfirmed; psychologically it has auxiliary rather than master status in the private development of a complete self.

Generally, anybody's complete self is constructed through the operation of what Mead calls the 'social process'. The two general stages of this process are, firstly, the response of the self to the attitudes of others towards the self and, secondly, that which Mead (1934, p. 155) calls 'their attitudes towards the various phases or aspects of the common social activity or set of social undertakings in which, as members of an organised society or social group, they are all engaged'.

The problem in organising the possible response to specifically *deviant* activity is that a contradiction arises between what law-abiding society thinks and the attitudes of the deviant social group. It is this contradiction (together with the practised protection against societal reaction) which prevents the agglomeration of 'elementary selves' in the usual way, and maintains the exclusivity of the part-time self. It is, then, precisely the attitudes of the righteous that, ironically, because they happen to contradict those held by the actor's reference group, themselves constitute the possible psychological conditions of successful infraction. As Mead puts it, these situationally specific elementary selves usually congeal to provide the balanced, societally respectable complete self. However, the fact that a salesman fiddles, steals or deals features for him (because of the failure of the social reaction to fiddling to override this contradiction) in biographical terms as what Goffman (1963, p. 89) refers to as a 'dead' diary fact: one totally ignored in his reflexive construction of his self. Thus, both the form and the content of identity production is ascribed to individual salesmen by the Wellbread organisation.

However, as I have shown in the discussion of stealing in Chapter 4, the management do not have it all their own way. They see themselves as facing a continuing crisis in the way that workforce thefts undermine their authority and challenge their moral position. Typically, this sort of moral alarm provokes a dualistic simplification of response by the respectable, coupled with a considerable dramatisation of the social forces allegedly at play. Divisions and moral boundaries become melodramatically etched, finer distinctions are withdrawn, and the 'enemy' is located in terms of moral images drawn from a very basic societal vocabulary. As Klapp (1954, p. 60) puts it, 'vilification movements' only recognise the good and the bad. Similarly, for the Wellbread sales management there are only two *proto*types of salesman. The sales manager told me 'There are the good and the bad, there are always some bad salesmen in the bunch, I know all the blokes personally in here and, well, there are villains and honest blokes, aren't there? Villains and others'. To define a member of the workforce as a 'villain', however carelessly done, amounts to permanent identity assassination. As one man bitterly complained 'There's a lot of blokes left here because of "shorts", as soon as you're short, they class you as a villain'. Of significance here is that such personal characteristics are held to be unalterably part of the personality of the individual so labelled. It is an unauthentic question to ask if somebody in the sales department is 'still on the fiddle'. Salesmen, like leopards, don't change their spots.

But the limited prototypical possibilities are insufficient to order life and interaction to the satisfaction of the salesmen. The managerial definitions are not ignored by the men. Instead they are redefined and reworked to produce a responsive vocabulary of salesmen 'characters', which are either variations on the 'villain' or 'other' moral prototype, or subtle blends of facets of each.

Salesmen 'characters' are rather like Cavan's (1966, pp. 79–87) 'bar characters'; internally consistent but inconsequential biographies which patrons prefabricate for the duration of drinking interaction. Bar characters are isolated part-time selves, although they are achieved rather than ascribed, and they are not necessarily situated in a particular tavern. In the dramaturgic sense, salesmen characters refer to the *personae* and not the actors; an aspect of a role (but not a role itself) which is locked irretrievably within the drama – here, that coming between management and salesmen. In sum, the seven common Wellbread salesmen 'characters' ('professional', 'rogue', 'Robin Hood', 'shark', 'wise straight', 'bent straight', and 'righteous straight') provide the salesmen with a set of abstract models revealing a common response to the shared problem of managerial prototyping.

Characters constructed as a response to managerial 'villain' prototype reflect concern amongst the salesmen with three core matters (Table 5.1): firstly, how good the illicit 'make' is; secondly, how

TABLE 5.1   The villain response

	Good make	Successful protection	Steal from other salesmen
Rogue	+	−	−
Professional	+	+	−
Robin Hood	−	+	−
Shark	−	−	+

TABLE 5.2   'Others': the straight response

	Make for company	Make for self	Acceptance of promotion
Bent-straight	+	+	+
Wise-straight	+	−	−
Righteous-straight	−	−	+

successfully it is protected from the victim's gaze; and thirdly, whether or not thefts from other salesmen are practised. Table 5.2 illustrates that the reactions to the 'other' prototype by straights and supervisors are based upon three quite different matters: the acceptance of promotion, the preparedness to fiddle for the company, and the willingness to 'make' for oneself. Individual salesmen's performances and practices are collectively judged in terms of these various melodramatic Achilles' heels, and they are allocated a bakery 'character' accordingly. Thus the vocabulary of characters provides a form of informal social control, as well as a significant aid to occupational self (and other) identification. But the characters also *mean* something themselves: the salesmen are perfectly well aware of the connotated meanings of their vocabulary. Table 5.3 analyses (after Klapp, 1962)

TABLE 5.3 Melodramatic components of characters

	Hero	Villain	Fool
Rogue	Smart operator	Rogue Flouter Deceiver	Rash, Nuisance Character Comic rogue
Professional	Smart operator Top dog Prima donna	Selfish-grabber	Show-off
Robin Hood	Benefactor Do gooder Good fellow	Rogue Flouter	Character
Shark		Trouble maker Flouter, Selfish-grabber, Suspicious isolate, Hidden traitor, Sneak-attacker, Renegade Chiseller, Parasite Pariah	Small-minded Nuisance, Upstart
Bent-straight		Suspicious isolate Hidden traitor Deceiver	Yes-man
Wise-straight	Conforming hero Moralist Diehard Defender	Suspicious isolate Shirker	Clumsy fool, Rigid fool, Simpleton Nobody, Second rater
Righteous-straight	Conforming Hero Moralist Stickler Crusader	Moral persecutor Suspicious isolate Renegade, Pariah	Weak fool, Stuffed shirt, Comic phoney High-minded, Mock-hero

the melodramatic components of each character inasmuch as they contain different proportions of the three basic societally dramatic roles – hero, villain and fool. The diagram is an attempt to capture not only the dramaturgic differences between characters, but also to display their sociological similarities.

In adopting a character, the salesman finds an occupational self. Because the characters are work specific, they provide a psychological

E

shield for the real self, warding off the psychic contamination that fiddling generates. But there are practical problems to be faced as well. From the endless list of methods of fiddling, dealing and stealing, the salesman who is 'in' character not only selects a variety of styles which, if regularly practised, would produce an equitable invisible income, but also he ensures that this collection is mutually discrete. Here the practical merges with the psychological: it is essential that discovery in the practice of one style should not automatically disclose the practice of others. This is the 'portfolio' effect; *all* characters at Wellbread's are equipped with a different practically protective portfolio of techniques. Some of the differences between them are outlined in Table 5.4 (on pages 124–5). The extent and nature of each portfolio might be said to represent the constructed tolerance of customers, and the personal limit at which dishonesty might begin to affect the 'complete' self. Admittedly, salesmen will know of many more techniques than they actually practise. In a sense, their selection presolves the problem of guilt, and ensures that their 'crimes' will, at least for psychological purposes, be 'part-time' ones. Techniques which might, for a particular individual, provide too heavy a burden of guilt after commission are discarded in favour of those for which psychological implications may easily be assimilated. So the salesmen have a built in allowance for the discovery and uncovering of one practice, without either affecting successful exploitation of other schemes or interrupting the continuous satisfaction of those conditions essential to smooth part-time crime. At the practical level, for example, when the government banned sale-and-return contracts in 1973, this hit some of the men hard. But as one 'rogue' (who had previously depended on fiddling returns) put it, fiddles, as well as contracts, can be changed: 'Still, I won't lose, I'll have to put the fiddle on the booking now . . . I shouldn't think I'll drop any, they'll pay for it somehow'.

At the psychological level, the practice of mutually sealed styles generates separated rather than summated impingement upon the self. In Goffman's terms (1974, p. 121), this practice foreshortens the potential backward and forward 'reach' that discrediting might have. The sub-elementary selves reflecting and operating portfolio component practice do not spread psychic contamination to the complete, 'honest' self. Possible psychological effects are nullified by tactics actually designed for more practical purposes. For example, one particular practice is delaying the booking on wholesale rounds. Salesmen are supposed to give each call a completed docket stub every day. If this can be waived, the chances of and for over-booking increase. But even for those calls who never expect or receive a docket, the falsified docket is rarely completed before the end of the day. Now, this is partially practical protection against spot checking. Should the customer suddenly realise that no docket has been left with the order, and ring the bakery to demand one, it would not be too late to fill the docket in correctly. Importantly, delay allows the salesman some psychological leeway. He may leave a decent delay before filling the docket with an incorrect amount to allow the customer, in some mysterious psychological way, to forget what was actually received. I once asked a wholesaler why he had filled in none of the dockets for his calls that day. He told me 'Well, if I filled them in each day, they'd all know what they'd had, wouldn't they? . . . I always think to myself "If I've forgotten what they had, they must have too" '.

'CHARACTERS' AT WELLBREAD'S

The 'Rogue'

The 'rogue's passport to privilege is his disarming grin, coupled with his tongue in cheek denials of dishonesty. A rogue, it is said, can resist anything but temptation. At Wellbread's, one 'rogue', for example, couldn't even resist selling his bakery cash bag to a milkman with a roving eye. Technically, the 'rogue' breaks all the rules restricting fiddling, but (and this is what distinguishes him from the 'shark') he can somehow mediate this moral harm by disarming the opponent. As Klapp (1964, p. 134) puts it 'Whatever he actually does, it is psychologically impossible to see him as a villain'.

'Rogues' possess sufficient interactional ingenuousness to be able to deny the deed, smile, and then, deprecatingly, admit it. One 'rogue' said to me 'Honestly, I can't make a thing on this round . . . well, not much anyway', and another 'They used to think that I had stuff off my brother [who was on a wholesale round] . . . but I didn't . . . well, only a few trays here and there!'. As one put it, nicely adopting the tone of injured wrongful indignation, 'I'm no fiddler . . . well, I might play the fiddle a bit, but not like some of the blokes up here, "——" plays the whole bloody orchestra!'.

On a practical level, the 'rogue's' portfolio is extensive and operates on the assumption that the most profitable approach is the percentage playing of all possible styles. 'Rogues' are particularly renowned for skill and dexterity in the practical arts of fiddling, for living by laughs, and for 'conning' well diddled customers into leaving them large tips at Christmas.

Generally, in financial terms, the 'rogue' portfolio pays handsomely. Willingness, for example, to push any 'sideline' often provides large dividends. One 'rogue' told me:

TABLE 5.4 Practical elements of portfolios

	Rogue	Professional	Robin Hood	Shark	Bent-straight	Wise-straight	Righteous-straight
Sales pattern	Very variable	High increasing	Medium-high static	Low decreasing	Slightly reduced	Medium static	Conscientious canvasser
Moral ceiling	Wholly unrestricted	Restricted to cash available	Variable in-round consumption and fixed ceiling	Unrestricted	Slightly lower than full-time roundsmen	No self-fiddles	No
Steals	Yes	Never	Stale bread only	Yes	Yes	No	No
Company fiddles	Yes	Yes	Yes	No	Yes	Yes	No
Private fiddles	Yes	Yes	Yes with regular fiddle calls	Yes	Yes	No	No
Inside deals	Whenever possible (tactical trade)	High strategic traffic (refuses trade)	Occasional and low (strategic traffic)	Never	Whatever is planned	No	No

TABLE 5.4 Practical elements of portfolios (continued)

	Rogue	Professional	Robin Hood	Shark	Bent-straight	Wise-straight	Righteous-straight
Sidelines (outside deals)	Anything (butter, tights)	High priced, stolen (radios, coats)	Purchased low value, high bulk, fragile (eggs, potatoes, tea)	No	If on van	Occasional like Robin Hood	No
Method of figuring take	Exact	Lax	Haphazard	Overtake (guessed)	Rough	No method needed	No
Organisational control	High	Efficient extensive	Lax Static	Static	Low	Lapsed control pattern	Static moralistic control
Perception of office	'On the Fiddle'	Incompetent	Does best	Malevolent	Incompetent	Benign	Benevolent
Handling of shortage	Complain	Powerful recheck rebuffal	Ignore	Accept deductions	Licensed	No deductions	Never occurs

He used to sell me tins of biscuits for 50p, and I used to sell them on the round for 75p . . . I had twenty four boxes one Christmas . . . I liked that army bloke, he used to give me butter, and I used to sell it . . . but one day, a woman said to me 'Here, that butter you sold me the other week, it had "NAAFI" written all down the side of it!' . . . so I thought I'd better pack that in . . . when I was serving that army place, I never touched the money I made, I just put it in a tin, and in the few months I worked for them, d'you know how much I made? . . . well, after I'd finished, I opened the tin, and put over £370 in the bank.

'Rogues' aspire to be 'professionals'. However, the two are permanently distinguished by the 'rogue's total lack of power, his refusal to believe that, in spite of his careful calculations, he could ever be short, and the subsequent injured righteousness which he adopts in the perpetual battle that he wages with the sales management. This righteousness is only characterologically supported by his refusal to believe he could be in the wrong. For the 'rogue', a short verdict at the end of the week 'is just not possible', because (as another said) 'there's just no way it could happen'.

The 'rogue's' comradely feelings towards other salesmen are matched by the disgust with which he views supervisors. If 'Robin Hoods' represent the traditional deferential worker (Lockwood, 1966) and 'professionals' the privatised worker, then the 'rogue' forms the proletarian core. As one 'rogue' put it:

You know, if they offered me that job [supervisor], I'd say 'No' thanks', and if they asked me why, I'd say 'Well, I don't want demotion!' . . . that's how much I think of *them*!

The 'Professional'

With enough sophistication, 'rogue' tactics can achieve 'professional' status on the large wholesale rounds. But with such maturity comes a humility of style. Bravado is replaced by thoughtfulness. One 'professional' claimed 'I'm still learning, see?', and another 'When I hear a new trick, I think "That's a good one, I'll have to remember that" '. Another put it 'You learn little things all the time, you're always learning, you never finish'.

The licence of the 'professional' is pure ability. In Klapp's terms (1964, p. 134) they are the melodramatic 'smart operator' – one who gets what he wants, always comes out on top – 'the modern version of the clever hero of folklore'. In the practical world at Wellbread's, the 'professional' is the cool, calculating expert. His status (which he stands to lose if caught) constructs a portfolio which substitutes the safety percentage play of dealing and fiddling for the risky and profitable gamble of the steal. One 'professional' only fiddled, saying 'I can make enough without stealing, same with dealing, I don't *watch* for it, but if anything comes up, I'll *have* it'. Another felt the same ('I don't steal, I can cover all the cash on over-booking'), but added 'Before, I was buying most of it from the dealers, I wasn't hardly touching the customers at all, dealing isn't as risky as fiddling, the risk is the most important'.

The 'professional' and the 'rogue' share a common loathing of supervisors but, crucially, whereas the 'rogue' plays the fiddling game almost for its own sake, the 'professional' coolly calculates all the risks and never makes any money that he cannot realise. Another distinguishing mark of the 'professional' character is the deliberate creation of trust by him in all his dealings – a tactic common amongst sophisticates in customer interactions, and noticed by both Mars (1973, p. 204) and Bigus (1972, p. 148). One of the Wellbread's 'professionals' claimed:

> He [the despatch manager] trusts me, he always has . . . he watches some of them, '——', for example, that bloke can't do a thing right for the manager, he used to be a bit of a 'rogue' when he was on retail . . . but I used to give him a tray back now and again, when I was issued too much, I'd go up to him, and I'd say 'Here you are, I'm honest, I give you a tray back when I've been given too much' . . . I didn't used to give him all of it back, mind you, only some, if I thought I couldn't get rid of it . . . he trusts me, I wouldn't say that he trusts me completely . . . but more than the rest.

The management by 'professionals' of large wholesale rounds provides them with relationships with good customers which are more significant than the relationships that these customers have with the Wellbread's management. The 'professionals' can thus threaten to leave (taking the customers with them) with great effect. One claimed, of life at the top, 'It's easier because you don't have to fight so hard and, another thing, they don't stop any money when you're short'.

The large 'make' of the 'professional' means that he can afford to operate via a system of kick-backs, sweeteners, and hush money (in much the same way that Davis, 1959, pp. 270–1, complains that taxi drivers are compelled to). Occasionally, staff in useful positions at the bakery are endebted, so that their services can be called upon at appropriate times. One used to distribute largesse (stolen cigarettes and soup) to all and sundry especially for unsolicited 'extras' ('give them something each time, and they won't mind the next time, will they?'), and another lent money to important but impoverished supervisors.

When he needed information, it could be got against (for example) 'that fifty pounds I lent him to buy that pricey car of his'. Customers are similarly entangled. One 'professional' said:

> If there's any trouble, I get on well with my customers, they'll back me up if I want them to, I know most of mine, and if I'm not sure whether or not I'm covered, I'll just ring one of them up and say 'You didn't pay me this week, O.K., Bill?', and he'll say 'Right, sure, mate'.

Partly through the artificial creation of trust and partly as a favour, 'professionals' rarely get caught in the spot checks that are sometimes carried out by the bakery management. Somehow, they always seem to know exactly when random and unplanned checks are due. Thus, the sales managerial office staff are left with virtually no control whatsoever over the 'professionals'. The office is believed by them to be wholly incompetent, and is 'fixed' forthwith. One 'professional' told me:

> They're [office staff] on the fiddle, I caught the chief accountant once, well, he was caught several times, I caught him on the round once, taking stuff out of the boot of his car, and putting it into somebody else's . . . I made sure that he saw me . . . I had never spoken to him before . . . but I blipped the horn and leant out of the cab . . . I never came short after that while he was the accountant . . . they're all fiddling in that office . . . no office could be as incompetent as ours is without a fiddle behind it.

If communication with the management is essential, the under managers (who are supposed to deal with the salesmen) are ignored. One 'professional' stated 'I never go to his sales meetings, they're a bloody waste of time. I told the senior manager "I haven't got time to waste listening to his [manager's] stupid ramblings" . . . I don't get on with him, I always go to the senior manager if I want something'. Whereas it is the power of the 'professional' that, for example, lowers his sales target (thus allowing him to make more commission), in the short term, it is mere long term attendance by the next 'character', the 'Robin Hood', that achieves the same result. By waiting patiently in the wings, the 'Robin Hood' manages to be around at the right time to benefit from any drop in the commission rates.

The 'Robin Hood'

As Klapp (1964, p. 134) points out, the dramatic immunity of the 'Robin Hood' lies in the fact that something he does pleases public sentiment more than his misdeeds shock. Because of this his crimes just seem like a technicality. Melodramatically, the 'Robin Hood' character is symbolised by the heroic 'Goodfellow', and 'independent spirit' traits, producing a character (as Klapp, 1962, p. 43 puts it) 'no prodigal but a plodder, not a fireball but a friend'. Like those in Sherwood Forest, one 'Robin Hood' Wellbread's roundsman claimed 'I never rob anybody unless they've got more money than I have . . . some of them, the old girls, I give them a bit back' and another told me 'I wouldn't take it off anybody who couldn't afford to lose it, even if they couldn't add up!'.

This rather lackadaisical approach to fiddle earnings (few of the 'Robin Hoods' ever bother to calculate accurately what they have made, preferring instead to allow the 'kitty' to subsidise mid-week consumption of beer, petrol and tobacco) is backed by a legendary static sales pattern coupled with a very low sales target. They never change their orders and never vary the sales pitch to increase sales. Nevertheless, they have normally done 'their' round for years, and have never been rerated. As one envious 'rogue' said of an aged 'Robin Hood' 'He's no fool, he can't sell anything, but I saw his wage packet, thirty-five pounds in fivers he had in it, and a couple of singles as well'. They are the least affected by the dynamic approach to selling taken by the manager and, generally, they ignore all special competitions, datums, targets and other office paraphernalia designed to boost sales. One 'Robin Hood' said:

> I've never had to pay any shorts, I never have any problems with the office, if I'm short one week, I pick it up the next, I don't worry about it . . . competitions? I *never* take any interest in them . . . if they plus them up, I don't worry . . . I never bother with them . . . I never have much to do with the management really, and they never say much to me.

The practical portfolio of the 'Robin Hood' is a regular, restricted, consumption related mixture of many possible styles. Outright stealing achieves a quite different meaning in the 'Robin Hood' context. Both stealing and reselling are redefined as 'recycling', and as 'public service'. One 'Robin Hood' who always helped himself 'to a few stales from up the passage when the manager isn't looking' claimed, in justification, that 'they only go to waste if I don't take them, or some poor sod gets them for "contract" . . . the bloke I sell them to, he only takes them for his dogs, and I only charge him half price . . . a dozen loaves a week doesn't hurt anybody does it?'.

But most 'Robin Hood' money comes, semi-legitimately, from customers, in the form of tips and sidelines. A supervisor describes how three 'Robin Hoods' get good tips:

Take old Bert, he's got one of the best rounds here, he cares, see? . . . he knows all his customers, and has known them for years . . . remember Rocky last year? he should have been on the club, but he came in special on Christmas Eve to get all his tips . . . he took about eighty pounds too . . . old Fred, he's another one, he had a real top round down at the coast, all the classy houses, he used to look after them, he even used to go and do the shopping for them, and before he went on holiday, he used to say to them all 'Be away on holiday next week, ma'am' . . . and they used to give him about ten bob, and say: 'Have a nice time, baker' . . . he used to make about sixty pounds out of that alone . . . like old Sam, they all think he's dim, but he's got it made . . . there was a couple of old ladies on his round, and he always used to fill the coal bucket up for them . . . one of them died, and left him about £400 . . . now, he's filling the coal bucket up for the other one and hoping for the best!

'Robin Hood' rounds are permanently stocked with sacks of potatoes, boxes of eggs, packets of tea, butter and cheap tights, all involving considerable extra effort for very low profit margins, often themselves eroded by high wastage and breakage. Of all the characters at Well-bread's, the 'Robin Hoods' are the most distinctive: older men, in cloth caps, serving the large retail country rounds. Both their style and their practical portfolio serve to distinguish them from the final salesman character – the 'shark' – with whom they share almost nothing.

The 'Shark'

The most divisive and disreputable act that a salesman can commit is to steal from his mates. Disgust would be levelled at any salesman who fiddled blind men or pensioners, but he would not be outlawed like the man who takes from his fellow workers. The 'shark' may accept scruples but, by treating both customers *and* other salesmen as 'fair game', totally and incompetently misreads the conditions of applicability of those scruples. Few 'sharks' really understand just why they have lost their 'licence'. One, for example, claimed in his defence 'There's people I don't fiddle, yeah, certain people, old age pensioners, people like that [I wouldn't] say "Couple of bob on her bill, she's blind" '. Another, grossly over-tipped at Christmas, said 'I even gave some of them [tips] back because I had treated them so rotten'.

But ordinary standard customer scruples are not the point. Witnessed stealing from another salesman marks a man at Wellbread's with the 'shark' taint for the rest of his occupational career. Melodramatically (Klapp, 1962, p. 58), the 'shark' crucially and irreversibly becomes the 'selfish grabber' and the 'malicious stranger'. Internal theft is quite beyond the pale; one 'rogue' expressed the dramatic horror particularly well:

> I'll take it from the firm . . . I don't mind that . . . but I'll tell you one thing, I'll never take it from a friend . . . that's one thing I could *never* do . . . not *nothing*! . . . some blokes do, you know.

It is not just a case of stopping men going onto one's van and stealing bread (although this can happen); the 'shark's' thefts strike at a more delicate and exposed organisational nerve: the inability of the salesmen to cross-check their rec. sheets systematically. Whilst most believe that the sales office, at worst, only makes benign mistakes, the exposure of one extensive, co-operative steal (where the financial accounts of innocent salesmen were debited to the value of the goods taken by 'sharks') made the whole sales force more suspicious of some of their fellow workers than of the management. It is not difficult to steal in these feared roundabout ways. As one 'shark' told me 'If I want biscuits, I can easily nick them by ordering them on somebody else's route number, and by going in early and taking them before anybody's about'.

If mistakenly over-issued with bread that they cannot get rid of, roundsmen are expected to share the surplus out amongst their friends. The 'shark' ignores this cohesive move and prefers instead to attempt to sell it, at reduced price, to any roundsman who can safely dispose of it. This clearly offends against the unwritten Wellbread's code. Subsequently, the 'shark' is not sufficiently trusted by the other salesmen to be allowed to take part in any deals that are going. The plight of one 'shark' was typical:

> I asked him [inside man] if he had any extra, but I wasn't bothered . . . and d'you know what he did? . . . he went and saw the manager straight away, didn't he? . . . and told him that one of his salesmen was asking for cheap bread . . . I don't know why, maybe he was set up to shop me or something.

Thus, the 'shark' becomes locked in irretrievable status deflation, living, in a sense, on borrowed time. He is not allowed in on the deals, so he has to steal more to make up for it. Because he steals, he further reduces his chances of participation in any future deals. Deterioration is swift. Of one man it was said 'He's a bit of a shark, he'd sell his own mother if he had a chance', and 'He's really carved this round up . . . it used to be a good one', and even 'Keep your hand on your cash bag when he's around'. The despised status of the 'shark' allows the management to proceed against him in ways that would not otherwise be tolerated. Salesmen often come short in their weekly takings.

'Sharks' sometimes get sacked for it, as in the following case, where the ostensible reason appears to be the number of cars owned by the man. The salesman claimed to have deposited ten pounds with the Well-bread's sales office, of which there was no official trace. The senior supervisor who sacked him told me:

> His sales were the same, and so were his debts, but his cash was down, that's how we knew . . . anyway, he runs four cars, and he's got a woman tucked away somewhere . . . well, I know what a job I have to run one home, let alone two . . . so he was obviously taking it out of the bag.

The 'Bent-straight' Supervisor

The 'bent-straight' supervisor wears his blue supervisor's coat super-ficially, and is a rogue underneath. His acceptance of promotion personally contaminates him, but his tacit and acknowledged agree-ment to share the men's private fiddles (and to practise them when acting as relief) provokes ambiguous reactions from the rest of the work force. Melodramatically, 'bent-straight' supervisors assume the para-doxical combination of 'traitor and sneak' on the one hand, with the 'yes man' trait on the other. Subsequently, as Klapp (1962, p. 84) puts it, 'it is hard to tell where he really stands, or who stands behind him, because of his shifting position'.

Sometimes a 'bent-straight' supervisor will use his position as supervisor to get allocated a fiddle profitable round. One told me that, if he was given a poor round by the under manager, he 'used to get a packet of Players out of one pocket and pass it to another, and look him in the eye, and he used to say "Which round do you want?" '. How-ever, most 'bent-straights' are content to just do what the regular man does. They understand the problems facing their salesmen, especially the need to show continuity of sales figures during holiday times. As one 'professional' commented 'The point is that if a supervisor jumps a round, he has to show a similar book to what the regular bloke does'. However, this is additionally difficult for supervisors. They have to attempt to maintain price, sales, and fiddle continuity without quite the same quality of trust relationship with the customer that the regular man has. As one 'bent-straight' supervisor put it:

> If it shows up, you could lose customers over it, couldn't you? . . . you've got to [fiddle] . . . but I don't *attempt* to go to the extremes that some of the salesmen go to . . . I try to find somewhere in between, keep the customer happy, and keep everybody else happy at the same time . . . if I'm on a journey and I know I've made five pounds, I won't keep five pounds . . . I'll leave a pound in to cover me.

But however hard they try, 'bent-straights' are never fully accepted. As one salesman acidly, but finally, commented 'When they're loading up beside you, out with you, they're certainly one of you, but when you're at the works, they're definitely one of *them*'.

The 'Wise-straight'

As Goffman (1963, p. 41) puts it, the 'wise' are those marginal men who know what goes on but do not actively take part in it. Before the 'wise', the practitioner 'need feel no shame, nor exert self-control, knowing that in spite of his failings he will be seen as an ordinary actor'.

Two distinct groups are seen as 'wise' in the bakery. They are either supervisors who are prepared to fiddle for the company, and not report the private infractions of others, or ordinary salesmen who are not prepared to fiddle for themselves. This second group is also a temporary resting place for all the neophytes and 'good boys' who have yet to demonstrate that they are long term employees deserving of proper, characterological classification. Thus 'wise-straights' are, in Klapp's terms (1962, pp. 46 and 75), *either*, as in the first case, 'group servants and defenders of order' *or*, as in the second, 'fools' discounted as 'nobodys'.

'Old woman' or 'bit of a nuisance' is the usual bakery slang for the 'wise-straight' supervisor, partly because of his reticence to indulge in private fiddles and partly because one's own business is harder to run in his presence. But as one supervisor astutely noticed, the second type of 'wise', the 'good boy', might be a 'con':

I told him to fiddle, but he said 'Oh, I don't know, I don't want to do that' . . . but he did it, or, I think he did, because he came two pounds over that week, next week, two pounds short again, mind you, he might be a faker . . . pulling our legs over this all the time.

The 'Righteous-straight'

The 'righteous-straight' is as status entrenched as the 'shark'. However, a period of tolerance by him, or a sufficient number of witnessed infractions, might move him to reclassification in the 'wise-straight' or 'bent-straight' categories. His personal and interpersonal uncontamination types him as a moral outcast, embodying what Klapp (1962, p. 41) refers to as the heroic trait of conforming moralist with the villainous moral persecutor twist.

Where the 'shark' of the last section takes the injunction to steal rather too seriously, the 'righteous-straight' makes a similarly incompetent situation reading, but takes the moral rather than the immoral aspect of his ambiguous occupational definition too seriously. Supervisors who do so are in a small but troublesome minority. The training officer at Wellbread's commented:

> Of course, the correct attitude is to say 'You will not over-charge the customer, this is the correct price, and that's what you will charge' ... that's something you should say, and something you should stick by, ... but only about one per cent of the supervisors *do* do that ... because the supervisor is doing the same thing [i.e. fiddling].

'Righteous-straights' are thought of as supervisors who take life much too seriously and who, furthermore, actually believe that the management wants them to behave in the superconformist way that they publicly espouse. Where the 'bent-straight' resolves the supervisors' occupational ambiguity by siding with the men and the 'wise-straight' supervisor by passively siding with management, the 'righteous-straight' actively pursues official managerial morality. Dalton (1964, p. 213) rather aptly calls such people 'rule devotees', and Peter and Hull (1966, p. 34) cynically but accurately spell out their organisational fate – the 'lateral arabesque' (or, pseudo-promotion). 'Righteous-straights' are commonly funnelled into a mock heroisation spiral, typically being sent (as I suggested in Chapter 2) grandly named to a depot where they can do no further organisational damage.

CHARACTER RELATIONS

As status crucially differentiates salesmen (in a sense, for example, that similarity of wages does not), personal status becomes tenuous and fragile, and any status challenges are treated with extreme touchiness. A 'professional' thus reports how a customer had unwittingly slurred his 'character':

> This morning I went in with six trays, and he was moaning, as usual ... said there was three missing, *three fucking loaves*! and me with eight other big calls to do before 9.00 a.m. ... when I got through the door, and he said that there was three missing, cor! ... that fucking annoyed me ... I only deal in *trays*.

On top of this sort of status conflict with the customer, similar troubles with other roundsmen are also possible. Retail salesmen serving the same domestic hinterland as the shops to which the wholesale drivers deliver depend for their living upon successfully eradicating the competition which inevitably arises in such an over-sold environment. One 'rogue' complained, for example, that a 'professional' serving shops in his area was selling some products for a penny or twopence less than he could. He added, morosely, 'I doubt whether it's worth getting the basket out twice a day down there'.

But these divisive and competitive fractures can be healed. For example, on one occasion that I witnessed, the 'professional' in the above case allowed the 'rogue' to clean his van out at the end of the day for stale bread worth 70p. Because wholesalers cannot personally profit from any 'make' greater than their 'take' calls, any product surpluses can be offered to retailers (at no loss) to ease structural strains. The basic difference between retailer and wholesaler price/ value interpretations can produce long lasting symbiotic relationships between those simultaneously serving the same customer constituency. When I tried to sell off some 'extra' bread at the depot (there is an unofficial rule that 'spare' should be given away free), I was kindly advised to 'find a retailer' to 'deal' with.

Procedures such as this help to maintain characterological boundaries and allow smooth and easy 'staying in character' for the salesmen. Unfortunately, however, managerial social control can occasionally stymie such created harmony. How do salesmen manage their characters in times of crisis?

The crises provided by periodic management 'clean up campaigns' (designed to inhibit stealing by the salesmen) can prompt character slippage. Here 'making' styles, usually dismissed with disgust, are temporarily adopted. One 'professional' who usually sneered at the 'Robin Hood' habit of taking a few 'stales' from the bakery each morning, added thoughtfully 'I *have* done it, I have done it in the past when things have been a bit tight, I've been and got myself a couple of trays of stales'. Another 'professional' pointed out that, when all else fails, alternatives are essential:

When '——' and the others were caught [inside dealers], it was madness, . . . it was murder for a few days, I mean, you have to cover what you have been getting, don't you? . . . otherwise it would show . . . especially at a time like that, when they're looking for that sort of thing.

If the management block a source of illicit inside supply, they usually then sit back and wait for hitherto unnamed salesmen buyers to increase their legitimate orders to satisfy their legal demand. Conversely, those salesmen with a suddenly dry illicit supply channel will frantically seek alternatives so as to avoid exposure. Inevitably, if deals foreclose, steals and fiddles will temporarily increase until things return to 'normal'. However, if salesmen resolve this problem by stealing from other salesmen, temporary character lapse will be seen as irremedial character change. A salesman can rapidly become defined as a 'shark'.

A similar effect can be created on the round. For example, the use of 'rogue' tactics on customers who have conventionally been accustomed to a 'Robin Hood' approach can deposit the salesman in a spiral of decreasing trust and status deflation. One man who did this did nothing that would have been seen as objectively wrong had his customers been used to 'rogue' service. But, faced with 'Robin Hood' expectations, 'he got to the point where the customers got suspicious, none of them did anything, but they all started checking him out, and he couldn't make any more'.

Although not so much of a problem for new recruits (who find a 'situated self', a 'character', awaiting them in the expectations of their customers), this can be particularly a problem for salesmen changing rounds in mid-career stream. Although the sales manager tries to 'fit' an existing roundsman to another round, this is not always successful, and if the situated self to which he comes differs from the one to which he has become used, conflict will result.

These untidy points raise an interesting issue. Just *how* can salesmen *change* their occupational 'characters'? Although some changes seem harder than others, this appears to be a structural rather than a personal difficulty. Any 'professional', for example, can become a 'shark' (as soon as he is seen stealing from another salesman) but no amount of sophistication can transform a 'shark' into a 'professional'. Similarly, it doesn't take much for a 'wise-straight' to become recast as a 'rogue' (again, a few managerially witnessed infractions would suffice), but characterological development in the opposite direction would be unthinkable. Why is this?

Two variables appear to operate to produce organisationally preferred directions of character-change, as well as some characterological culs-de-sac. They are, firstly, the perceived *tensility* of the self implied in managerial prototypes. The 'villain' prototype self is relatively rigid, although the selves of 'others' are considered to be more flexible. Thus, it is simple to become a 'villain', but correspondingly difficult to escape that classification once it has been publicised. As Fig. 5.1 shows, a second variable comes from the nature of the men's reaction to this prototyping. The 'characters' formed in response to managerial typing have an intrinsic meaning. Thus, *defamation* may create permanent 'outcasts' (the 'shark' and 'righteous-straight' characters are seen as being the irremedial master status of the holder) or defamation (as with the other characters) may merely produce temporary or remedial 'membership' which is relatively easy to disavow as it is only seen as an auxiliary status of the holder.

These distinctions allow us to understand the possibility of change between characters. I have already discussed the crucial effects of

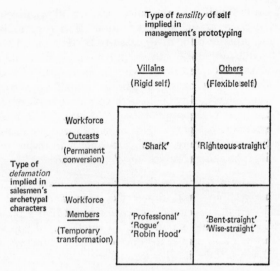

Fig. 5.1 Character change

imputed self tensility (in the discussion of prototyping on page 119). What effects do differences in the men's reactions to prototyping have? Of those considered to be workforce 'members', those with a rigid official self ('professional', 'rogue' and 'Robin Hood') might simply be recharacterised as 'shark', although they would have considerable difficulty changing their public selves to become an 'other' (a 'wise-straight' or a 'bent-straight'). These latter two 'member' characters, on the other hand, do have a flexible public self and they can easily move to become more upright (as a 'righteous-straight') or less so, as a 'rogue', 'professional' or 'Robin Hood'. Thus 'member' characters can be disarmed fairly easily. One man, who had operated with success on a 'Robin Hood' round, recalled his smooth transition to 'professional' status:

> A lot of the old girls, I used to let them have stale bread for the birds and that sort of thing . . . I'd let them have it, and not charge them . . . things like that, I never used to make a lot on retail, about a fiver a week, I suppose, when you change rounds, it isn't *that* much different. [When I was being retrained] I expected him to do it [fiddle], and I was watching him, but the *amount* surprised me.

Those seen as work force 'outcasts' are believed to be irremediably typed. To change character, the 'shark' or the 'righteous-straight' would need to benefit from either collaborative structural changes in the social control policy of the sales force or, alternatively, by personally leaving the actual work situation. It is easy to become an 'outcast', and equally difficult to cease to become one. However, the relatively flexible public self of the 'righteous-straight' would eventually allow the men to relocate him as 'wise' or 'bent' if he ceased to report the infractions of others, or began to fiddle himself. On the other hand, the 'shark' combines rigidity of self with permanence of conversion, and thus finds character change impossible. As Klapp (1962, p. 2) suggests, it is 'an inescapable category – once so categorised, he can change his social identity only by moving on'. One salesman trying to exchange a 'shark' biography for a 'professional' one found:

> I've had many a barney with the despatch manager, he's always calling me a 'thief' and things like that, and '——' [the sales manager] said the other day, when I showed him a photograph of my son 'Fancy having a dad who's a thief!' . . . I suppose he was joking, but he's said that to me once or twice . . . he says things, and you just have to take it with a pinch of salt.

CHARACTER MANAGEMENT

How do these characters fare in dealing with the real day to day financial problems of being a roundsman? As I have already explained, a reconciliation sheet of debits and credits (a 'rec.') is prepared for each roundsman every week. Each rec. ends with a personal verdict for the salesman: his balance may have 'come out' exactly, or, more likely, he is either 'over' or 'short' of the requisite balance. How do the salesmen deal with these difficulties?

Firstly, it is practically impossible to 'come out'. In fact, in the history of the sales department at Wellbread's, no salesman has ever exactly matched his debits with his credits. As the sales manager put it 'To do a journey and to come out spot on is nearly impossible'. This is optimistic. Should chance befall a salesman, and his rec. 'come out', this would not pass the eagle eye of the sales office. As a senior supervisor put it:

> You know, if one of my blokes ever came out exactly right [in the rec.], I'd sack him on the spot . . . it's impossible, and if somebody did it, I'd suspect that he was on the fiddle with the office . . . he must be . . . it's impossible.

Because the management believe that office calculations are infallible (the training officer told me 'They don't make mistakes in the office, it's impossible, because the work is checked') the frequent salesman claims that 'Oh well, they've made a mistake in the office' are treated as unfounded.

Secondly, coming 'over' merely depicts bad calculations by retailers, as they should simply be able to deduct the cash that they have made. Most wholesale rounds, however, have only a fixed amount of ready cash (from the limited supply of cash calls) to which the weekly 'make' must be regularly and accurately matched. If a salesman's 'make' regularly exceeds his 'take', he is merely wasting time making money that he cannot realise and which automatically swells the coffers of the firm. Most salesmen therefore try to plan 'making' arrangements to tie in neatly with predictable 'take' levels. For example a 'professional' claimed that he had turned down several potential inside deals because, if he had accepted them all, it would have meant that he would have had to get rid of thirty pounds' worth of 'extra' every day. He commented 'You just keep coming "over" and that's no good to you, you can't get it out'. Another man accepted all offers for the sake of good relations, but told me 'It's a waste of time really, I can cover all I can get out already'.

It is pointless for the salesmen to collect a series of 'over' verdicts as a sort of savings for use in times of future shortage, as large 'overs' usually mysteriously vanish from personal round accounts as the management take them to balance shortages on other rounds. One 'rogue' claimed 'I came about £220 over by the end of the season, well, they "evened it out" and, in the end, I just broke even'. A 'professional' felt similarly bitter (he lost £300 in 'overs') but he added 'Still, if you're down in the book, they'll help to balance it up'.

To consistently come 'over' is the mark of a 'rogue' on a big round. Unable to resist the sport, he continues to make money for the firm even when he cannot realise it himself. This can provoke awkward questions, as one 'rogue' remembered:

> When you come over, they just take it off and pay somebody else's debts with it, that happened to me . . . I came about £225 over one year, just before they cleared the books, and they took it all off, and left me with nothing . . . I got furious, and went and saw '——' [the accountant] and said 'Why should you take it all off?' and he said 'If you don't shut up, I'll want to know how you came so much over'.

The 'professional' *can* resist the sport. One turned down an inside deal for what he called 'purely financial' reasons. He added 'I haven't got the sort of stores where I can get rid of an extra tray a day, that's why I don't go into the bakery and steal it, I can't get rid of it'. Another 'professional' told me:

I never turn down the advantage of fiddle . . . well, it depends on the circumstances at the time, I suppose . . . if I've made enough to cover all the cash calls, then it's a waste of time doing any more like '——' does [a 'rogue'] . . . he'll fiddle as much as he can all the time . . . he'll come thirty pounds over each week, it's a waste of time really . . . it's just money for the company.

Various strategies have been evolved by the Wellbread's salesmen to aid those suffering from a chronic and regular shortage of available cash on their rounds. Most experienced wholesale roundsmen have *imaginary shops* (like the executives' 'dummy corporation') where the firm thinks that the salesman calls at a shop, but there isn't one and the salesman pockets the percentage discount, and, more frequently, *anonymous shops* (the salesman serves a call that the management knows nothing about, covers the order by under-booking elsewhere, and pockets all the cash from that call). One 'professional' claimed 'Everyone here's got their own little calls . . . I've got three, and there isn't a wholesaler who hasn't', and two more salesmen admitted to 'calls on the side that they don't even know about', even 'six . . . actually, that nobody knows about'.

If a call checker is bent, but has no access to organisational cash, an alternative strategy (where there is a will but, alas, no other way) is to *exchange for kind*. I was told by a 'rogue':

Well, see, one of the managers in the shops, then, offers him some bread for some groceries or something . . . I do it all the time, over here, they're only too glad to do it most of the time, it doesn't bother them, if I want a couple of bottles of drink or anything, I give them a couple of loaves . . . but I go outside and book them!

Periodically, when they have sufficient but otherwise 'untakeable' cash in their hypothetical 'make' kitty, some of the 'professionals' *close a shop*. This means that the docket bill is presented to the shopkeeper in the usual way, but instead of collecting the money and turning it over to Wellbread's in the conventional way, the money is pocketed by the salesman, and the firm is told that the shopkeeper closed up for that week to go on holiday. One 'professional' told me that he had 'closed a shop' one week, pocketed the fifty seven pounds payment, and torn up the invoice, because he'd 'been "over" for weeks, see? I'd been counting it up, and I thought I'd come "short" to even it out'. This worked, but he added 'Trouble is you can't close them too often', or the sales office would get suspicious.

Perhaps more dangerous, but at least an alternative way of getting cash in a tight situation, is *conversion*. This is not a regular practice and is only enacted by 'rogues', one of whom told me when I complained that I hadn't got sufficient cash on my round:

> You shouldn't let that worry you! . . . look, if you have a cash call, and he pays you twenty pounds by cheque, just pay that in and take ten pounds from somewhere else, as long as you can cover it, you're O.K. . . . if they say anything, all you have to say is 'Well, he only owed ten pounds, but he wanted ten pounds cash, so I let him give me a cheque for twenty pounds' . . . not that they will want to know, but just in case they do, you're covered . . . you can always cover it at the other end too if you want, I do sometimes, I get on well with my customers, they'll back me up if I want them to.

The policy of *carrying forward* (often called 'lapping' elsewhere – the suppression of paper profits in order to allow them to emerge later to suit accounting practices), has some short term utility amongst salesmen. It was described to me by a 'professional': 'Look, if you've made a lot one week, and can't get it out, make sure you have a lot of stock on the van, and don't book it on Saturday night'. In this way, 'made' money is carried, as stock, to be used later. A short term and dangerous policy is that of *delaying payment* (presenting bills to customers in the usual way, but pocketing the money. The call is reinvoiced by the bakery the following week, but then the salesman delays the payment of another call to deflect suspicion from himself, and pays the outstanding amount owed on the first call. It is a procedure that, once embarked upon, ends in almost certain entrapment.). A supervisor told me of a salesman who had quite accidentally been caught doing this. 'He could cover a lot of fiddling but couldn't get any cash. He didn't want to return it to the bakery for credit, because this would have been a black mark on his sales record. When the manager went to his house to see him one day "He had loads of bread round there! He had it stockpiled all along the sides of his house, everywhere! Even in the shed!". In the absence of any available cash, he eventually resorted to *delaying*. He took:

> Money from one of the shops, and put a ticket in to the firm saying that they hadn't paid, then next week, when they got a bill for a balance they had already paid, he paid it off out of somebody else's money . . . then he borrowed some more from somebody else . . . in the end, he owed about £300.

A third problem, actually more awkward to negotiate than either coming 'out' or 'over', is that of coming 'short'. Few of the salesmen accept the management's procedures for dealing with their shortages, and most define the subsequent pay packet deductions as clearly being class based retaliative punishment. I asked the assistant manager how Wellbread's handled 'shorts'. He told me:

> We don't do it by any hard and fast system, we have to have a think about it, and if a bloke is coming short regularly, and the total that he is short keeps building up, I'll get him in here, and say to him 'Look, if this doesn't come out right next week, we'll have to knock a couple of quid off'.

If deductions are actually made, the salesmen have three choices: they can *accept it, use it,* or *fight it.* Some accept it only if they happen to agree with it. One man claimed to me 'If I *am* short, then fair enough, I don't mind if they *do* take it out of the wages . . . I always think back to myself, and say "Did I have that much out?". If I did, then fair enough'. Another salesman thought that deductions could not only be used, but used systematically to the benefit of the salesman. He remembered a man 'who used to be a fiver short regularly, *every* week, consequently they used to stop him a fiver every week, but actually he was gaining about two pounds tax on it'.

As far as the third choice goes, different 'characters' specify different preferred procedures for fighting attempted wage packet deductions. The 'rogue' sometimes counter-attacks by *back dipping* (a spiral wherein whatever is deducted is simply retaken out of the cash bag). One man said 'They took six pounds out of my wage packet, so *I* just took six pounds out of the bag'. Alternatively, he may *threaten to leave.* One 'rogue' reported:

> Yeah, the first time I was stopped, they had me in the office, and I was stopped about two or three pounds, so I said I was going to give a week's notice . . . so they let me off . . . but they did it again, so I handed in my notice again, and they said the same thing, and I got the money back.

'Robin Hoods', in contrast, are left very much on their own, and are trusted to allow their accounts to *even out* in the long term. One 'Robin Hood' told me that he 'never bothers' with his rec., 'I just take it and look at the bottom, and think "Oh, dear", or "Oh, that's a surprise", or something like that, I don't worry about it'.

'Professionals', like 'rogues', fight tooth and nail to avoid deductions, but from a position of power and sophistication, rather than mere bitterness. A 'professional' rather blandly told me that, whenever he was short, he just assumed that it was an office mistake, because 'they always cock the calculations up in the office'. 'Professionals' usually either have the ability to cross check the calculations, or to demand that a supervisor check all the office work until a mistake is found.

The 'shark', on the other hand, because of his relationships with other salesmen and his public image, is virtually defenceless against the deductions system (see, for example, what happened to the 'shark' who owned too many cars chronicled in the quote on page 132). Any attempts by the 'shark' to use 'rogue', 'professional', or 'Robin Hood' strategies will just get him the sack.

Coming 'short' again brings the salesman up against the issue of the relative credibility of rec. calculations. As I have already mentioned, managerial calculations are sophisticated, specialised and high status. The salesmen's hurried unofficial computations cannot match the symbolic weight of the managerial figures. But recs. are a *moral* as well as a mathematical issue. Each salesman gradually builds himself an organisational moral profile reflecting his personal history of recon-ciliation performance. Now the management (who genuinely feel that sales life should 'add up' symbolically as well as mathematically for the work force) face an organisational problem in satisfying the crucial rationale of departmental solvency. Whilst 'shorts' amongst the sales force are so regular in toto, they are relatively unpredictable with particular members of the sales force. Accordingly, managerial success in publicly establishing reconciliation verdicts for the salesmen will be more ably and easily obtained if some degree of labelling regularity (i.e. the same salesmen each week) can be implanted into rec. verdict production procedures. Of course, the management do not see rec. procedures as creating rec. victims, merely as tracing them. The sales manager told me:

> If it's the roundsman's fault, I blame myself, I take a look in the mirror . . . I do a bit of self analysis . . . I tell myself that I've slipped up somewhere in his training . . . it's not always that poor bastard's fault . . . you've got to pick the right man in the first place.

Nevertheless, the 'poor bastards' are at a particular disadvantage. The managerial conceit concerning their auditing capabilities generally eliminates their double checking, and thus successfully avoids the only process which could expose errors. One salesman believed that pressure of work on the office girls (together with their knowledge that the salesmen have agreed to pay for mistakes) means that 'if they find a rec. sheet that works out at six pounds short, they know they can make us pay it, and that cuts out their double check and their treble check'. Accordingly, the moral concern with calculation that salesmen feel becomes concentrated upon prior accuracy of methods of calculating the fiddle 'take', rather than post hoc debates over relative validity. This concern with 'figuring the take' becomes an issue dependent upon the salesman's 'character'.

At one extreme, the 'Robin Hood' affects total disinterest in the rec. At the other, the 'rogue' maniacally calculates every penny he 'takes' or 'makes'. One 'rogue' claimed that 'When I'm out on the road, I put it all down in a little notebook' and another 'I've got it all written down on the roof of the cab, I always write it down somewhere . . . sometimes, I do it on the windscreen and rub it off at the end of the day'. He added 'I tot it all up and that's what I take out of the bag, all except the halfpennies, I leave them in, and that covers me for a cup of tea and a roll if I go into a café'. These methods may be accurate, but they will not be accepted by management – *however* they are computed. One 'rogue' even bought an electronic calculator! He claimed 'I'm going to work the whole lot out, just to see what they do'. 'Professionals', on the other hand, use satisfactory 'guesstimation' as ultimately more cost effective than endless and pointless calculations. One 'professional' claimed that 'I know roughly in my head, say, X amount of trays', and another said that 'I always say to myself, at the end of the week, "Have I had a good week?" '. Another 'professional' had a simpler solution 'I never write it down like some of them do, I just take all the cash!'.

A history of puzzled inability to cross-match the financial verdicts produced by both parties generally encourages most of the salesmen, in the long run, to drop the time consuming tactic of exactly matching 'make' with 'take', and to settle instead on the pro rata rule of 'leave a bit in', on top of sufficient financial cover, leaving the settlement of any issues arising to reconciliation debate.

Apart from these difficulties of 'figuring the take', greater problems for salesmen are generated by the managerial refusal to disclose relevant information about a salesman's personal financial standing. Some calls are invoiced directly, by post, by the sales office, and this prevents separate computation by the salesmen involved. More importantly, although salesmen believe that they are supposed to have unfettered access to the standing sum of their weekly verdicts, they are systematically denied access to the 'big book' where weekly recs. are summated. When salesmen request a look at their standing balance entered there, the request is always denied. One salesman claimed that he was always told 'Oh, I don't know, 'I don't know where the book is', or 'You're all right'. Another salesman said that when he asked how much in credit he was, the manager 'just says "Enough", so I say "How much is enough?", and he says "I haven't finished it yet", and he tells you to come in next week'.

One salesman suggested that the only way to find out the exact amount that one was in credit was to 'take a dip' (in the bag) of a regular amount over consecutive weeks, until told that the round was short. He told me 'You never know whether you're short or over . . . all you can do is "take a dip", and wait until they suddenly tell you that you're short, then you know where you are'. On many occasions, persistent demands for rechecking are ignored by the management. Anyway, even rechecking itself rarely establishes anything that the salesmen believe to be true. One salesman claimed that he had not only not seen his 'big book' total for a long time, but also he had not even seen a rec. for seven months. Another man added that, because the management adopt the 'attitude that it will work itself out next week', by the time the salesman can be sure that it won't, it is too late and too hard to trace the first error. Even more eerie, a 'professional' came seventeen pounds short one week, and had the whole sum docked from his wages. He 'spent two hours going over it, and found it all, *plus a bit more*, how could I do that? . . . *and* they never put it in the "big book" '.

Thus, each man's personal experience with the reconciliation system sours his erstwhile respect for it. Even superficially acceptable verdicts become suspect. One man told me 'Well, the funny thing was, I came *exactly* £3.96 short two weeks running'. It is only within the context of suspicion that this would become pregnant with the meaning that this man attached to it. Another claimed, quite logically, 'They [the office] must be on the fiddle . . . they take money out of the wage packet, right? . . . where the hell does that go?'. Sometimes rechecking the managerial verdicts produces bizarre results. Paradoxically, discovering managerial mistakes often saddens rather than gladdens the salesmen. Occasionally they get the feeling that, if only they checked a bit more thoroughly, the management would owe them money! One salesman recalled 'They made me twenty six pounds short last week, so I went and got the rec. and, in ten minutes, I'd found thirty three pounds . . . ridiculous isn't it? . . . if I'd found twenty six pounds, all right, but how the hell could I find thirty three pounds?'. When another man discovered that he and his mate were coming alternatively short by the same amount, they complained to the management. 'Then for the next six weeks, they both came short in the same week, then the next week, they both came over.' An astute salesman challenged an orthodox process. He had claimed twenty six pounds for cake waste, but had only noticed sixteen pounds entered as waste on his rec.:

> So I saw the supervisor, and asked him if he had put it all down . . . and he said 'I saw the manager, and we've worked something between us' . . . what the fuck does that mean? . . . what have they 'worked' between them . . . either you've got twenty six pounds' worth of cake waste, or you haven't.

In terms of the core premise of the sales department (that in weekly terms, the department must remain solvent), these assumptions are justifiable bearing in mind the amounts actually stolen from the bakery by the salesmen every week, and the quantities siphoned off by the inside dealers. Most of these latter losses, though, are lost to the despatch department. Accordingly, the book balancing tricks of the sales management, are compounded by the 'juggling' of the despatch manager. One of the senior sales managers told me to 'Watch —— (despatch manager) like a hawk if I was a salesman. It's your money he's playing with when he is doing your returns . . . if he doesn't put them down properly, you're going to be short the next week'. Ultimately, a salesman wishing to recompute his debit/credit balance each week faces the daunting task of not only cross-checking all the office figures (on his fingers), but also adding the financial outcomes of all the (invisible) managerial dirty tricks into this. I don't know how this could be done, and I met no salesmen who claimed to be able to do it.

Nevertheless, rather than unqualified acceptance of managerial reconciliation, salesmen define the accounting business as an issue of *moral*, rather than mathematical control. The auditing process is defined, by the salesmen, as one of *amoral* 'construction', cunningly contrived about criteria *other* than truth and accuracy. One exceptionally perceptive salesman suggested that these criteria are primarily presentational, and furthermore, are individually 'constructed' to suit particular characters:

> Look, they can just stick on any charges they like, he [the manager] can put on an extra charge, or miss a credit . . . mostly, you've got credits to come, as nine times out of ten you never get all the cakes you order . . . *and he knows I'm just slaphappy* . . . I chuck the tickets away each morning, never keep them to check off with the rec. . . . he's got to rectify *his* books, he's got to bring them straight, if he's so much down, he's got to get it back . . . he hits particular rounds each time . . . what happens is, the girls in the office might think it's correct, but he will go into the office *before* they're all [i.e. the recs.] written out, and change the figures . . . *you don't want an untidy rec., do you?* . . . that would make anybody suspicious, if it was all crossed out, and stamped all over . . . if a credit is crossed out, you would ask what it was for . . . but *a nice tidy rec.* goes a long way with me . . . he goes into the inner office and tells the girl that it's not supposed to be in there [i.e. that a credit is not supposed to be entered on the rec.] and she knocks it off . . . and he'll only do to blokes he knows won't be believed . . . Take '——' [the 'shark' from page 132] he was too much of a liar to know when he was telling the truth, nobody believed him about anything . . . *and the manager knew that nobody would believe anything he said* . . . and they never fully explain the system to

new blokes . . . they show them the rec. and the bloke *doesn't even know what he's looking for* . . . he [the manager] knows that the blokes are more interested in getting off home, not sitting here for a couple of hours trying to work it out . . . in all, they make it far too complicated, so that *you can't understand it.*

The organisational necessity (so defined by the management) of weekly financial balancing of individual salesmen's accounts creates an official routine of *moral* 'character' construction overlaying standard managerial prototyping. This serves to satisfy the normal organisational ends of controlling the work force. Recs., considered as weekly *moral* statements, are added to the 'big book' which lists periodic melodramatic definitions, and generates an ongoing average, moral profile for each 'character'.

In this chapter I have discussed normal times, and some difficulties that 'characters' generated in such situations might have when, for indirect reasons, the supporting environment temporarily fails to extend such support. I have considered the 'public negotiation' of self in the execution of 'part-time' crimes. How do the salesmen manage 'private preservation' of part-time selves in situations designed to make those part-time selves full-time? I shall face this question in Chapter 6.

6 Motives: Private Identity Preservation—Getting Caught and Getting Off

MOTIVES

For salesmen at Wellbread's, portfolio practice (character enactment) routinely satisfies practical and psychological 'cover' needs. Normally the part-time self remains psychologically partial, and can be taken for granted. However, the fiddling salesman faces a procedural dilemma: successful commerce requires the maintenance of routine and yet, on the other hand, fiddling is an intrinsically unprotected practice which constantly exposes the practitioner to the possibility of entrapment. The acid test of the part-time criminal is his ability to deal with the problematic threat of entrapment (and not just mundane everyday sales life) without psychological disintegration or encapsulation. Without a workable part-time self, fiddling would be impossible. If getting caught translates the part-time self into a full-time self, then fiddling would lose its crucial psychological meaning as 'trifling'. How do the salesmen sustain their fiddling self as partial in the face of others' attempts to promote that self to full-time status?

It is *conversation* which is the context of this attack and defence of the salesman's part-time self. This is where the special sociological sense of 'motive' comes in. When I talk of the salesmen's 'motives', I shall not attempt somehow to look behind their verbal and symbolic restructuring of events to elucidate the so-called 'real' motives of fiddling. Rather than address the conventional question of '*Why* do they do it?', I shall instead concentrate upon illuminating those practical and psychological processes which would allow us to answer '*How* do they do it?'. Instead of making the conventional distinction between 'his' and 'the' motives (Peters, 1958, p. 34), I shall just see how 'his' motives help the salesman to stay 'good' in difficult situations. This interest in the social function of motives and in the creation and maintenance of the self involves seeing motives as a linguistic matter, and the defences of partial selves as verbal ones. It is not that motives cannot be seen as 'causes', or that, as Lyman and Scott (1970, p. 3) put it, linguistic motive deliberation always precedes an action, but rather that the actual *meaning* of motives for the individual lies exclusively in his linguistic statement of them, whether that statement is constructed before or after the questioned act.

This opens another point: as Mills tells us (1940, p. 905) the conversational ground condition of both motive imputation and motive avowal *is* the 'question'. Further, as Peters (1958, p. 29) says, 'We only ask about a man's motives when we wish, in some way, to hold his conduct up for assessment'. To combine the two, in Mills' words, 'motives are words . . . they stand for anticipated situational consequences of questioned conduct'.

There is another refinement. Verbalisations are also *situated*; different situations have differently appropriate 'motives'. The profession and confession of motive obviously depend on the vocabulary of motives available to the individual. For example, there is a specific vocabulary of phrases and accents which the salesmen at Wellbread's use in conversation with those who question their honesty. Of course, the post facto profession of these linguistic motives is not necessarily strategically ulterior, as the possibility of making such statements may be crucial in guiding the release of physical energy allowing the action in the first place. The possibility of getting away with saying 'It was a mistake', if questioned, might allow the roundsman initially to fiddle the customer. So the discussion of motives might also throw extra light upon the initial decision to fiddle (through such 'identification' with socially available reasons that might be acceptably verbalised after the act takes place) and to the processes which might account for the maintenance of a non-deviant, 'good' partial self in the face of the commission of deviant actions (through the 'neutralisation' of morality).

But these two processes, 'identification' and 'neutralisation', are conceptually untidy and intransigent, and cannot be simply and uncritically adopted to explain the situation of the salesmen at Wellbread's. 'Identification' was proposed by Foote (1951, p. 14) to fill what he termed 'an unanalysed hiatus between words and acts, of mystery as to just *how* language does in fact motivate'. Whilst the principle of identification helped, for example, to understand 'compulsive' criminals (through diffuse identification, solitary deviants assemble behaviouristic rationalisations, as a means of identifying themselves as 'out of control' or 'overcome'), by releasing them from the miasma of unconscious motivation, it instead entangled them in accusations of malevolent provision of ulterior motives.

The second process, 'neutralisation', was, on the other hand, proposed by Matza and Sykes (1957) as benevolent in principle. In a later formulation, Matza (1964, p. 61) explicitly denies that deviants articulately seize upon and exploit loopholes in the law. Instead, the structure of the criminal law paradoxically invites the individual to neutralise his normative attachment to it. How is the 'moral bind' of the law weakened? Matza suggests that 'the criminal law is especially susceptible to neutralisation because the conditions of applicability, *and thus inapplicability*, are explicitly stated'. Accordingly, this liquidation of the 'oughtness' of norms neutralises the actor's sense of illegal infraction (which had been attached to the projected act) and allows him to 'drift' into committing the offence. But there are some problems with the concept of 'neutralisation'. Consider an initial statement by Matza and Sykes (1957, p. 251):

> Disapproval flowing from internalised norms and conforming to others in the social environment is neutralised, turned back, or deflected in advance. Social controls that serve to check or inhibit deviant motivational patterns are rendered inoperative, and the individual is freed to engage in delinquency without serious damage to his self image . . . they are [also] viewed as following deviant behaviour and as protecting the individual from self-blame and the blame of others after the act.

Three general weaknesses appear here. Firstly, eclecticism in *timing* (can neutralisation act before *and* after the act?); secondly, non-specificity of *audience* (does neutralisation operate on self *and* others?); and thirdly, over-extensiveness of *arena* (can neutralisation refer both to practical *and* psychological consequences?).

A separate confusion (and additional limitation) arises in Matza and Sykes' typology of 'techniques' of neutralisation. Their classification comprises the *denial of responsibility* ('I didn't mean it'); the *denial of injury* ('I didn't really hurt anybody'); the *denial of the victim* ('They had it coming to them'); the *condemnation of the condemners* ('Everyone's picking on me'); and the *appeal to higher loyalties* ('I didn't do it for myself'). These social but 'unrecognised extensions of defences to crimes' are derived from standard defences to 'defensible' accusations. However, on their own admission (Matza and Sykes, 1957, p. 252), this arbitrary division into five categories is a matter of 'convenience'. It is difficult to tell which parts of their analyses are specific to juvenile delinquency and which more generally applicable, and the typology fails to be either parsimonious or comprehensive when faced with the alternatives given in English courts. There, Hart (1952, p. 147) suggests, an accusation can be challenged in two ways. Firstly, by a denial of the facts, and secondly, by a 'plea that although all the circumstances on which a claim could succeed are present, yet, in the particular case, the claim or accusation could not succeed because other circumstances are present which bring the case under some recognised head of exception'. Hart cites the multiple criteria for excluding or reducing liability in criminal cases as 'mistakes of fact, accident, coercion, duress, provocation, insanity, and infancy'. The presentational form of a defence cannot be decided a priori of a particular case. The same exception might be a justification, an excuse, or a mitigation upon different occasions. Hart (1968, p. 16) comments 'Though the central cases are distinct enough, the border-lines between justification, excuse and mitigation are not'.

In an attempt to improve Matza and Sykes' formulation, Scott and Lyman took up the last point with what they feel is the more basic category of 'accounts'. An account is (Scott and Lyman, 1970a, p. 93) 'a statement made by social actors to relieve themselves of culpability of untoward or unanticipated acts'. Accounts (techniques of neutralisation in a different order, and under a different name) fall into two separate types. Firstly, *justifications*, or 'accounts in which one accepts responsibility for the act in question but denies the pejorative quality associated with it' (Scott and Lyman, 1968, p. 25); and secondly, *excuses*, which are 'accounts in which one admits that the act in question was bad, wrong, or inappropriate, but denies full responsibility'. The difficulties with this formulation (it ignores two alternative pairings of pejorativeness and responsibility, especially the 'confession' (Hepworth and Turner, 1974, p. 47) defining the act as bad, but accepting responsibility for it) are not fully resolved by Goffman, the final significant contributor to the debate within linguistics on motives.

Goffman's early (1955) concern with ritual strategies of corrective 'face work' designed to neutralise threats to the self occurring as disruptions to the expressive order later emerged (1961a) as implication control moves (explanation, apology, joking, or righteous indignation), designed to realign self-information with self-conception. Somewhat later, Goffman (1971, p. 149) settled upon a 'single ritual idiom of remedial moves [which] must be called on whether a toe has been accidentally stepped on or a destroyer accidentally sunk'. This idiom is composed of three *'devices'*; accounts, apologies and requests. Accounts can be one of five relevant *'pleas'*, and can arrive in one of three *'terms'*; explanation, excuse or pretext. Apologies include the usual Goffman grovel procedures, and requests are timed just a little better. Surprisingly, Goffman's final typology has an eclectically inclusive air, and is particularly vague about the actual effects upon the selves of the participants. Rather than synthesise other typologies, Goffman expansively includes them all.

None of these theorists has produced a typology sufficiently clear or exhaustive to cope with the use of motive by the salesmen at Wellbread's. To remedy this deficiency, I have produced a logically inductive typology of linguistic defences of the self which is at least relevant to life at Wellbread's. The two basic sets (or 'terminologies') of self-maintaining lingualisations are summarised in Table 6.1.

The crucial element of the defensive, apologetic form of the terminology (the left hand side of Table 6.1) is its mode of expression. To apologise is to perform penance and promise restitution and ultimately, as Goffman (1971, p. 145) puts it, 'apologies represent a splitting of the self into a blameworthy part and a part that stands back and sympathises with the blame giving'. However, whilst there is full admission of the pejorativeness of the act in operation, there is disputed agreement over full responsibility for its commission. Firstly, the '*flat*' denial of responsibility (1a in Table 6.1) requires substantiation of the actor's claim that the act either wasn't done, or that the accused didn't do it.

Secondly, '*defeats*' of the allegation (2a in Table 6.1) require that the accused show that acceptable circumstances or states of mind warrant partial excuse of the act, and this technically reduces the charge. Although some self-abasement is still necessary, the allegation needs restructuring. Whilst the act may still be deplored, the individual's responsibility has been excluded.

Thirdly, some occasions can be so defended that, although the act is still deplored and the actor held responsible for it, there still remain grounds for total offence '*reduction*' (3a in Table 6.1). If successful, a mild punishment follows a reduced guilty plea. Accounts using 'reductions' are often personalised. Through selective recounting of past events and their amalgamation in a nicely reconstituted semi-fictional biography, the accused tries to consolidate current reduced liability claims. These defensive biographies (defined by Goffman, 1961, p. 139, as 'a view of himself that he can usefully expound in current situations') tend to view the actor as an object, and thus a matter for excusing. The prime example, the 'sad tale', is again provided by Goffman (1961, p. 140) who tells us that 'if the facts of a person's past and present are extremely dismal, then about the best he can do is show that he is not responsible for what has become of him'.

Other defensive biographies are the 'apologia' (of which Goffman, 1959a, p. 140, says 'the person's line concerning self defensively brings him into appropriate alignment with the basic values of his society); together with 'atrocity tales' and 'trickster stories' (Goffman, 1963,

TABLE 6.1 Self-maintenance terminologies

	Defensive (retreating) lingualisations	Offensive (attacking) lingualisations
	Morality neutralising	Morality rejecting
	Shameful penitence	Righteous indignation
	(Strategic alliance)	(Principled opposition)
	Apologetic justification	Radical justification
	(Disputing responsibility allegations)	(Disputing pejorativeness imputations)
	Restitutive	**Retaliatory**
	Self-inclusion pleas (deviance)	Self-exclusion pleas (politics)
1 **Denial**	(a) 'Flat' denial of total responsibility	(b) 'King Edward' denial of total pejorativeness
2 **Qualified admission**	(a) 'Defeats' of allegation (Denial of responsibility) (1) *Circumstantial excuse* (Projection) Act Adjustment to defeat fault: non-conventional situation claim (2) *Psychological excuse* (Introjection) Actor Adjustment to defeat imputability: non-theoretical actor claim/fiat	(b) 'Ignore' accusation (Counter denunciation) (Condemnation of condemners) (Denial of victim) (Denial of injury, persons) **Principled justification** Universal counter-statement
3 **Mitigated admission**	(a) 'Reductions' of logical punishment (Denial of injury, objects)	(b) 'Balance' accusation **Situational justification** Particularistic defence (Appeal to higher loyalties)
4 **Full admission**	(a) Active: with full explanation (Submit to mercy of judge)	(b) Passive: non-participation (Refusal to acknowledge judgement)

F

pp. 33, 37) wherein current personal situation is explained by extreme mistreatment or sheer deceit by others in the past.

Fourthly, the '*active*' full admission (4a in Table 6.1), whilst simple to describe, is not a technique which the salesmen at Wellbread's find useful.

The offensive, attacking, radical form of the terminology, on the other hand, is principally organised from the oppositional subculture (Matza, 1964, p. 41), and characterised by *righteous indignation*. A display of righteousness has a similar format to the apology. But here (the right hand side of Table 6.1), it is the *accuser*, rather than a split off part of the *self*, who is abased. In these terms, the '*King Edward*' denial (1b in Table 6.1: the name derives from an apocryphal story about a potato seller challenged with selling falsely described goods. He replied 'Of course they're King Edwards. And anyway, what do you expect for twopence a pound?') actually denies the act in question, but asserts that its commission would be a good thing. Because of the nature of the relationship between justifier and accuser, '*ignoring*' (2b in Table 6.1) and '*Balancing*' (3b in Table 6.1) an accusation with lateral pleas is unlikely to be successful, apart from perhaps moderating stringent punishment. '*Passive*' non-participation in the proceedings (4b in Table 6.1) is taken as tacit admission of guilt but total rejection of the legitimacy of the accuser.

Offensive styles (as do defensive styles) have recounting resources as well as accounting ones. Appropriate biographies here are justifying rather than apologising ones. The actor begins to feature as hero rather than as victim. Goffman (1959a, p. 140) suggests, for example, the 'success story', where the individual manages 'to present a view of his current situation which shows the operation of favourable qualities in the past, and a favourable destiny awaiting him'.

How do salesmen at Wellbread's use these lingualisations in conversations with those who question their honesty, and therefore their motives? Basically, they do so at two levels. Firstly, the immediate concern of the fiddling salesman is the public, practical consequences of sales life. At the purely material level, he needs some sort of practical 'cover' that will prevent actual physical apprehension by others. The part-time self requires an 'alibi', a 'presented piece of biography that ordinarily would not have become part of one's biography at all' (Goffman, 1963, p. 89), to deflect blame from others. But, secondly, some private psychological 'cover' must be provided to protect the real self from psychic contamination by the partial self of work. To prevent the self-apprehension of shame, the fiddler must find an 'alias' for his work self and so ensure his psychological status as a stable part-time criminal.

Accordingly, I will look firstly at *'alibis'* (public covers for others, or the neutralisation of blame), and secondly, at *'aliases'* (private covers for the self, or the neutralisation of shame). The operation of 'alibis' and 'aliases' by salesmen at Wellbread's successfully sustains their partial identities in times of potential crisis.

ALIBIS

For sophisticated fiddlers, provision of public cover can partially be a *prior* matter of strategic blame deflection. Firstly, then, an 'alibi' can be provided by sheer cunning. Experience teaches salesmen at Wellbread's that the typical customer accusation will be crude and unthinking. Accordingly they may, as one 'rogue' recalled, build alibi cover backwards in time:

> I always add a bit onto the monthly accounts, they never know, but you have to be careful that they're not checking . . . so what I do is tell the period that it's for . . . the best thing is to alter the length of the month . . . know what I mean? . . . say they really owe £5.63 . . . then say to them 'That'll be £6.44 please', and if they're checking on you, if they've kept a note of what they've had, just say something like 'Well, it's not an exact month, see, it's five weeks!' . . . or, tell them that it's not *right* up to date, and then carry an extra bit over to next time . . . then you've covered, see? . . . you've got to cover yourself.

To prevent the initial formulation of suspicion is, after all, better and more conducive to good customer relations than to allow sour feelings to curdle into accusation. A second technique is never to leave oneself without a 'reserve story' (Goffman, 1966, p. 20). At Wellbread's this means, as one man put it, 'Short change them, yeah, I often do that, but don't over-charge them' (as the latter would provide verbal evidence of offence). Thirdly, another man thought blame best deflected by the adoption of chosen styles of personal presentation. When I asked him why he never smiled, he replied *'What? . . . smile? . . . smile? . . .* if you smile round here, they think you've made money or something; smile and they'll search your van'. The fourth and final technique is what Davis (1959, p. 270) calls the 'psychological' approach. One astute salesman said:

> What I always do is talk about what *they* want to talk about when we're checking the stuff in, there's one girl who's mad on speedway, so I go on about speedway all the time . . . there's another one who's sex mad . . . so I go on about all the bits of stuff that I've seen bending

down as I drive around the town . . . and the bloke at Robinson's, he's always moaning at something . . . I'm diddling him left, right and centre, but I'm moaning all the time, and he loves it . . . when I go, and I've done him for about fifteen pounds . . . he shouts 'Cheerio, boy', and gives me the thumbs up sign.

But 'alibis' are generally constructed *after* the event. What is then crucial about practical, public cover is its relative success rather than its particular timing. I will first describe successful (covered) alibis, and then unsuccessful (discovered) ones.

Success: Getting caught – 'close ones'

Sometimes customers seem to think that it is sound commercial logic to warn their visiting bread salesmen about their dishonesty, but sheer moral extravagance to push things any further. Questions about the actor's intentions are irrelevant to the smooth running of commercial social control, and superseded by concentration on ensuring future restitution. It is sometimes even conceived to be a matter of little concern that the loss suffered by the customer is a result of deliberate swindling or unintentional mistake. In fact, since future prevention is the crucial issue, belief in accident proneness is more likely to lead to increased checking procedures in the future, than an established case of fiddling: a rather nice commercial irony.

Customers are usually prepared to allow their suspicions of malpractice to be refuted on most occasions, specifically to allow the commercial routine to continue. This gives 'getting caught' (always, in effect, getting *off*) a symbolic and ritual quality. This does not mean that customers pass up the chance to comment on the situation, being unwilling to sacrifice the chance of offering moral superiority displays and lectures upon proper commercial practice.

In game terms, the verbal contribution of the salesman successfully transforms a pretence awareness context ('both interactants are fully aware but pretend not to be', Glaser and Strauss, 1964, p. 10), or a suspicion awareness context ('one participant suspects the true identity of the other or the other's view of his own identity, or both') into an effectively *closed* context. The game element might be simultaneously seen as cleverly managed recovering moves in an information game (with opaqueness being restored to the interaction) and as a routinely successful corrective 'face game'. Goffman (1955, p. 9) defines face work as 'the actions taken by a person to make whatever he is doing consistent with face'. Face is 'the positive value a person effectively claims for himself by the line others assume he has taken during a particular contact'. The ritual order is re-established by neutralising such threats through participation in a series of ritual moves. Scott and Lyman (1970b) have extended Goffman's (1955) analysis, and suggest the following typical moves. Firstly, *initiation* ('an occurrence that openly damages the identity of one of the persons') and secondly the *challenge*, 'which calls attention to the offensive deed, designates the person responsible, and calls for an admission of responsibility or a statement or deed of exculpation'. Finally, there is the *response*, which is a statement typically selected from either the offensive or the defensive range of the self-maintenance terminology outlined in Table 6.1.

Although the nature of the initiation move varies situationally, initiation indicates a breakdown in practical cover arrangements, and not a change in the techniques of fiddling. For some unspecifiable reason the performance facade begins to thin, and the customer begins to perceive discrepancies between the impressions that the salesman 'gives' and those he 'gives off' (Goffman, 1959, p. 14). As Matza (1969, p. 152) puts it, this opens 'the intricate and sensitive network of gestural clues: shifting eyes, tell-tale expression, nervous avoidance, assiduous interest, informational slips, and everything else that composes the sensibility of suspicion'. In these conditions, the customer can present a warning to the salesman by either pretence or suspicion.

Firstly, then, *pretence* warning is communicated through the *vague accusation*, whereby face encounters are initiated by notifying acknowledgement of a morally disturbing event as justification for attack, but withdrawal just prior to the challenge proper. One form of vague accusation is the 'cautionary tale'. Here, the customer co-opts a piece of folk wisdom from what Goffman (1963, p. 104) calls 'the morality which we employ to keep people in their places', and presents it to the roundsman in the hope that he will 'get the message' and not misbehave in the future. Regrettably, salesmen accept the tale as personal verification that the customer telling the tale has been (and thus may be in the future) successfully fiddled. I once had a conversation with a customer who not only 'cautioned' me, but also managed to meta-communicate to me that she would not, after all, be able to catch me if the caution failed. She said:

My bills seem to be getting bigger nowadays . . . about twelve pounds, instead of what they used to be . . . about nine or ten pounds . . . you're not adding a bit on, are you? . . . I don't know, I never check it . . . I hope you're doing it properly, I don't know what all the prices are nowadays.

One of the salesmen explained how pointless it was for customers to indulge in this sort of purging of their worries:

Take the manager of Johnson's, the first time he came, he said 'You've got to watch all bakers and cake deliverers, because they're the biggest twisting bleeders under the sun!' . . . which is stupid really because he's the greenest of any of them . . . they're always the easiest, the ones who say that sort of thing . . . they're saps, because they can't be bothered to check you . . . they think that's enough, just to warn you.

Another form of the vague accusation is the 'warning story'. Here, the customer similarly indicates that she is not going to pursue the matter to the courts, but whilst she indicates that she is aware of quite what has happened, she is prepared to *act* as if a mistake has occurred. Goffman (1959, p. 227) refers to this tactic as an audience 'hint': 'It is through hints that the audience can warn the performer that his show is unacceptable, and that he had better modify it quickly if the situation is to be saved'.

Secondly, a salesman can be warned by notification of *suspicion*. The challenge may be, firstly, the *hidden accusation*. Here, apprehensiveness replaces apprehension in a very subtle way. Moral opprobrium can be satisfactorily conveyed, and yet the inferred guilt is unchallengeable without publicly acknowledging the accusation. To do the latter is to admit the guilt on the basis that only the guilty would be sufficiently sensitive to notice the accusation.

One of the Wellbread's salesmen commented of one of his calls 'Well, there's one of my shops, he's never actually *accused* me of fiddling him . . . but he makes sure that he checks it when I'm looking'. The same man said of the bakery despatch manager:

Whenever I come in in the morning, my rack is stood by itself . . . when I go to check it off, he says to me 'No need to check that, I've already done it' . . . well, as it happened, on one of the trays, two large browns were spaced out funny, and sure enough, I was a couple short, when I told him, d'you know what he said? . . . 'Fucking marvellous, as soon as you come back from holiday, bread goes missing'.

An interpretative error by customers (rather than a moral decision) produces the second type of suspicion warning: the *hasty accusation*. In this case, customers actually bent upon entrapment have not waited for the accumulation of sufficient proof. A customer once said to me 'You're not cheating me like the other one did, are you?' thus allowing me both an easy denial and an insight into the customer's ignorance. Several of the salesmen remembered times when they had been caught with their pants not really down, under circumstances (as in this last case) where, to pursue the metaphor, the customer's slip begins to show.

Responses to either of these challenges (the pretence or suspicion warnings) are rarely offensive as this might precipitate a moral reaction from a customer hitherto prepared to forget the issue altogether. Sometimes the morally offended can be persuaded to reconsider the accusation, and tactical righteous indignation is deployed when suspicion needs cooling. If stealing has become an issue at the depot, then (since future practical and social relations depend upon it) efforts will be made to get the accuser to retract the accusation. For example, although the despatch manager privately told me that 'You've got to have 100 per cent proof, it's a man's character you're talking about, you've got to be sure', one of his salesmen commented, of a separate occasion when this rule had apparently been waived:

He'd better stop making accusations like that, or I'll get a solicitor's letter . . . like I had to when he started saying things like that before.

Away from the bakery, with customers, righteous offensive denials are only used on those occasions when it is considered that the only way to stop accusations interfering with everyday business is to threaten counter-suit, or to stress bluntly the unfactual nature of the accusation. One salesman tried to halt the flow of innuendo by asking the suspicious customer ' "Are you accusing me of fiddling, then?" and he said: "Yes" . . . what the hell could I do? I just left. He said he was going to ring the bakery but he never did'. When a shopkeeper threatened to report another man, he 'just said "Oh well, please your fucking self", and drove off'.

The most useful offensive tack is to 'ignore' the accusation, and, in effect, deny the injury. Typically, this takes the form of a strategic 'fight back'. One salesman claimed:

The manager said [after a relief had been on] 'Well, he never put sixty in there, you can't get sixty on that shelf' . . . well, I could drop Alf [the relief] in the cart, so I said to the manager of the shop 'Clear that shelf and I'll show you how to get sixty on there' . . . I managed to get sixty on, but he still didn't believe me, he said 'It wasn't as full as that' . . . I told Alf so that when he goes again, he can put sixty on . . . if he can't, then we'll have to make another excuse, he'll have to say 'I'm sorry, I read the wrong note, it was fifty not sixty'.

More regularly, however, on such occasions, the offender agrees with his moral label in the encounter, and instead attempts a form of face work. Rare, but just possible, is *avoidance* face work, wherein contact with the person threatening one's face is reduced. For example, one man claimed:

> Whenever he [a fiddled army sergeant] sent for me, I used to start to sweat around the collar, one of the corporals used to say to me 'Hang on a minute, the sarge wants a word with you' . . . I used to sweat, and say 'Some other time, I'm in a hurry this morning'.

But in these situations, although anger may cool, the situation has to be faced eventually, when *corrective* face work will be needed. Defensive work here centres upon 'defeats'. The flat denial is morally careless and might anger the offended, and admission is wholly unnecessary. The nature of the defeat is conceived by salesmen to be just 'talk'. Talk, as Scott and Lyman (1968, p. 24) put it, has the 'ability to repair the broken and restore the estranged'. Talk prevents the free running of alarm and stalls the mobilisation of customer anxiety. It becomes clear to the cynical roundsman that the actual content of 'talk' isn't too important. With alarmed customers I was told by other roundsmen to 'pretend to look surprised' or 'have a ready made excuse'. To confront accusations of fiddling, I was told 'As long as you keep talking to them, they'll take anything, just keep talking, that's all, give 'em any excuse, and they'll believe it, they'll believe anything'.

Successful talk renders the indignant unconscious of any infringement. Based upon verbal dexterity and presence of mind, the acute salesman is able to suggest that, with Goffman (1971, p. 309), 'Although things look strange, they are really explicable and, furthermore, explicable in a way that will remove cause for concern'. Talk that allows a potentially disturbing event to be assimilated into the normal sphere is thus, on the same terms, 'good'.

Much less frequently, psychological defeats of imputability are employed. By *fiat*, the trainee salesman has a special excuse by virtue of his temporary role (see Chapter 2), and more accomplished members of the work force occasionally plead variations on the 'I don't know what came over me' theme. One man reportedly had strategically periodic bouts of flu. He told me 'When she [customer] asked me about it, I told her that I'd had flu all the previous week, and I pretended that I didn't know what I was doing'.

The very nature of positing a defeat, of course, assumes that financial restitution will automatically be made. Only customers, salesmen feel, are prepared to fight over the odd packet of biscuits, and most of the men give the customer the benefit of any available doubt on the basis that any shortfall on their sales accounts can be balanced elsewhere, or at the same call upon future days.

What counts practically, then, is not so much the nature of the account offered to customers, but its effect. Distinctions may exist between malign and benign mistakes, but for practical purposes, one only has to establish that a mistake has been made. I have dealt with the successful deflection of blame. What happens when deflection attempts fail?

Failure: Getting caught out – 'slip ups'
As Scott and Lyman (1968, p. 26) put it 'The excuse of accident is acceptable precisely because of the irregularity and infrequency of accidents occurring to any single actor'. The folk fear of the fiddler is that design or accident will correlate a sufficient number of suspicions, thereby translating theoretical dishonesty into empirical guilt. Cross-checking is not routinely done by customers, and thus the fiddler's moral world is predicated upon the theoretically fragile (albeit empirically tough) assumption that others will only have 'small information' (Goffman, 1974, p. 448) about his activities. This usually but not always occurs. For example, when an originally minded office clerk at Wellbread's decided to cross-check bread despatched to salesmen with that invoiced for each journey, the salesmen got together and complained to the management who prevented the woman in question from completing her investigations.

The relevant empirical conditions for concrete and unnegotiable discovery are thus either the *longitudinal* or the *lateral* check. The longitudinal check is successful if the customer has collated and summated an inordinate number of mischievous mistakes, a list with which she can face the roundsman. The customer's 'list on the larder wall' terrifies retail salesmen at Wellbread's. I was warned to avoid fiddling one customer, for example, as 'she has all the prices chalked up on the wall'. Similarly, a customer once told me 'I always write down what I have on the fridge door so that I don't get cheated . . . when the other baker used to add it up, it always used to come to more than I made it, I think he used to add it on'. Wholesale men, on the other hand, face the possibility that they are being cross-checked over long periods without their knowledge. Regrettably, salesmen always have to take the customer's naïvety and stupidity on trust. One salesman told me:

> I've been caught out, and have had to pay them back . . . I mean caught *properly*, over a period of time, that's what you've got to watch for, when they try and catch you over a *period of time* . . . otherwise, you can just say it was a mistake.

Customers can also unwittingly get together and happen to entrap the salesmen through the lateral check. One man expressed this as the 'coffee morning fear': he was continually worried that all his customers might meet over coffee and accidentally reveal to one another that their baker was charging them all different prices! Wholesale men might suffer from haphazard canvassing. One said:

—— [Sales manager] went to one of my calls last week, to see if everything was alright . . . and the fucker told him that he had forty two pounds' worth of stuff every week from me, well, he came back and saw that I only booked him for about twenty pounds . . . he told —— [supervisor] that 'something funny was going on' . . . prat!

There is thus a pragmatic as well as a dramaturgical reason for the proper scheduling of sales performances, and for the maintenance of audience segregation. It is not just that (as all performances do) the sales performance contains what Goffman (1959, p. 143) calls 'latent secrets' (i.e. 'facts about almost every performance which are incompatible with the impression fostered by the performance but which have not been collected and organised into a usable form by anyone') but rather that the audience of customers is structurally 'weak'. This means a type of audience whose members are not in face to face contact with one another during the performance, but who later come together to pool their criticisms of it.

Peculiarly, offensive replies *are* possible to solid accusations of this nature. For instance, the classical 'pilferer's plea' might be offered. A pilferer's plea contains hidden 'weasel words' (words which cunningly evade the spirit but not the letter of the law) which sound innocuous enough but do, in fact, legally protect the pilferer. For example, at Wellbread's, one could plead 'I asked the despatch man whether he wanted the bread, and he replied "You can have the whole bloody lot as far as I'm concerned, mate" '. The joke answer is set up, and subsequently used in defence.

More likely from the salesmen are varieties of mitigated and fulldefensive admission, since denial would be somewhat impractical and possibly inflammatory under the circumstances. One wholesaler reported:

I got caught proper soon after I started, I had to carry on where the other bloke left off, or it would have looked bad . . . it was a bit embarrassing going back there at first, but she just seemed to think of it as amusing, she seemed to treat it as a victory . . . he had told me to take some old loaves out, and put them on top and book them, but she'd marked them all, put little crosses on them! . . . I just had to admit it, there wasn't anything else I could say.

On occasions such as this, little more than mere restitution (exact compensation for the amount lost) is necessary. However, if wily customers are prepared to retaliate in kind, they can claim that much more was lost than their one act of checking can demonstrate. In these cases, the salesman has to bribe the customer to keep quiet. One of the senior supervisors was particularly adept at arriving at an agreeable settlement, and was used informally by the more sophisticated salesmen specifically for that purpose. One wholesaler told me that a fellow salesman 'got caught heavily the other day, he phoned —— [the senior supervisor] up, and the manager never got to know about it . . . and the supervisor went down and sorted it out'.

Although it is extremely unlikely that an aggrieved customer will actually take a salesman to court (never in living memory at Wellbread's), the salesman faces the embarrassing necessity of having to return to the scene of the previous entrapment every day. Luckily, the commercial necessity of routine face re-engagement absorbs residual indignation and guarantees eventual return to normality, albeit to a re-normalised setting. As Gross and Stone (1970, p. 175) suggest 'Embarrassment occurs whenever some central assumption in a transaction has been unexpectedly and unqualifiedly discredited'. But although the exposure of one participant as having unacceptable moral qualities is potentially shattering, even the wounded party feels a structural sympathy (for having brought misfortune on another) and a necessity to deny his own implication (maintaining the embarrassment similarly sustains the fact that he is, or was, a fool) which satisfactorily normalises the setting. The residual knowledge, however, always exists. As Goffman (1956b, p. 104) puts it 'The individual is likely to know that certain special situations always make him uncomfortable and that he has certain "faulty" relationships which always cause him uneasiness'. The salesman's round is exactly this. There are always a few awkward calls which are served awkwardly, formally, stiltingly, and haltingly. One man claimed, for instance, of one call 'It's embarrassing serving him now, but he never seems to notice', recognising that the effect of embarrassment can persevere long after the embarrassment itself has cooled.

Thus public life can be adequately managed by the work self, the part-time self, of the fiddler. Even provable occasions of theft do not allow apprehension to spread embarrassment into the inner, basic layers of the self. But is self-maintenance *privately* manageable?

ALIASES

Crucially the private, psychological management of danger has two forms: *prior* denials of responsibility (a rhetoric of self-adjustment) and posterior denials of pejorativeness (a rhetoric of self-reconciliation). However, before- and after-ness is an existential rather than a temporal issue. Importantly, the adjustment rhetoric may, in fact, be formulated or conceptualised by the actor *after* an act takes place, but is *seen* by him as being causally *antecedent*. Implied here is the idea of 'toying' with an act (Rock, 1973, p. 66), or rehearsing the consequences in one's imagination. The reconciliation rhetoric, on the other hand, might have been called upon for self-maintenance *before* act commission. It nevertheless involves a conception of the future as releasing the self to act *in* the present, and a conception of self as having already acted, and as having personal reflective knowledge of self as actor.

Before: Inoculation (Self-adjustment)

Self-protection from shame which proceeds from self-inoculating adjustment will either depend upon neutralising the salesman's self or upon neutralising the activity of fiddling. The application of what Cressey (1953, p. 95) calls 'key neutralisations' is intended either to adjust the actor to the act, or the act itself. In either event, Cressey continues, 'Such ideologies adjust contradictory personal values in regard to criminality on the one hand and integrity, honesty and morality on the other'.

The theoretically possible limits of adjustment for salesmen are indicated by the restrictions that they place on their deviant activity. The very nature of their 'portfolio' (discussed in Chapter 5) describes the limits above which dishonesty might begin to infect the real self. This seems to be a general phenomenon. Cameron (1964, p. 168), for example, noting that many shop-lifters prefer to steal goods that they might have been able to afford (most such offences occur in the bargain basement) rather than filch expensive items that might pose problems of psychological management back at home.

Salesmen at Wellbread's typically experience 'honesty lapses' of the same nature. For instance, one said 'You might have a good day, you really go daft [laugh], erratic, and then you start to worry about it the following day, thinking "I didn't half sting them well yesterday" [laugh], feeling sorry for them, and you start to think "I'll knock a bit off today" '. More likely than this sort of guilty paying back, and in order to be able to use reconciliatory justifications at a later stage, the salesmen pursue a policy of situational honesty. Most men don't fiddle the small, corner shops. Losses here are too real, their effects too obvious, and the relationships with the shopkeeper sometimes too close. One man reported 'Sometimes when you do a little one [fiddle a corner shop] it hurts, I mean you've only got to do them for a loaf, and that's their whole week's profit gone'. Sometimes the small shops are not fiddled because the chances of getting caught there are so much higher, and the partial honesty policy is also thought to increase the chances of customers honestly returning bread that they might have been given in error. Recalling these benign occasions allows the salesman righteously to conceive of himself as not all bad. This use of the 'metaphoric ledger' (from Klockars, 1974, p. 151) in which good events are set against the bad is useful in some personally reflective moments. This possession of scruples plays a crucial part in the reflexive construction of self. One salesman was mindful of the dangers:

> I don't do it all the time . . . you've got to have respect for some people, otherwise life would be unbearable, wouldn't it? . . . that would be defeating the object as far as I'm concerned, you'd be just one big fiddle, that's all your life would consist of, you have to have a break now and again, to know that somebody is *actually* paying for what they've got . . . it would make me feel evil if I did it too much.

Shared scruples (such as the maxim at Wellbread's of 'don't steal from your mates') act simultaneously as restrictions upon actual practice and psychological defence against self-apprehension qua criminal. The rhetoric of adjustment adapts the apologetic justification framework with a format which Lofland (1969, p. 86) calls 'conventionalising':

> By 'conventionalisation' is meant the practice of continuing to believe that the general class of deviance in question is wrong and subjectively unavailable, but managing to avoid defining the actual act as an instance of the subjectively unavailable class.

Adjustment may be achieved in one of two ways. Firstly, by adjustment of the *actor*, which amounts to a denial of full responsibility by psychologically excusing the self on the grounds of the denial of imputability. Secondly, through the application of various definitions, it is possible to adjust the fault component of the *act* in question as a form of circumstantial excuse.

Firstly, by *actor* adjustment, the self manages periodic release from the moral bind of the law. In the specific industrial context of Wellbread's we might see this guilt reduction by the use of such statements as 'The company expects it' as a particular example of the neutralising technique that Matza and Sykes refer to as the denial of responsibility, and which Matza (1964, pp. 82, 89) later redefines as the negation of responsibility:

> Extenuation is granted because the actor did not cause the act. Thus, the accused is released from legal responsibility . . . Thus intent, the

mental element in crime, periodically vanishes. When it does, the moral bind is broken, and one may drift.

Typical denials of full responsibility at Wellbread's are 'I couldn't help it [it started by accident, and now it's a habit]'. Most of the salesmen feel that the nature of their socialisation into the firm (outlined in Chapter 2) means that, once they realise what was required of them, it is too late to extricate themselves from the firm without making sacrifices. One man's comment was typical:

> When I started I didn't know anything about it [fiddles] . . . before you sign on, they let you think that only a fool would make mistakes, and come short in the money, but they've got you by the short and curlies, by the time you realise that you *can't* check everything, it's too late, you've agreed to pay shortages.

Once initiated into the black arts of fiddling, however, the salesmen believe that practice reflects basic and unchangeable human traits. This nicely mirrors a common pattern amongst performers, also emerging amongst salesmen as, for example, the feeling that sales genuineness is an acquirable trait. Most of the salesmen profess to a belief that fiddling is habit forming, and that it represents (in the words of one man) 'Greed . . . it's greed, isn't it? Let's face it, everybody will make an extra couple of bob if he can'.

A second classic responsibility denial theme is 'I was told to do it'. The Wellbread's salesmen take this literally and feel it particularly bitterly. One claimed 'They used to say "Put a penny on here, and a half on here" . . . it was the firm what made me change' and another, more explicitly, that 'It's the company that *make* you . . . what you are, because *they're* twisting *us*!'. Another man put it directly:

> Their attitude towards everything and the way that they treat you, that made you feel, 'Oh, all right, if you're going to rob me, I'm going to rob you'.

A third, commonly felt, but rarely expressed feeling is that 'If I don't do it, somebody else will [I'm only a pawn]', and a fourth feeling, 'It isn't really me [it's only work]' is also privately felt at Wellbread's, but not often mentioned.

The second major adjustive device transfers attention from the actor to the act. Here, the personalised plea of '*I'm* insignificant' becomes directed at the act, and emerges as '*It's* insignificant'. Appeals to psychological defeats change to pleas for circumstantial mitigations. The underlying technique of neutralisation here is the denial of injury (inasmuch as it refers to objects) or, as Matza (1964, p. 161) later defines it, the assertion of tort:

> Other acts are not so self-evidently wrong. They do not so obviously warrant the intervention of the state, and thus their prohibition is a topic of debate and discussion both among experts and the ordinary citizenry. These acts are in effect *mala prohibita*.

Here the actor contrasts his admission that he committed the act with the moral argument that his particular case had trifling consequences of a non-moral nature. The bread salesmen not only use the very word 'fiddle' (in its sense as a trifling sum) to cover very large amounts; they also continually and rather archly refer to the total 'take' as 'the odd bob or two', 'a few coppers', 'enough to buy a cup of tea', or 'enough for a packet of fags'. Each of these statements serves to produce a verbally shared conception of the amounts involved as being petty ones. Also, the cash bag (which contains money belonging solely to the company) is generally referred to as the 'kitty', which serves to neutralise the otherwise morally threatening and possibly psychologically disturbing nature of appropriations therefrom. Overall, the shared definition that fiddling is 'just to cover mistakes', although technically misleading, has obvious psychological utility. It is ironic that the justifications that the firm teach the men to psychologically cover fiddling for the company is used by them to also cover fiddling for the self.

Taken as a whole, however, the vocabulary of adjustment is unable to cover satisfactorily the self in private *after* the commission of the act. A separate category of definition, the rhetoric of *reconciliation*, is needed to cope with the implications of the *knowledge* of the self as violator.

After: Insulation (Self-reconciliation)

The psychologically divorced proceedings of day to day work allow the creation of a part time self: the fiddling self. The nature of the relationship of the core self to this special self (through the strategies of inoculation before the act, and insulation after it) means that in the social processes that make up identities, the part time self has mere *partial*, or elemental status. Whereas inoculation prevented self-apprehension through the deflection of disapproval before the logical occurrence of the act in question, insulation acts by post hoc protection from disapproval. Separating reflected knowledge of self as violator from one's 'natural' self (separating the judged act from the self *it*self) amounts to the neutralisation of internalised *social*- rather than *self*-control.

At Wellbread's, a certain amount of self-*camouflage* is provided by the sheer procedural similarity in skills between fiddling and selling. The immersion of fiddling in work means that the fiddler has no tell-tale insignia of deviant identification. The only 'original' act that a salesman commits (i.e. one that is not used in legitimate selling) is the wholly private and occasional act of transferring sums of company money to his own pocket. The structure of the fiddle adds another layer of insulation around the practice. Its tactical essence is non-discovery, its practice is isolated, and by virtue of the practical 'covers' which form a part of its analytic structure, it is (if successful) untraceable. As Rock (1973, p. 80) suggests, fiddling is the sort of deviancy which is 'likely to be socially invisible when, to the unwary, it seems to be a natural part of some conventional setting'. Within the victim population, the 'known aboutness' (Goffman, 1963, p. 67) is slight, and its 'obtrusiveness' (the extent to which it interferes with the ongoing interaction) imperceptible. The nature of the fiddle gives it characteristics similar to situations that Goffman (1971, p. 133) terms 'situational delicts'; infractions where the victim is not only unaware of the date of the offence and the identity of the culprit (e.g. if a housewife discovers a 'shortage' in her purse, who shall she blame?), but also raises the issue as to whether any infraction has in fact occurred. Thus the almost total absence of stigmatising interaction occurring between the fiddler and his victim/customer reduces the need for extensive overt practice of insulation techniques. However, during the sales act, the practitioner is inwardly participating in rituals of silence, affective and informational neutrality, and thus neutralisation.

Camouflaging the participation of the work self in evil is essential for the successful adoption by the rhetoric of reconciliation of the radical mode of justification. Reflected denial of involvement allows simultaneous denial of the pejorative quality of the action and the successful liberation of the salesman's self from the throes of guilt. Adequately to 'ignore' possible accusations, retaliative counter-denunciation is essential. Neutralisation here combines the condemnation of condemners, the denial of injury (persons), and the denial of the victim. Matza (1964, pp. 101, 172) later defines these more explicitly as, on the one hand, the sense of injustice, 'a simmering resentment – a setting of antagonism and antipathy – within which a variety of extenuating circumstances may abrogate the moral bind to the law' and, on the other, as the assertion of tort, wherein 'the wrong can be conceived of as a private transaction between the accused and the victim'. Cumulatively this amounts to the total defeat of crime by disputing its basic logical meaning. By attempting to demonstrate that the number of deviant practitioners is so obviously large, then, as Young (1970, p. 41) puts it, the common-sense meaning of crime as statistical abnormality, fails.

The first sense of *counter-denunciation* is 'we all do it'. The bread salesmen believe, almost to a man, that fiddling is inevitable, widespread, and thus justifiable. One said to me 'Look, in every job, where there's a loophole, there's a fiddle' and another, in more detail:

> Well, the way I look at it is this: you've got to look after yourself . . . everybody is doing it, this probably comes as a shock to you, that *everybody* is doing it, even the shops where you're doing it, they're doing it to somebody else . . . perhaps even just to the tax man, and the government is doing it to another government, it's just part of life . . . thinking *that* eases your conscience.

The practice is also believed to be sanctioned explicitly by actual participation in the fiddle by bakery supervisors, who regularly 'show a similar book' (take similar amounts from the kitty when they are on relief work). As a pilferer in Horning's study (1970, p. 57) suggested 'Well, you can't feel very guilty when you know that even the supers approve'.

Coupled with this second sense of 'they do it higher up' (the first sense was 'we all do it'), is a third feeling of 'they do it to us'. Some of the salesmen at Wellbread's merely feel that they are recouping money that they lose elsewhere and that the whole fiddle business is one eternal round. One man said, with a note of desperation:

> You *have* to do it, everybody overcharges *you*, I know, because we have the milkman and the paper boy call at ours, and even now, the milkman charges me a bit extra every week . . . all door to door selling is the same.

On top of this, there is always the elusive feeling that some of the customers are 'trying it on'. A specific focus for this sense of retaliatory injustice is the feeling that the management is deliberately robbing the sales force. Virtually every roundsman believes that the manager steals money from them as a matter of sales policy, and most of them feel that they, at least, are in the possession of actual proof. One claimed, a little bitterly 'They're all fiddling in the office, no office could be as incompetent as ours without a fiddle behind it', but for many no real reasons are present, just maniacal belief. For example, one salesman said 'I wish I knew what they were up to in the office, I *know* they're on the fiddle somehow'. Some men do, however, seem to have latched on to discrepancies which can only be explained in one way. One man, whilst out on the round, claimed to have seen the chief accountant of Wellbread's 'Taking stuff out of the boot of his car and putting it into someone else's'. Another simply claimed 'Take cake waste, that *must* be a fiddle . . . why were they cutting it?'. A third claimed better evidence:

I've seen it . . . I've gone into the office some days, and the super-visors are working out the competitions, and they say 'Oh, that can't be right' and they knock it off . . . not the datums, they clip the sales . . . it makes you suspicious.

The sense of retaliation is also fed by the cynicism that comes naturally with the adoption of the selling role from constantly dealing with stupid people. Here the sense that 'they deserve to lose it' is born. One man said 'I just say that the bloke [customer] is a bloody fool if you can get away with it' and two more that:

I look at it this way, if they're stupid enough to let you do it, then they deserve to have it done to them.

Mind you, I only used to do it to awkward customers, the ones that used to make me run back to the van for things . . . sort of retaliation.

Another classic sense of retaliation derives from the definition of the victim as rich enough to easily withstand the loss, or sufficiently well insured to reclaim it (see in Mars, 1974, for example, the knowledge that dockers have of the insurance claim possibilities which the ship-owners from whom they pilfer have). One of the salesmen at Well-bread's, speaking for many of the men, said 'You don't feel so guilty with the big stores . . . you know it's wrong, but you know that they are allowed wastage'.

A closely related sentiment to that of 'they can afford it' is 'nobody suffers'. A pilferer who talked to Horning (1970, p. 55) suggested 'It's like a corporation . . . it's not like taking it from one person . . . the people justify it by saying that the corporation wouldn't be hurt by it . . . they just jack the price up and screw the customer'. This feeling is particularly appropriate to the salesman's preference at Wellbread's for fiddling large shops. Why is this? Cahn (1955, p. 199) suggests that the following maxim applies: 'As soon as the owner becomes too large or too impersonal to permit an imaginative interchange with him, even very honest men may act as though they were blind to his rights'. This suggestion is nicely translated into action prescription by Smigel and Ross (1970, p. 7) as 'Lack of moral rules specifying the relationship between individuals and corporations'. For the inside man, Cort (1959, p. 340) does a similar job. He suggests that the employee is faced with 'mere figures in a ledger, which have no moral meaning', and which can be falsified without confronting any scruples.

Giving final breath to counter-denunciation is the feeling that either 'their inactivity sanctions it' or 'their lack of enforcement consistency invites it'. I have already quoted the puzzled recruit who said of the management of Wellbread's 'They seem to think that taking bread from them is wrong and fiddling their customers is right'. Another claimed:

> They know what goes on, and they don't do much about it . . . —— [managing director] worked up from the ranks . . . he knows all about it.

These extensive direct attacks are 'balanced' by mitigating self-admissions which merely affect a tangential, glancing blow at the feelings which the rhetoric of reconciliation is designed to overcome. Where 'qualified admission' involves (at this level of self-development) a variety of forms of counter-denunciation, 'mitigated admission' appeals to higher loyalties. Generally, Matza (1964, p. 158) talks of the appeal to higher loyalties in terms of conflicting customary convictions which:

> Merely hold the offence to be mitigated; the act is still wrong, and warrants official intervention; but *less wrong* because it was motivated and inspired by sentiments that in a different context everybody would consider fine and noble. Thus, the illegal behaviour obscures an ethical act.

In the factory, this feeling adopts the twin economic themes of 'we need it' and 'we deserve it'. 'We need it' relates low pay with the management's known knowledge of the fiddle. The men that talk in these terms are overtly recognising the invisible portion of their wages (see Ditton, 1976a). One said to me 'Thirty pounds a week, do you think that's good? When you have to get up at three in the morning in mid-winter? . . . six days a week'. A supervisor agreed 'I wouldn't come in at the times and work the hours that these blokes do, I think they've got to be "rewarded" for it'. Another man put it blandly:

> I don't bother about it at all . . . I just think of it as subsidising my wages, that's all.

'We deserve it', on the other hand, combines estimations of work done with definitions of acceptable standards of living. Two salesmen told me:

> It is a sort of general feeling . . . I know that it's a bad attitude to take [laugh] . . . it's like if someone threw a stone through my window, and then I start doing it, just because everybody else does, . . . but you can't live on the normal wage . . . that's why it really is *need*.

> I don't like to do it . . . that's all there is to it . . . it's part of the job as far as I'm concerned . . . I've got to do it because everybody else does.

Thus, by exhaustive conversion of the self-maintenance terminology, the specific fiddling self of the salesman is both inoculated from and insulated against the moral implications of rule infraction, and from the knowledge of the self as a rule breaker. When this psychological level of self-protection is added to the practical self-protection gathered in conversations with customers who doubt the salesman's identity, the stability of the part-time self is privately and publicly assumed.

7 Conclusion: Fiddling—A Subculture of Business

Fiddling is *not* morally and normatively supported by a contra-culture; one in qualitative opposition to the main themes of society. As I showed in Chapter 3, fiddling is contextually dependent upon the legitimate structure of 'service'. Further (hinted at in Chapter 4), stealing and dealing are only sensibly distinguished as inventory issues, and (explored in detail in Ditton, 1976a) the full range of 'part-time' crimes at Wellbread's are most realistically considered as an (albeit invisible) part of wages. Fiddling is, then, on these terms, normatively contingent upon a *subculture*; one developed as a reaction to wider societal values. In this broader sense, fiddling is a subculture of legitimate *commerce* itself.

Paradoxically (or so it might seem), fiddling shares many structural and substantive features with business, differing from business solely in the relative emphasis attached to these values. It is in *this* sense that, as Clinard and Quinney (1967, p. 195) put it 'Occupational crime cannot be fully understood without reference to the structure and values of society'. Fiddling is *not* in opposition to these values; salesmen at Wellbread's do not believe that fiddling will eventually overthrow the capitalist economy. Although, as Mills (1951, p. 164) delicately puts it 'They are not captains of industry, but the corporals of retailing', they fully believe themselves to be in the same commercial army. The customs of the fiddling subculture are delicately balanced between legitimate and criminal activity, making fiddling what Matza (1961, p. 105) calls a 'subterranean' version of the conventional culture of business.

It is this very basic structural and normative similarity between business and the fiddle which produces the ambiguous (but generally) benevolent societal reaction to fiddling which practitioners experience. Matza (1969, p. 105) notices that subterranean versions of culturally acceptable conventional traditions commonly produce a public reaction 'subject to faddish oscillation ranging from sympathetic tolerance to outright suppression'. In practical terms, for fiddlers, the pendulum permanently and stiffly points at 'indulgence'. Fiddling, in this sense, only superficially undermines societal goals. Ultimately, the very same norms which support the conventional activity (business) also support the subterranean version (fiddling). But what are these norms? It is not just that fiddling is business-like, that selling is essentially based on confidence swindling, or that the two are irrevocably mixed. Whilst we may agree with a sentiment adapted from Ecclesiastes ('As a nail sticketh fast between the joinings of the stones, so doth sin stick close to buying and selling', quoted in Geis, 1968, p. 8), there is something more. Fiddling, like selling, *epitomises* the capitalist 'spirit'. The subculture of fiddling reflects the sort of dutiful anti-hedonism (what Weber, 1930, p. 57, called 'The universal reign of absolute unscrupulousness in the pursuit of selfish interests in the making of money') which provides the normative bedrock of capitalism.

But how can *one* normative structure simultaneously support both selling and its (superficially apparent) antithesis, fiddling? Basically this is because the structural norms of commerce are really qualified guidelines for a zone of acceptable activity, rather than categorical imperatives demanding particular courses of action. Matza and Sykes (1957, p. 251) refer to this as the 'flexibility' of conformity prescriptions, indicating that their applicability is not limited to particular circumstances. Matza (1964, pp. 62–3) also notes that beneath surface differences the subculture is, in fact, buttressed by beliefs flourishing in the legitimate normative sphere and that, ultimately, 'the continued existence of the subculture is facilitated and perhaps even dependent upon support and reinforcement from conventional sources'.

The conventional normative structure is milked for subcultural support through the neutralisations portrayed in Chapter 6. The fact that some accusations can be 'defeated' percolates to the subcultural strata. As Matza (1964, p. 70) puts it 'Criminal law is especially susceptible of neutralisation because the conditions of applicability, and thus inapplicability, are explicitly stated'. This overt invitation to neutralise allows the subculture unwittingly to broaden the conditions of inapplicability, producing what Matza and Sykes (1957, p. 257) refer to as 'unrecognised extensions of defences to crimes'. Thus the fiddler can interpret some cultural support through simply interpreting and situating the law. But neutralisation is not a process that needs to be re-created, de novo, by each deviant. Neutralisations are ready made, processed, and delivered through the channels of symbolic communication. Stocks of neutralisations, posing as motives, are culturally stored and exist as shared 'habits of thought' (Hartung, 1965, p. 135), creating what Lofland (1966, p. 88) calls a 'pool of publicly legitimated platitudes'. The verbalisations derived from these popular ideologies are assimilated and internalised by individuals, and publicly or privately regurgitated at motivationally appropriate intervals.

To return to commerce: what values are extracted and extended by the fiddler? Conventional business manages to succeed only by practising one set of values whilst publicly espousing another. The justifying philosophies of organisations are rarely their working ones. To take just one example, 'profit maximisation' is the justifying philosophy of the managerial class. Actual working use of such an ideal would be economic disaster: over-production would create a glut. So, illegal cartels are often constructed (see, for example, 'The Incredible Electrical Conspiracy', Smith, 1961) as the inevitable and regrettable result of unrestrained capitalism. The fiddler, exasperatingly, actually *operates* upon the basis of capitalism's *justifying* philosophy. To paraphrase Matza, the fiddler misinterprets the conditions of applicability (i.e. justification only) of the philosophy of capitalism, and naïvely sees the philosophy as a set of practical, procedural rules. In other words, the fiddler makes an incompetent reading of the philosophy (see Fig. 3.1). Absurdly, the fiddler believes that, just because the values of business may be attached to the practices of crime, this is enough in itself. Schur (1957, pp. 301-2) accurately summarises the stock of values common to both crime and business. The fiddler reads this *coincidence* of support for a *similarity* of support:

> One system of values which may foster crime, and particularly fraud, in our society, is that relating to the phenomena of salesmanship. As Sutherland notes, 'the confidence games are based essentially on salesmanship'. To a great extent, our society is built on salesmanship, and the term implies much more than the mere sale of material goods. In an era when an increased premium is being put on 'idea men', the ability to 'sell a bill of goods' [in the figurative sense as well as the literal] takes on added importance. It is just this ability which the successful 'con man' must demonstrate. Closely related to 'selling a bill of goods' is the cultural stress on 'putting across' one's 'personality' . . . These socially sanctioned attributes are the very hall-mark of the experienced swindler.

It is in these terms of general societal membership that the fiddler makes an incompetent, naïve, literal reading of the support that he can expect from society as a whole for fiddling. It is the precise structural powerlessness of the (blue collar) salesman which makes his use of such

values bizarre, absurd, and misplaced. However, this is not an inno-
vatory usage. Core business values have sedimented at the blue collar
level as a subtle, wry, reflection of the sentiments from which they were
initially derived. Lofland (1966, p. 99), for example, quotes 'Honesty
is the best policy, *but* business is business, and a businessman would be
a fool if he didn't cover his hand' as typical of the way that business
has tried to interweave the moral and commercial orders. But such
sentiments were meant for private rationalisation and not for public
presentation. The subterranean adherent not only misreads the
conditions of applicability of these warped maxims (they are not for the
working class), he also mistakes their epistemological status and sees
them (literally) as reality, rather than as (metaphoric) reflection. Thus,
traditional sardonic comments upon the unintended consequences of
business practice, such as 'It's a dog eat dog world', 'May the best man
win', 'Business is business', 'We are not in business for our health', 'No
business was built on the beatitudes', 'Patriotism is a very beautiful
thing, but it mustn't be allowed to interfere with business' (Sutherland,
1949, pp. 174, 240, 246), and 'Look after number one', are taken by
the fiddler to be the guiding rather than the qualifying moral precepts
of action. Popular ideology is taken by the fiddler to sanction crime.
Cressey (1953, p. 97) adds:

'Some of our most respectable citizens got their start in life by using
other people's money temporarily', 'In the real estate business there
is nothing wrong about using deposits before the deal is closed', 'All
people steal when they get into a tight spot'.

In particular, fiddling at Wellbread's is psychologically supported by
extending the excusing conditions of selling – specifically, the caveat
emptor rider. Accordingly, employees at Wellbread's as salesmen (and
not just in 'service') can select large portions of justifying rhetoric from
cultural interpretations of business. Taylor (1971, p. 105) adds:

So, for example, stealing money may be made easier for salesmen by
the presence in the culture of the phrase 'making a bit on the side'.
A bank clerk, however, can hardly assume himself as he contemplates
dipping into the till that others would accept a similar motivational
account for his contemplated behaviour.

The subterranean rationalisation of the selling process recreates the
historic form of 'booty' capitalism. At Wellbread's, for example, the
price paid for a loaf of bread depends not on elaborate costing procedures, but instead upon the amount of money that a particular
salesman can extricate from a particular customer on each occasion.
Thus the disturbing reflection or caricature of ordinary business that

fiddling represents calls for an ambiguous and oscillating public reaction, allowing practical escape and private insulation. It is the precise absence of power backing the fiddler's production of reality definitions that fails to donate the quality of 'exoneration' (Robin, 1974, p. 259) from stigmatisation accorded to rascally industrial and corporate activity.

Available support for practical and private self-maintenance is thus traceable to the way that crime is intricately enmeshed with everyday society. The subculture of fiddling is not supported by contra-values, but instead by an exasperating combination of caricatured redefinitions of core values.

But there is a final problem. I have shown how fiddling may seem to be a reasonable activity to recruits and how solitary salesmen may find psychological support for continuing to fiddle in the 'special' context of service. I have portrayed the practical and melodramatic mechanisms which preserve the 'part-time' self of the fiddling salesman both in mundane and extraordinary situations. The last hurdle for the fiddler is to engineer satisfactory consumption of the 'spoils' of fiddling without guilt infecting the real, complete self of the salesman. How does he manage this?

FIDDLING: THE SPOILS AND THE GUILT

Who can the salesmen at Wellbread's entrust with the knowledge that they are also fiddlers? Generally, the salesmen keep tight control over information about their 'part-time' crimes outside the work situation. Information release, when it does occur, is usually only to the wife, who provides accommodative informational support, rather than any threat of blackmail. However, the salesman faces yet another dilemma here. To be overly secretive about his fiddling would be to force the self to demand to know the reasons for secrecy, thus permeating the existential membrane between the 'work' and 'real' selves. They all did, be it noted, tell *me* about their fiddling. As Henry (1976, p. 191) so cleverly deduces, some control (yet not too much) is necessary to balance psychological and practical demands (just here contradictory). Rather than being either 'open' or 'secretive' about his work life, the fiddler is 'careful' about such information.

In any case, paradoxically, whereas for some deviant activities, loot dispersal can provide obvious indications to others that the individual has a suspect source of income, the fiddler's income is sufficiently small and regular (in most cases) to be immersed totally in the family budget. It is also very stable – a feature which aids morals as well as budgets. Thus, rather than increased spending power indicating immorality to inquisitive neighbours, the fiddler's ability to provide better for his family is taken as indicative of his very morality!

However, within the fiddler's knowledgeable world, all finances need good management irrespective of the legality of their origin. Purchase of a new car, for example, is imbued with guilt in the eyes of peers who *are* in the know. Such purchases are dominated by the fact that the fiddle, however indirectly, contributed to it. When one of the salesmen bought a brand new Mercedes, it had, as one salesman reported, unfortunate consequences:

> You should have seen —— [sales manager] . . . went mad . . . he said 'What? Second-hand?' and '——' said 'No, "M" registration, actually' . . . well, the fucking manager hit the roof, he said 'Right, the hospital's coming off your route, and so's the co-op.'

The salesman with the new car explained to me:

> It gets awkward . . . living in this fucking great house, and now that car, when I'm out in it, and one of my customers sees me, I always say 'It's the manager's' . . . they suspect you because of your standard of living . . . I inherited the money . . . I know it looks bad . . . I know that they all think I must be on the fiddle.

Control of one's moral identity in the bakery can also be punctured by events. Another salesman reported 'If you take too much out (i.e. come short), they'll start looking around your car to see if you've bought any new tyres'. In addition to this, situations can occasionally make spoils handling impossible. On the very day that one inside dealer was sacked for 'stealing', he arrived to work in another unmistakably new car!

Obviously, if the consumption of spoils can be successfully concealed (apart from the rather extraordinary instances that I have just described) both from the public and from the real self, then the chances of self-apprehension as deviant, and resulting guilt, are reduced. Do salesmen feel 'guilty' about their fiddling at all?

Although the successful routine public honouring of salesmen's accounts means that reality rarely intrudes to break down the defensive ideology, and although biographies and accounts are rarely checked against alternative documentation, it is inevitable that the meaning of the fiddle spreads somewhat and permeates brief periods of the conventional existence of the salesman. The problem is, as Matza (1969, p. 151) puts it, that:

> When among the right-minded, the subject may sense his transparency . . . the possibility of hiding from righteous scrutiny – of

being opaque – is subverted by the conscious existence of society in mind.

There are times when living a double life is profoundly brought home to the fiddler, although they do not lead the embezzler's classic 'two lives' (Jaspan and Black, 1960, p. 27) or have the forger's 'Jekyll and Hyde' character (Lemert, 1958, p. 116). Although the processes of socialisation (which I outlined in Chapter 2) that salesmen undergo are designed to alleviate misplaced guilt, the two realities cannot always be held apart, and friction results. For instance, recruits typically experience initial shock. Their comments echo fairly standard feelings. One said 'It shocked me at the time, he didn't tell me *why* I had to do it'; another 'It *did* shock me at the time, he told me to do it if I wanted to cover shortages'; and a third 'I used to worry in case I might get caught sometimes . . . when I first started'.

Socialisation is never fully successful and occasionally even the experienced men feel guilty. One told me 'Yeah, I do, I worry too much . . . I feel guilty about doing it' and another that guilt was currently less of a problem than it could be or, in fact, was:

Yeah, I did . . . I still do see it as immoral . . . although I don't think nothing of it . . . really . . . that's nasty, bloody horrible thing to do . . . I don't feel so guilty about it now, although it still strikes me as a bit immoral.

Generally, however, residual guilt is sufficient for most of the men to dislike the fiddle ('I don't like going into a shop and fiddling them . . . but I *have* to do it') and themselves for doing it. Guilt at this level is alleviated by various counter-denunciations (especially 'they deserve it') which are proudly collected in gullibility testimonials, and shared with peers. The availability of shared support for illegality strengthens psychological resolve. Group defence is particularly common amongst pilfering factory workers. As Horning (1970, p. 62) suggests, factory wisdom is transmitted in folk tales, which consist of 'congeries of episodes about pilferers'. Every salesman I spoke to at Wellbread's seemed to have a gullibility testimonial of a past event in which a salesman figured heroically. These tales were repeated to me as examples of great fiddles that had been pulled off or, more seriously, as illustrative of moral maxims or indications of the limits of group tolerance and the initiation of social control.

FIDDLING, AND THE 'ULTIMATE' GUARANTEE OF 'PART-TIME' CRIME

In conclusion, and looking momentarily at the broader category (introduced in Chapter 4) of 'part-time' criminals, there is a sense in which it is ultimately the weak social reaction to fiddling which preserves the 'partial' self. On the one hand, whilst practical protection creates psychological safety per se, private protection may be possible even whilst the body is publicly shamed and incarcerated. Sometimes, with other 'part-time' crimes, law enforcers perceive the societal reaction, rate the effects as harmful, and subsequently aid the offender's self-insulation. Physician narcotic addicts, for example (Winick, 1964), normally have hushed-up trials, and offenders, although convicted, may refute or publicly denounce the sentence. Similarly, after conviction, the General Electric vice-president (quoted in Geis, 1967, p. 112) reportedly 'issued a statement to the press, noting that he had to serve a jail term "for conduct which has been interpreted as being in conflict with complex antitrust laws" '.

Cressey (1953) also reported that several convicted embezzlers found that they could maintain original protective self-conceptions even behind bars. Humphreys (1970, p. 134), in a study of homosexual encounters in public lavatories, adds that this is usually psychologically managed by donning what he calls the 'breastplate of righteousness', a sort of thick shield of super-propriety, against which one can balance and cover the odd indiscretion.

Psychic investment may become so heavy in secondary selves that the logical strata of the self may get permanently obscured. In Humphrey's sample, one fellator was a full-time clergyman (presumably posing problems in the unbiased establishment of which 'me' is the 'real' one) and the problem arises excruciatingly when both selves appear to demand all the actor's time.

The psychological consequences of exposure as a deviant depends upon the *nature* of skill development. Firstly, skills that are developed individually are backed by private insulation that is much better than public cover. Secondly, those developed subculturally, on the other hand, create an extensive public cover battery coupled with minimal private insulation. This disparity becomes particularly apparent during apprehension situations. The sorts of skills which are successful at adjusting and reconciling self-conceptions in private are insufficient for the public avoidance of legal liability. Individually developed private accounts are not publicly legitimate, although they may seem privately effective and reasonable. Public challenges of 'part-time' deviance, then, will not be routinely rebuffed with the simple verbalisation of private inoculations and insulations.

The situation of possible apprehension is adequately dealt with by the fiddler at Wellbread's because of his cynical disbelief in the 'truth' of the public accounts that he gives. Apprehension situations thus do not, for the salesman, precipitate shocking redefinition and realignment of the public and private self. The fiddler 'learns that a defensible picture of self can be seen as something outside oneself that can be constructed, lost, and rebuilt, all with great speed and equanimity' (Goffman, 1961, p. 151). Although to some extent the degree of self-shock that will be felt on apprehension will depend on the quality of the information of a discreditable nature within the person's biography (Humphreys, 1970, p. 134), over-insulation of the self denies the theoretical possibility of apprehension and thus idle inner debate cannot prepare the self. In this way, as Cameron (1964, pp. 150–63) puts it, the shock of entrapment hits 'self-made' deviants particularly hard. Adult shoplifters caught in their 'part-time' occupation frequently resort to 'the lies, rationalisations and alibis characteristic of children', with some continuing to feel that 'although they are adults they are, in fact, acting as naughty children, and not really criminal'. Cameron notices that the eventual realisation of self as criminal is:

> Often accompanied by a dramatic change in attitudes and by severe emotional disturbance . . . 'This can't be happening to me' . . . 'This is a nightmare' . . . 'Oh, why, why can't I find out that it isn't so'.

Apprehension also forces changes in the insulation procedures that allowed the infraction in the first instance. Cressey (1953, p. 100) notes 'Those who realise that they are "in too deep" are forced to recognise that their reasoning in regard to borrowing has been "phony" or that they have been "kidding themselves" '. For the fiddler, it is the inability of wounded others to disclose the partial self of the salesman which aids him. Manipulation of practical accounts (and non-alignment of practical outcomes with self-sustenance) means that public or private discrediting work does not spread the deviance, in a psychological sense, to the complete, real self.

For salesmen at Wellbread's, the control context of fiddling is *commercial* rather than *legal*. Typically, the reaction to discovered theft is tolerance. As Cavan (1964, p. 235) puts it, 'It represents a practical adjustment of legal behaviour to meet certain inconveniences and exigencies of socio-economic life'. Added to systematic failure to sanction offenders effectively and publicly is a general resistance to notifying future prospective employers of a sacked employee that he has been suspected of a criminal offence, or that any unofficial action has been taken against him. This is not born out of an altruistic desire to allow an employee to start afresh after penance for a 'mistake', but rather out of a more cynical regard for possible legal reprisals which might be sparked off if unofficially handled misdemeanours are mentioned in testimonials. In fact, 'caught', for the employee thief, rarely means 'court'. As Clinard and Quinney (1967, p. 207) put it,

'Employee thieves, obviously, are among the least stigmatised offenders'. Martin (1962, p. 86), for example, found that the larger firms in his sample prosecuted forty one per cent of cases, and smaller firms only twenty four per cent. Robin (1967, p. 689) discovered that shops only take seventeen per cent of their employee thieves to court. Although the success rate at court is generally high (Robin cites ninety six per cent), the judicial disposition of occupational thieves is typically non-penal. Crime at work is rarely a moral issue: it is more normally viewed instrumentally as an economic issue. The courts are rarely invoked to deal with employee miscreants although, when they are, they do so leniently.

In brief, if *legal* control may be characterised as having a moral basis, guilt orientation, formally bureaucratic style, 'fine', technical-judicial decision making, and public hearings; then, in contrast, *commercial* social control has a calculative basis, a profit orientation, an eclectic ad hoc-ness in its decision making procedures, and a particularly 'rough' sense of justice. At Wellbread's, the managing director is prosecuting counsel, judge and jury. For example, one dismissed inside dealer told me:

> So I went in there [managing director's office] and there were these two security men from head office, in there with him . . ., well, he told them they could wait outside, and there was just him and —— [bakery manager] in the corner scribbling notes. —— [managing director] said to me 'I've got a signed statement here alleging that you and the said —— [alleged accomplice] took sixty two pounds' worth of cake on 3 October, do you plead guilty, or not guilty? . . .' Well, the first thing I said was 'What a load of rubbish, let me see that statement' . . . so he let me see it, see, but he kept his finger over that bit where it was signed . . . Then I said 'Before I go any further, I want to see my solicitor', and he said 'Well, in that case, we will have no option but to go to the police' . . . Then I thought a bit, see, and I thought 'Well, if they do that, the amount of stuff I've nicked in my time, I might get twelve years!' . . . so I said 'Well, I admit to that, except for the bit which includes ——, I did it by myself'.

Most offences are summarily and immediately dealt with ('Put that bloody loaf down!', 'Don't you try and fiddle me') and laughingly dismissed. Those few which are defined as theft proceed to the managing director where they receive even more summary (but considerably less amusing) treatment. Consider the bizarre case of a wholesale salesman, interviewed by the managing director:

He said to me that my name had been mentioned to him, about discrepancies between certain dates, and I said to him 'I was on holiday for two of those dates' . . . and he said 'Don't make excuses!' . . . so I just shut up! And he said 'If your name is mentioned again, you're going to take a long walk up the road'.

Accordingly, as a form of deviance, fiddling instances are always practically 'primary' (Lemert, 1964, p. 17). In other words, fiddling 'at best has only marginal implications for the psychic structure of the individual'. Fiddling is what we may term 'ultimate' deviance; it *cannot* become 'secondary' in Lemert's sense (when deviant action and meaning is recognised to include the social reaction to primary infraction). If it did, then it would cease to *be* 'fiddling' (in its psychological sense as trifling). Practically, any salesman processed by the legitimate courts would be unable to return to work and practise fiddling in the 'secondary' sense for good commercial insurance reasons.

Thus public enforcement is private *re*-enforcement of 'partial' and 'part-time' deviant selves. Since secondary deviation is not a possibility (for the reasons just outlined), then this additionally experienced deviance is 'ultimate' deviation. It is not quite primary (in the psychological sense that would be appropriate to shoplifters who have never been caught) and yet enforcement attempts do not force realignment of partial and real self levels which would precipitate secondary deviation. Instead, enforcement regrounds and empirically and publicly embeds hitherto private definitions.

Since theft is so basically contradictory to the ideal values of capitalism (and business), there will not, in the future, be mass rallies or public meetings for fiddlers to attend, to protest their self-consciousness, and to tactically adopt a secondary deviation pose as a strategy for eventual release from stigmatisation. 'Fiddlers Lib' would not gather much support from the fiddlers themselves, let alone their victims.

The features which guarantee the practical 'part-timeness' of fiddling at Wellbread's serve also to produce and maintain its psychological 'partiality'. The structural features of the commercial control setting most emphatically do *not* produce the conditions of identity degradation suffered by 'classical' criminals. Following Garfinkel's (1956) check list of the essential conditions of successful self-degradation; the caught, but 'non-court' fiddler is *not* defined as 'out of the ordinary'; neither the theft nor the thief is naturally treated as an example of a phenomenally extraordinary batch of similar occurrences. Contrary to public denunciation, there is no social metaphysic demanding a perceptive similarity between audience and denouncer, and no great show is made of rallying ultimate societal values to the defence of the prosecution.

'Ultimately' (both in the lay sense and in the special sense outlined above), the fiddling bread salesman at Wellbread's manages to preserve his self and conduct his occupational life, as well as his private life, as a 'good' citizen.

Bibliography

Barthes, Roland (1957), *Mythologies* (St. Albans: Paladin).

Barthes, Roland (1964), *Elements of Semiology* (London: Cape).

Bateson, Gregory (1936), *Naven* (Stanford: Stanford U.P.).

Bateson, Gregory, Jackson, Don D., Haley, Jay and Weakland, John H. (1956), 'Towards a Theory of Schizophrenia', *Behav. Sci.*, **1**; included in Bateson (ed.) 1972.

Bateson, Gregory (1971), 'The Logical Categories of Learning and Communication'; included in Bateson (ed.) 1972.

Bateson, Gregory (1972) (ed.), *Steps to an Ecology of Mind* (St. Albans: Paladin).

Becker, Howard S. and Strauss, Anselm L. (1956), 'Careers, Personality and Adult Socialisation', *Am. J. Sociol.*, **62**, pp 253–263; included in Becker, 1970.

Becker, Howard S. (1960), 'Notes on the Concept of Commitment', *Am. J. Sociol.*, **66**, pp 32–40; included in Becker, 1970.

Becker, Howard S. (1963), *Outsiders* (New York: Free Press).

Becker, Howard S. (1964) (ed.), *The Other Side* (New York: Free Press).

Becker, Howard S. (1968b), 'Conventional Crime: Rationalisations and Punishment', from: *Orthopsychiatry and the Law*, M. Leavitt and B. Rubenstein (eds) (Wayne State UP) pp 192–212; included in Becker, 1970.

Becker, Howard S. (1970), *Sociological Work: Method and Substance* (London: Allen Lane).

Bensman, J. and Gerver, I. (1963), 'Crime and Punishment in the Factory: The Function of Deviancy in Maintaining the Social System', *Am. Sociol. Rev.*, **28**, pp 588–598.

Bigus, Odis E. (1972), 'The Milkman and his Customer', *Urban Life and Culture*, **1**, pp 131–165.

Birenbaum, Arnold and Sagarin, Edward (eds) (1973), *People in Places* (London: Nelson).

Brim, Orville G. and Wheeler, Stanton (1966), *Socialisation after Childhood* (New York: Wiley).

Bryant, Clifton D. (ed.) (1974), *Deviant Behaviour: Occupational and Organisational Bases* (Chicago: Rand McNally).

Bukowski, Charles (1973), *Post Office* (Los Angeles: Black Sparrow Press).

Burns, Tom (1953), 'Friends, Enemies and the Polite Fiction', *Am. Sociol. Rev.*, **18**, pp 654–662.

Cahn, Edmond (1955), 'Cheating on Taxes' from E. Cahn, *The Moral Decision* (Bloomington: Indiana University Press); included in Geis (ed.) 1968.

G

Caldwell, Robert G. (1958), 'A Re-examination of the Concept of White Collar Crime', *Fed. Prob.*, **22**, pp 30–36; included in Geis (ed.) 1968.

Cameron, Mary O. (1964), *The Booster and the Snitch* (New York: Free Press).

Caplovitz, David (1963), *The Poor Pay More: The Consumer Practices of Low-Income Families* (New York: Free Press) 2nd edn.

Caplovitz, David (1965), 'The Merchant and the Low Income Consumer', *Jewish Social Studies*, **27**, pp 45–53; included in Geis (ed.) 1968.

Cavan, Ruth S. (1964), 'Underworld, Conventional and Ideological Crime', *J. Crim. Law, Criminol., Police Sci.*, **55**, pp 235–245.

Cavan, Sherri (1966), *Liquor Licence: An Ethnography of Bar Behaviour* (Chicago: Aldine).

Chesney, Kellow (1970), *The Victorian Underworld* (Harmondsworth: Penguin).

Clinard, Marshall B. and Quinney, R. (1967), *Criminal Behaviour Systems: a Typology* (New York: Holt, Reinhart and Winston) 2nd edn.

Clinard, Marshall B. (1969), *The Black Market* (Chicago: Patterson Smith).

Cohen, Albert, Lindesmith, Alfred and Schuessler, Karl (eds) (1956), *The Sutherland Papers* (Bloomington: Indiana University Press).

Cohen, Stanley and Taylor, Laurie (1972), *Psychological Survival* (Harmondsworth: Penguin).

Conant, Louise (1936), 'The Borax House', *The American Mercury*, **XXVII**, pp 169–174.

Cort, David (1959), 'The Embezzler', *Nation*, April 18, pp 339–342.

Cressey, Donald (1953), *Other People's Money* (Belmont: Wadsworth).

Curtis, S. J. (1960), *Modern Retail Security* (Springfield: C. C. Thomas).

Dalton, M. (1964), *Men Who Manage* (New York: Wiley).

Daniel, W. W. (1963), 'A Consideration of Individual and Group Attitudes in an Expanding and Technically Changing Organisation', *M.Sc.(Tech) Thesis*, Unpub (Manchester University).

Davis, Fred (1959), 'The Cabdriver and His Fare: Facets of a Fleeting Relationship', *Am. J. Sociol.*, **65**, pp 158–165.

Deutscher, I. and Thompson, E. J. (eds) (1968), *Among the People: Encounters with the Poor* (New York: Basic Books).

Ditton, Jason (1972), 'The Problem of Time: Styles of Time-Management and Schemes of Time-Manipulation Amongst Machine-Paced Workers', *Working Paper No. 2*. Durham University.

Ditton, Jason (1972a), 'Absent at Work: Or How to Manage Monotony', *New Society*, 21 December, pp 679–681.

Ditton, Jason (1974), 'The Fiddling Salesman: Connivance at Corruption', *New Society*, 28 November, pp 535–537.

Ditton, Jason (1975), 'Moral Horror vs. Folk Terror: Class, Output Restriction and the Social Organisation of Exploitation', *Soc. Rev.* (Forthcoming).

Ditton, Jason (1976), ' "The Fiddler": A Sociological Analysis of Forms of Blue-Collar Employee Theft amongst Bread Salesmen', *Ph.D. Thesis* (University of Durham).

Ditton, Jason (1976a), 'Perks, Pilferage and The Fiddle: Invisible Wages and the Hidden Economy', *Mimeo* (University of Durham).

Emerson, Frank E. (1971), 'They Can Get It For You BETTER Than Wholesale', *New York Magazine*, **4**, pp 34–39.

England, K. A. D. (1973), 'A Consideration of the Alienated Condition of Shopworkers in the Retail Trade', *Mimeo.*

Flew, Anthony (ed.) (1952), *Logic and Language*, 1st Series (Oxford: B. Blackwell).

Foote, Nelson N. (1951), 'Identification as the Basis for a Theory of Motivations', *Am. Sociol. Rev.*, **16**, pp 14–22.

Garfinkel, Harold (1956), 'Conditions of Successful Degradation Ceremonies', *Am. J. Sociol.*, **61**, pp 420–424.

Geer, Blanche, *et al.* (1968), 'Learning the Ropes: Situational learning in four occupational training programs'. In I. Deutscher and E. J. Thompson (eds) (1968).

Geis, Gilbert (1967), 'The Heavy Electrical Equipment Antitrust Cases of 1961', from Clinard and Quinney (1967) (eds), in Geis (ed.) 1968.

Geis, Gilbert (1968) (ed.), *White Collar Criminal* (New York: Atherton).

Gennep, Arnold van (1908), *The Rites of Passage* (London: R.K.P.).

Giles, F. T. (1954), *The Criminal Law* (Harmondsworth: Penguin).

Glaser, Barney G. (1965), 'The Constant Comparative Method of Qualitative Analysis', *Soc. Probs.*, **12**, pp 436–445; included in McCall-Simmons (ed) 1969.

Glaser, Barney G. and Strauss, Anselm L. (1964), 'Awareness Contexts and Social Interaction', *Am. Sociol. Rev.*, **29**, pp 669–679.

Glaser, Barney G. and Strauss, Anselm L. (1967), *The Discovery of Grounded Theory* (London: Weidenfeld and Nicolson).

Goffman, Erving (1952), 'On Cooling the Mark Out: Some Aspects of Adaptation to Failure', *Psychiatry*, **15**, pp 451–463; included in Arnold M. Rose (ed.) 1962.

Goffman, Erving (1955), 'On Face Work', *Psychiatry*, **18**, pp 213–231; included in Goffman 1967 and Goffman 1969.

Goffman, Erving (1956a), 'The Nature of Deference and Demeanor', *Am. Anthrop.*, **58**, pp 473–502; included in Goffman, 1967.

Goffman, Erving (1956b), 'Embarrassment and Social Organisation', *Am. J. Sociol.*, **62**, pp 264–274; included in Goffman, 1967.

Goffman, Erving (1957), 'Alienation from Interaction', *Hum. Rels.*, **10**, pp 47–59; included in Goffman, 1967.

Goffman, Erving (1957a), 'On the Characteristics of Total Institutions', Revised from paper given to *Symposium on Preventative and Social Psychiatry*, Walter Reed Army Institute of Research, Washington D.C., 15–17 April 1957, pp 43–84; included in Goffman, 1961c.

Goffman, Erving (1957b), 'The Underlife of a Public Institution: A Study of Ways of Making out in a Mental Hospital' (Paper to A.S.S., August 1957); included in Goffman, 1961c.

Goffman, Erving (1959), *The Presentation of Self in Everyday Life* (Harmondsworth: Penguin, 1959 edn.).

Goffman, Erving (1959a), 'The Moral Career of the Mental Patient', *Psychiatry*, **22**; included in Goffman, 1961c.

Goffman, Erving (1961), *Encounters* (Harmondsworth: Penguin).

Goffman, Erving (1961a), 'Role Distance' in Goffman, 1961 and Goffman, 1969.

Goffman, Erving (1961b), 'Fun in Games' in Goffman, 1961.

Goffman, Erving (1961c), *Asylums: Essays on the Social Situation of Mental Patients and Other Inmates* (Harmondsworth: Penguin).

Goffman, Erving (1961d), 'The Medical Model and Mental Hospitalisation: Some Notes on the Vicissitudes of the Tinkering Trades', in Goffman, 1961c.

Goffman, Erving (1963), *Stigma: Notes on the Management of Spoiled Identity* (Harmondsworth: Penguin).

Goffman, Erving (1966), 'Expression Games: An Analysis of Doubts at Play'. Revised from *Strategic Interaction and Conflict* (ed.) K. Archibald, 1966; included in Goffman, 1969.

Goffman, Erving (1971), *Relations in Public: Microstudies of the Public Order* (Harmondsworth: Penguin).

Goffman, Erving (1974), *Frame Analysis: An Essay on the Organisation of Experience* (Harmondsworth: Peregrine).

Gold, Ray (1952), 'Janitors vs. Tenants: A Status-Income Dilemma', *Am. J. Sociol.*, **57**, pp 486–493; included in Birenbaum and Sagarin (eds) 1973.

Gross, E. and Stone, I. (1970), 'Embarrassment and the Analysis of Role Requirements' in Stone and Farberman (eds) 1970.

Haberstein, Robert W. (1970) (ed.), *Pathways to Data* (Chicago: Aldine).

Hart, H. L. A. (1952), 'The Ascription of Responsibilities and Rights' in A. Flew (ed.) 1952.

Hart, H. L. A. (1968), *Punishment and Responsibility* (Oxford: Clarendon Press).

Hartung, Frank E. (1965), *Crime, Law and Society* (Wayne State Univ. Press).

Henry, Stuart (1976), 'Stolen Goods: The Amateur Trade', *Ph.D. Thesis*, Unpub. (University of Kent).

Hepworth, Mike and Turner, Bryan S. (1974), 'Confessing to Murder: Critical Notes on the Sociology of Motivation', *Brit. J. Law Soc.*, **1**, pp 31–49.

Horning, Donald M. (1970), 'Blue-Collar Theft: Conceptions of Property, Attitudes Toward Pilfering, and Work Group Norms in a Modern Industrial Plant', in Smigel and Ross (ed.) 1970.

Howton, F. William and Rosenberg, Bernard (1965), 'The Salesman: Ideology and Self-Imagery in a Prototypic Occupation', *Soc. Res.*, **32**, pp 277–298.

Hughes, Everett C. (1962), 'Good People and Dirty Work', *Soc. Probs.*, **9**, included in Becker (ed.) 1964.

Humphreys, Laud (1970), *Tearoom Trade* (London: Duckworth).

Jackman, Norman R., O'Toole, Richard and Geis, Gilbert (1963), 'The Self Image of the Prostitute', *Soc. Quart.*, **4**, pp 150–161.

James, William (1890), *The Principles of Psychology* (2 vols) (New York: Dover).

James, William (1902), *The Varieties of Religious Experience* (London: Fontana) (1974 edn.).

Jaspan, Norman and Black, Hillel (1960), *The Thief in the White Collar* (New York: Lippincott).

Kirkland, John (1911), *The Modern Baker, Confectioner and Caterer* (London: Gresham Pub.).

Kitsuse, John I. (1962), 'Societal Reactions to Deviant Behaviour', *Soc. Probs.*, **9**, included in Becker (ed.) 1964.

Klapp, Orrin E. (1954), 'Heroes, Villains and Fools as Agents of Social Control', *Am. Sociol. Rev.*, **19**, pp 56–62.

Klapp, Orrin E. (1962), *Heroes, Villains and Fools: The Changing American Character* (New Jersey: Prentice-Hall).

Klapp, Orrin E. (1964), *Symbolic Leaders: Public Dramas and Public Men* (Chicago: Aldine).

Klockars, Carl B. (1974), *The Professional Fence* (London: Tavistock).

Laird, Donald A. (1950), 'Psychology and the Crooked Employee', *Man. Rev.*, **39**, pp 210–215.

Lemert, Edwin M. (1953), 'An Isolation and Closure Theory of Naive Check Forgery', *J. Crim. Law, Criminol., Police Sci.*, **44**, pp 296–307; included in Lemert, 1967.

Lemert, Edwin M. (1958), 'The Behaviour of the Systematic Check Forger', *Soc. Probs.*, **6**, pp 141–148; included in Lemert, 1967.

Lemert, Edwin M. (1962), 'Paranoia and the Dynamics of Exclusion', *Sociom.*, **25**, pp 2–25; included in Rubington and Weinberg (eds) 1968.

Lemert, Edwin M. (1964), 'Social Structure, Social Control and Deviation', from Clinard (ed.) 1964; included in Lemert, 1967.

Lemert, Edwin M. (1967), *Human Deviance, Social Problems, and Social Control* (New Jersey: Prentice-Hall).

Leonard, William N. and Weber, Marvin Glenn (1970), 'Automakers and Dealers: A Study of Criminogenic Market Forces', *L. Soc. Rev.*, **4**, pp 407–424.

Levens, G. F. (1964), '101 British White-Collar Criminals', *New Society*, March 26, pp 6–8; included in Geis (ed.) 1968.

Lockwood, David (1966), 'Sources of Variation in Working Class Images of Society', *Soc. Rev.*, **14**, pp 249–267.

Lofland, John (1966), *Doomsday Cult: A Study of Conversion, Proselytization, and Maintenance of Faith* (New Jersey: Prentice-Hall).

Lofland, John (1969), *Deviance and Identity* (New Jersey: Prentice-Hall).

Lofland, John (1974), 'Styles of Reporting Qualitative Field Research', *Am. Soc.*, **9**, pp 101–111.

Lyman, Stanford and Scott, Marvin B. (1970), *A Sociology of the Absurd* (New York: Appleton-Century-Crofts).

Mack, John A. (1964), 'Full-Time Miscreants, Delinquent Neighbourhoods, and Criminal Networks', *Brit. J. Sociol.*, **12**, pp 38–53.

Marcuse, Herbert (1964), *One Dimensional Man* (London: Sphere).

Mars, Gerald (1973), 'Chance, Punters and the Fiddle: Institutionalised Pilferage in a Hotel Dining Room', in M. Warner (ed.) 1973.

Mars, Gerald (1974), 'Dock Pilferage' in Rock and McIntosh (eds) 1974.

Martin, J. P. (1962), *Offenders as Employees*, Vol XVI of the Cambridge Studies in Criminology (London: Macmillan).

Matza, David and Sykes, Gresham (1957), 'Techniques of Neutralisation: A Theory of Delinquency', *Am. Sociol. Rev.*, **22**, pp 664–670; included in Wolfgang *et al.* (eds) 1962.

Matza, David (1961), 'Subterranean Traditions of Youth', *Annals Am. Acad. Soc. Pol. Sci.*, **338**, pp 102–118.

Matza, David (1964), *Delinquency and Drift* (London: Wiley).

Matza, David (1969), *Becoming Deviant* (New Jersey: Prentice-Hall).

Maurer, David W. (1940), *The Big Con* (New York: Bobbs-Merrill).

Maurer, David W. (1955), *Whiz Mob* (Connecticut: College and Univ. P.).

Mayhew, Henry (1862), *London Labour and the London Poor* (London: Griffin, Bohn and Co).

Mead, George Herbert (1934), *Mind, Self, and Society* (Chicago: Univ. Chicago Press).

Mills, C. Wright (1940), 'Situated Actions and Vocabularies of Motive', *Am. Sociol. Rev.*, **5**, 1940, pp 904–913.

Mills, C. Wright (1951), *White Collar* (Oxford: O.U.P.).

McCall, George J. and Simmons, J. L. (1969), *Issues in Participant Observation: A Text and Reader* (London: Addison-Wesley).

McIntosh, Mary (1971), 'Changes in the Organisation of Thieving', in Stanley Cohen (ed.) 1971.

MacIntyre, Alasdair (1973), 'The Essential Contestability of some Social Concepts', *Ethics*, **84**, pp 3–9.

Nettler, Gwynn (1974), 'Embezzlement without Problems', *B. J. Crim.*, **14**, pp 70–77.

Newman, Donald J. (1958), 'White-Collar Crime', *Law. and C. Probs.*, **23**, pp 735–753.

Orwell, George (1933), *Down and Out in Paris and London* (Harmondsworth: Penguin).

Pepinsky, Harold E. (1974), 'From White Collar Crime to Exploitation: Redefinition of a Field', *J. Crim. Law Criminol.*, **65**, pp 225–233.

Peter, Lawrence and Hull, Peter (1966), *The Peter Principle* (London: Pan).

Peters, R. S. (1958), *The Concept of Motivation* (London: Routledge Kegan Paul).

Polsky, Ned (1967), *Hustlers, Beats and Others* (Harmondsworth: Penguin).

Quinney, Richard (1963), 'Occupational Structure and Criminal Behaviour: Prescription Violations by Retail Pharmacists', *Soc. Probs.*, **11**, pp 179–185; included in Geis (ed.) 1968.

Quinney, Earl R. (1964), 'The Study of White Collar Crime: Toward a Reorientation of Theory and Research', *J. Crim. Laws, Criminol., Police Sci.*, **55**, pp 208–214.

Richstein, Kenneth J. (1965), 'Ambulance Chasing: A Case Study of Deviation and Control within the Legal Profession', *Soc. Probs.*, **13**, pp 3–17.

Riis, Roger William and Patric, John (1942), *Repairmen Will Get You If You Don't Watch Out* (Garden City: Doubleday Doran).

Robin, Gerald D. (1965), 'Employees as Offenders: A Sociological Analysis of Occupational Crime', *Ph.D.* Unpub. (University of Pennsylvania).

Robin, Gerald D. (1967), 'The Corporate and Judicial Disposition of Employee Thieves', *Wis. Law Rev.*, **642**, pp 685–702; included in Smigel and Ross (eds) 1970.

Robin, Gerald D. (1974), 'White Collar Crime and Employee Theft', *Crime and Delinquency*, **20**, pp 251–262.

Rock, Paul (1973), 'Phenomenalism and Essentialism in the Sociology of Deviance', *Sociol.*, **7**, pp 18–29.

Rock, Paul (1973a), *Deviant Behaviour* (London: Hutchinson).

Rock, Paul (1973b), *Making People Pay* (London: Routledge Kegan Paul).

Rock, Paul (1973c), 'News as Eternal Recurrence', in S. Cohen and J. Young (eds) 1973.

Rock, Paul and McIntosh, Mary (eds) (1974), *Deviance and Social Control* (London: Tavistock).

Rogers, Joseph and Buffalo, M. D. (1974), 'Neutralisation Techniques: Toward a Simplified Measurement Scale', *Pacific Sociol. Rev.*, **17**, pp 313–331.

Rose, Arnold M. (1962) (ed.), *Human Behaviour and Social Process* (London: Routledge Kegan Paul).

Ross, H. Lawrence (1960–61), 'Traffic Law Violation: A Folk Crime', *Soc. Probs.*, **8**, pp 231–241.

Roy, Donald F. (1955), 'Efficiency and "The Fix": Informal Intergroup Relations in a Piece-Work Machine Shop', *Am. J. Sociol.*, **60**, pp 255–266.

Roy, Donald F. (1970), 'The Study of Southern Labor Union Organising Campaigns', in R. W. Haberstein (ed.) 1970, pp 216–244.

Rubington, Earl and Weinberg, Martin S. (eds) (1968), *Deviance: The Interactionist Perspective* (New York: Macmillan).

Sarbin, Theodore R. and Adler, Nathan (1970–71), 'Self-Reconstitution Processes: A Preliminary Report', *Psy. Res.*, **57**, pp 599–616.

Schuck, Peter (1972), 'The Curious Case of the Indicted Meat Inspectors', *Harpers*, **245**, pp 81–88.

Schur, Edwin M. (1957), 'Sociological Analysis of Confidence Swindling', *J. Crim. Law, Criminol., Police Sci.*, **48**, pp 296–304.

Scott, Marvin B. (1968), *The Racing Game* (Chicago: Aldine).

Scott, Marvin B. and Lyman, Stanford M. (1968), 'Accounts', *Am. Sociol. Rev.*, **33**, pp 46–62; included in Filstead (ed.) 1972.

Scott, Marvin B. and Lyman, Stanford M. (1970a), 'Accounts, Deviance and the Social Order', in Douglas (ed.) 1970.

Scott, Marvin B. and Lyman, Stanford M. (1970b), 'Game Frameworks', in Lyman and Scott (ed.) 1970.

Sherlock, B. and Cohen, A. (1966), 'The Strategy of Occupational Choice: Recruitment to Dentistry', *Soc. Forces*, **44**, pp 303–313.

Shoemaker, Donald J. and South, Donald R. (1974), 'White Collar Crime', in Bryant (ed.) 1974.

Skipper, James K. and McCaghy, Charles H. (1969), 'Stripteasers: The Anatomy and Career Contingencies of a Deviant Occupation', *Soc. Probs.*, **17**, pp 391–405.

Skipper, James K. and McCaghy, Charles H. (1972), 'Respondents' Intrusion upon the Situation: The Problem on Interviewing Subjects with Special Qualities', *Soc. Quart.*, **13**, pp 237–243.

Smigel, E. O. and Ross, H. L. (1970) (eds), *Crimes Against Bureaucracy* (New York: Van Nostrand Reinhold).

Smith, Richard A. (1961), 'The Incredible Electrical Conspiracy', *Fortune*, April, pp 132–180, May, pp 161–224. (Abridged in Wolfgang *et al*, eds. 1962.)

Solzhenitsyn, Alexander (1968), *One Day in the Life of Ivan Denisovich* (Harmondsworth: Penguin).

Spencer, John C. (1965), 'A Study of Incarcerated White-Collar Offenders', in T. Grygier, H. Jones and J. C. Spencer (eds), *Criminology in Transition* (London: Tavistock, 1965), pp 251–264; included in Geis (ed.) 1968.

Stone, G. and Farberman, H. (1970) (eds), *Social Psychology Through Symbolic Interaction* (New York: Ginn-Blaisdell).

Strauss, Anselm (1959), *Mirrors and Masks: The Search for Identity* (New York: Free Press).

Strodbeck, Fred L. and Sussman, Marvin B. (1955–56), 'Of Time, The City and the "One-Year Guaranty": The Relations between Watch Owners and Repairers', *Am. J. Sociol.*, **61**, pp 602–609.

Sudnow, David (1967), *Passing On: The Social Organisation of Dying* (New Jersey: Prentice-Hall).

Sutherland, Edwin H. (1937), *The Professional Thief* (Chicago: Phoenix).

Sutherland, Edwin H. (1949), *White Collar Crime* (New York: Holt, Reinhart and Winston).

Sutherland, Edwin H. (1956), 'Crime of Corporations' from Cohen, Lindesmith and Schuessler (eds) 1956; included in Geis (ed.) 1968.

Taylor, Brian (1974), 'Supermarket Semiology: Order and Significance in a Classificatory System', *Mimeo* (University of Aberdeen).

Taylor, Laurie (1971), *Deviance and Society* (London: M. Joseph).

Thompson, E. P. (1971), 'The Moral Economy of the English Crowd in the Eighteenth Century', *Past and Present*, **50**, pp 77–136.

Trice, Harrison M. and Roman, Paul Michael (1969–70), 'Delabeling, Relabeling and Alcoholics Anonymous', *Soc. Probs.*, **17**, pp 538–546.

Velarde, Albert J. (1975), 'Becoming Prostituted', *B. J. Crim.*, **15**, pp 251–263.

Warner, Malcolm (ed.) (1973), *The Sociology of the Workplace* (London: Allen and Unwin).

Weber, Max (1930), *The Protestant Ethic and the Spirit of Capitalism* (London: Unwin).

Webster (1934), *New International Dictionary* (London: Bell).

Weinberg, Martin S. (1966), 'Becoming a Nudist', *Psychiatry*, **29**; included in Rubington and Weinberg (eds) 1968.

Winick, Charles (1964), 'Physical Narcotic Addicts', in Howard S. Becker (ed.) 1964.

Wolfgang, Marvin E., Savitz, Leonard and Johnston, Norman (1962) (eds), *The Sociology of Crime and Delinquency* (London: Wiley).

Young, Jock (1970), 'The Zoo-Keepers of Deviancy', *Catalyst*, 5, pp 38–46.

Zeitlin, Lawrence R. (1971), 'Stimulus/Response: A Little Larceny Can Do a Lot for Employee Morale', *Psychology Today*, 5, pp 22, 24, 26, 64.

Index